A Surve...
the new testament

By W. W. SLOAN

About the Author

THE PROFESSOR of Bible and religious education, Elon College, Elon College, North Carolina, has had a varied career as teacher, preacher, and world traveler.

A native of Prospect, Pennsylvania, Dr. Sloan was educated at the College of Wooster, McCormick Theological Seminary, and Northwestern University, receiving the Ph.D. degree from the latter.

After teaching at the American Mission College, Alexandria, Egypt, Dr. Sloan became director of religious education at the First Congregational Church, Appleton, Wisconsin, later serving churches in the middle and far west. He has taught at several middle western colleges.

Dr. Sloan is a member of the Bible Speakers Bureau, Department of English Bible, Division of Christian Education of the National Council of Churches of Christ in the U.S.A.

He is the author of numerous articles for religious magazines and for World-Book Encyclopedia. He also has written Sunday school material for several publishers.

The setting of the New Testament, the experience and teachings of Jesus, and the problems met by the early church are discussed. Dr. Sloan has utilized newspaper experience, extensive travel, knowledge of the questions laymen and students ask with biblical scholarship in composing a very readable companion volume to his popular "A Survey of the Old Testament."

A Survey of
the
New Testament

W. W. SLOAN

225
SLO

New Testament
Survey, N.T.

1966

LITTLEFIELD, ADAMS & CO.

Totowa, New Jersey

Paper 1966 ed.
302 pp.

1966 Edition
By LITTLEFIELD, ADAMS & CO.

Printed in the United States of America

Contents

Preface

1. How We Got Our New Testament — 3
2. "Many Have Undertaken to Compile a Narrative" — 15
3. The Palestine of Jesus' Day — 27
4. Mark's Gospel Account — 36
5. "Unto Us a Child Is Born" — 39
6. "The Devil Tempted Him" — 48
7. "You Have Heard That It Was Said" — 56
8. "Piety Before Men" — 63
9. "Nothing Without a Parable" — 68
10. "Thy Kingdom Come" — 78
11. "Who Is the Greatest?" — 83
12. "This Day Our Daily Bread" — 90
13. "Show Us the Father" — 95
14. "Lord, Teach Us to Pray" — 100
15. "Remember the Sabbath Day" — 106
16. "Jews Have no Dealings with Samaritans" — 111
17. "To Entrap Him in His Talk" — 118
18. "The Works That I Do" — 124
19. "Though He Die, Yet Shall He Live" — 130
20. "Even the Spirit of Truth" — 136
21. "The Son of Man Must Be Killed" — 140
22. "Let Him Be Crucified" — 145
23. "This Jesus God Raised Up" — 153
24. "Speak No Man in This Name" — 161
25. "Seven Men of Good Report" — 169
26. "Who Was I to Withstand God?" — 175
27. "We Turn to the Gentiles" — 184
28. "Come Over to Macedonia" — 191
29. "To the Church of the Thessalonians" — 200
30. "Paul an Apostle . . . Through Jesus Christ" — 209

31. "I Belong to Paul"   214
32. "To All God's Beloved in Rome"   222
33. "Ready to Die at Jerusalem"   229
34. "What Has Happened Has Served to Advance the Gospel" 236
35. "A Prisoner for Christ Jesus"   244
36. "What Must Soon Take Place"   253
37. "He Continues a Priest Forever"   263
38. "Be Doers of the Word"   270
39. "God Is Love"   277
40. "Be a Good Minister of Christ Jesus"   282
41. "Grow in the Grace and Knowledge of Our Lord"   290
    Review Assignments   296
    Name Index   299

Preface

"You search the scriptures because you think that in them you have eternal life," Jesus is reported to have said (John 5:39). In his search, the average layman wants to know what biblical scholars have discovered about the book of books. He wants this knowledge in simple terms which he can understand. There are many scholarly books well written but indulging in technical words and comparatively unimportant details. This is true of books dealing with the Old Testament and those about the New Testament. At the request of students and teachers, laymen and pastors for a book that puts scholarship into easily understood terms I wrote A SURVEY OF THE OLD TESTAMENT. This was published by Abingdon Press in 1957.

Requests have come from all parts of the English speaking world for a similar book about the New Testament. When the man interested in the background and teaching of the New Testament is asked, "Do you understand what you are reading?" he is forced to give the answer the Ethiopian eunuch gave, "How can I, unless some one guide me?" (Acts 8:30-31)

This book is not a substitute for the New Testament. It is a guide to be used in studying the Christian scriptures. The portion of the New Testament discussed should be read with each chapter. It is well to use the more easily understood Revised Standard Version. It is hoped that readers will be like the noble Beroeans who searched "the scriptures daily to see if these things were so" (Acts 17:11).

Gratitude should be expressed to my students and parishioners whose questions and suggestions are reflected in this book. Numerous college teachers have read multigraphed editions and suggested improvements. The North Carolina college teachers of religion drew up a set of criteria for a Freshman and Sophomore text which I have carefully followed. But above all others, my wife, Bessie Pickett Sloan, assistant professor of Romance Languages at Elon College, deserves recognition for her belief in me, her patience, and her forebearance. Four visits to the lands of the Bible have proved helpful.

W. W. Sloan

CHAPTER 1

How We Got Our New Testament

"Remembering the words of the Lord Jesus, how he said" (Acts 20:35); "I received . . . what I also delivered to you" (1 Cor. 11:23). These quotations introduce us to the first New Testament. Words and deeds of Jesus handed down by memory constitute the beginning of our Christian scriptures. For the early church the Hebrew writings which had come into general acceptance as religiously helpful were the only scriptures. These were read at Christian services, but were supplemented by stories about Jesus and statements he was remembered to have made.

Various Christian individuals or groups began to gather together such materials as they thought useful in instructing those interested in the new religion. By A.D. 150 there was almost universal acceptance of the four writings we call our four gospel accounts. However, they were not thought of as parts of one book. Other accounts were accepted by some of the churches. A writing called "The Teaching of the Lord through the Twelve Apostles to the Heathen" or more commonly "The Teaching of the Twelve Apostles" was popular. In Egypt "The Gospel According to the Hebrews" and "The Gospel According to the Egyptians" were in use before the four accounts we now read reached there. In Syria a bit later the gospel record used was "The Diatessaron," a combination of the four gospels into one. As late as A.D. 423 we find a Syrian bishop reporting that he had gathered together two hundred copies of the Diatessaron and replaced them with the "gospel of the four evangelists". The "Gospel of Peter", the "Gospel of Thomas" and others were popular here and there but were soon rejected by the church.

Another group of Christian writings early came into popular use—the letters of Paul. 1 and 2 Thessalonians, Galatians, 1 and 2 Corinthians, Romans, Philippians, Colossians, and Philemon were almost universally used. The letter to the Ephesians was com-

3

monly added to the list. Some groups added Hebrews; others rejected it; still others used the book but did not attribute it to Paul. By A.D. 200 most churches added 1 and 2 Timothy and Titus to their collection of useful Christian writings.

When "The Acts of the Apostles" became separated from "Luke" it came to be quite generally accepted as a part of the collection, connecting the gospels and the writings attributed to Paul.

However, these writings were not thought of as constituting Christian scriptures in contrast to Hebrew scriptures. The first attempt to make a list of writings which should constitute a recognized Christian collection was made by a leader named Marcion about A.D. 145. Marcion was eager to separate the church from Jewish influence. He believed the Hebrew scriptures should not be used. To take their place he made a collection consisting of his own edited version of the gospel according to Luke and ten letters of Paul (including Ephesians which, however, he called Laodiceans). To this he added a book of his own which attacked the Jewish religion as contradictory to Christianity. His attempt to have Christians abandon the Hebrew scriptures met with very little success.

When did these Christian writings start being considered as scriptures? We find two references within the Bible itself. In 1 Tim. 5:18 we read "the scripture says", followed by two quotations, one from Deuteronomy and the other from the Gospel according to Luke. This Timothy statement seems to have been made during the time of Marcion. In what is believed to be the last book of our Bible to have been written, 2 Peter 3:16 states that some people misuse the writings of Paul "as they do the other scriptures". Writing at Rome about A.D. 150, Justin quoted New Testament writers with the words "It is written" just as he did Old Testament writers.

About A.D. 185 a bishop of Antioch referred to the Hebrew scriptures and the gospels as "inspired by one spirit of God". On another occasion he referred to Paul's writings as "the divine word". About the same time another writer gave a list of the books of the "Old Covenant" or Old Testament. Did this imply a New Testament? Although the word "scriptures" had been used in reference to Christian writings it was not until A.D. 192 that

4

an unknown writer mentioned "the word of the New Testament".

By this time Christians began to prize writings attributed to other apostles: Peter, John, Jude. They were also including in their lists of Christian writings apocalypses or books with secret meanings only understood by those who had the key. The three most often used were "The Revelation to John" which eventually came to be quite generally accepted, "The Revelation to Peter", and "The Shepherd of Hermas". The letter of Clement of Rome to the Corinthians and the letter attributed to Barnabas were included in the Christian scriptures used in Egypt.

A little after A.D. 200 Origen, the Christian leader in Alexandria, Egypt, wrote: "The canonical books as the Hebrews have handed them down, are twenty-two, corresponding with the number of their letters". He then listed a balancing number of twenty-two "acknowledged" New Testament books. His list included the four gospels, fourteen letters attributed to Paul, Acts, 1 Peter, 1 John and the Revelation to John. Origen also listed seven "disputed" books: Shepherd of Hermas, Barnabas, 2 and 3 John, Jude, James and 2 Peter. This is the earliest list in which the last two books appear. The copy of the Bible found in St. Catherine's monastery in the Sinai desert in 1859 and made about A.D. 350 has as its New Testament the same twenty-nine books listed by Origen.

The general or "catholic" letters bearing the names of Peter, James, John and Jude eventually came to be accepted by the church as parts of the Christian scriptures. Books which we now do not consider as belonging to the New Testament came to be given a secondary position by most of the churches. However, two of the books we use were very slow in gaining popular approval. The apocalypses had served their purpose. Many people felt they were no longer of great value. The Revelation to Peter and the Shepherd of Hermas disappeared from lists of "canonical" books despite claims of their supporters that they had been written by the Apostle Peter and a friend of Paul (Rom 16:14). Many people, especially along the eastern part of the Mediterranean Sea, where numerous apocalypses had been written, wanted to treat the Revelation to John in the same way. Although it eventually came to be included in their Bible, Eastern Orthodox churches yet today never assign any portions of it to be read. Among churches farther to the west the letter to the Hebrews was almost as unpopular as the Revelation to John was in the east.

In A.D. 325 the father of church history, Eusebius, made a list of "acknowledged" New Testament books which is the same 22 as that of Origen, except that he was not certain about the Revelation to John. After it in his list he put the phrase, "if it really seems proper." He then gave a list of "disputed" books: James, Jude, 2 Peter, 2 and 3 John. He followed this by a list of books he had rejected: the Acts of Paul, the Shepherd, the Revelation to Peter, the letter of Barnabas, and the Teaching of the Apostles, "and besides, as I said, the Revelation to John, if it seems proper, which some, as I said, reject but which some class with the accepted books." He then more vehemently rejected another list of books which some people had included in the scriptures but which he felt were heretical: the gospels of Peter, of Thomas, and of Matthias, and the Acts of Andrew and John.

In A.D. 367 Athanasius, then bishop of Alexandria, made his list of New Testament books which is the same as the "accepted" list of Eusebius except that he seemed to have no question about the Revelation to John. The church council meeting in Hippo in northern Africa in A.D. 393 considered our present list of New Testament books as scripture. Four years later the Synod of Carthage declared that nothing should be read in the churches as divine scripture save those books it listed. Its New Testament list is the same as ours. This date, A.D. 397, is generally considered the birth date of the official New Testament canon; this term comes from a Greek word meaning norm or standard. However, several lists of New Testament books made by church leaders after A.D. 397 do not entirely agree. The New Testament commonly used in Syria for several hundred years had but twenty-two books. On the other hand the New Testament of the Ethiopian church had thirty-five books.

Christians came to think of the New Testament as the witness to Christ of the apostles. Books which seemed to have no relation to the early apostles were rejected. Mark and Luke were not considered apostles, but Mark got his major material from Peter, and Luke was closely associated with Paul. Similarity to the names of apostles helped gain acceptance for writings which bore the names of John, Peter, James, and Jude. Authors of other writings in the second and third centuries attempted to gain authority by associating with them the names of apostles, especially Peter and Paul. However, they were rejected by the early church, which failed to find in them significant apostolic witness.

With the exception of the Diatessaron all the books we have discussed were originally written in Greek. However, starting about A.D. 200, Greek came gradually to be replaced by Latin. In various sections of the Mediterranean world parts of the Bible were translated into Latin. Some of this translation was poorly done. Some was only a paraphrase. The church was dissatisfied with this. It decided that there should be an official, carefully made translation. A leading scholar, Jerome, was appointed to this task. His Latin Bible, called the Vulgate, a word meaning usual or common, was completed in A.D. 407. He expressed some doubt about Hebrews and 2 and 3 John but included them. Although other Latin translations were used by some church groups Jerome's official translation came to be "the Bible". His use of our twenty-seven New Testament books may have done more to make them the accepted books than did the church councils.

Shortly before the Synod of Carthage someone composed a book which he called Paul's letter to the Laodiceans. Many churches included this in their Bible for several hundred years. It is even found in some of the earlier Old English and German translations. Except for this Laodicean letter no serious attempt has been made to add other books to the New Testament. However, in the nineteenth and twentieth centuries several crude fictions have appeared which their sponsors claimed to be ancient manuscripts. One of these was called, "The Unknown Life of Jesus" or "The Life of Saint Isa, Best of the Sons of Men". Another was "The Letter of Jesus Christ".

For many centuries the Latin was the only Bible used in western Europe. In time none but the well educated were able to read it. It became largely a book for priests alone. A church synod in 1229 forbade laymen to have any book of the Bible other than the Psalms and prohibited any translation of the Bible. The Greek New Testament was looked down upon as inferior to the Vulgate. However, especially among German people and in the British Isles, there were many who would not accept this prohibition.

We are chiefly interested in how we got our Bible in the English language. The story of the English Bible goes back to about 660 when an illiterate herdsman named Caedmon developed the ability to turn Bible stories told him by monks into songs in the local language. These songs began to interest people in the Bible. Someone translated the Psalms into Anglo-Saxon and a bishop translated the gospels, although neither was well done. A scholarly monk named Bede wrote numerous books, but his great contribution was a careful translation of the gospel of John. He died a few minutes after completing his translation. This was in 735. One hundred and fifty years later King Alfred the Great translated small parts of the Bible from Latin and ordered that the entire Bible be translated. He declared that, "All the freeborn youth of my kingdom should employ themselves in nothing till they can read well the English Scriptures." After his death his translation program was abandoned.

The church had not objected to these early translations, but with the coming of the revival of learning which led to the Renaissance the church began to be challenged. It felt that if people were allowed to read the Bible they might become even more critical of the authority of the church.

Yet it was a churchman, John Wycliffe, born in 1320, who, with some assistance, made the first translation of the entire Bible into English. This was during the time of the poet Chaucer. He sent out "poor priests" over the land to read his translation of parts of the Bible to the common people. Many of them were arrested and imprisoned, but an interest in the Book was aroused. The printing press had not yet been developed. Copies were all made by hand and were quite expensive. We have the record of a load of hay being given in exchange for the loan of a Bible. Threats to Wycliffe's life were made, but he died in bed in 1384, just after completing his translation. A few years later the church had his body dug up and burned, and the ashes thrown into the river. This whole action advertised the Bible. Although Wycliffe's Bible was banned, it was read in secret and many copies of it were laboriously made.

It was another 140 years before further work of any extent was done on making the Bible available to the people of the British Isles. Wycliffe's and all previous translations had been made from Latin Bibles which by then were very inaccurate copies of ancient translations. The conquest of Constantinople by the Turks caused Greek scholars to flee to western Europe. This revived an interest in Greek. At about the same time printing from movable type was developed. A Dutch scholar, Erasmus, had a Greek New Testament printed in 1516. He revived an interest in the Bible by making his own Latin translation. This was the first satisfactory Latin translation since Jerome eleven hundred years earlier. Erasmus lectured on the Bible in Cambridge, England.

The language of the British Isles had changed so much since the time of Wycliffe that a young English priest and scholar, William Tyndale, under the influence of Erasmus determined to translate the New Testament into the English of his time and have it printed. He said he would make it possible for "a boye that dryveth the plow" to know more about the Bible than did the priests. Tyndale was one of the most scholarly men of his day, being a complete master of Hebrew, Greek, Latin, French, Spanish, Italian, and probably German, as well as English. The bishop of London forbade Tyndale to make a translation. Tyndale also knew that no English printer would dare to publish it. Therefore he fled to Germany, where with the assistance of Martin Luther he completed a translation into English and secured a printer. Church authorities learned of Tyndale's activity and destroyed the printing shop. Tyndale escaped with his manuscript. In 1525 he managed to have several thousand copies printed. Friends helped smuggle these into England in bales of cloth, sacks of flour and other merchandise. The bishop of London ordered that all copies be collected and publicly burned. In time the man in charge of these bonfires reported that he had destroyed ten thousand copies but believed there were that many more which he could not find. Tyndale worked on a translation of the Old Testament and improved his New Testament but was imprisoned by church authorities and in 1536 was burned at the stake. As he died he is reported to have prayed, "Lord, open the King of England's eyes."

This prayer was soon to be answered. Tyndale had a convert, Miles Coverdale, who completed Tyndale's translation and made some changes in what Tyndale had already done. He knew very little Hebrew and found it necessary to work with Latin and German translations. However, he learned how to flatter the king and queen, with the result that a few months before Tyndale was burned at the stake Coverdale published the entire Bible in English in England. Shortly later another compilation of Tyndale's work appeared over the name Thomas Matthew. This had the approval of the king who ordered that every church in England secure a copy of it and have "the same set up in summe convenient place within the church that ye have the care of, where-at your parishioners may most commodiously resort to the same and rede it." In St. Paul's Cathedral in London six copies were chained to reading desks and great crowds flocked there to hear the Bible read in English. "Thomas Matthew" proved to be a pen name for John Rogers. When Mary came to the throne of England as a staunch Roman Catholic, she had Rogers and three hundred others put to death for their support of the English Bible.

However, before the time of Queen Mary, another Bible was published which was an attempt to use the best of Tyndale, Coverdale and Matthew (or Rogers) . This was ordered to be placed in every church. A penalty of forty shillings for each month of disobedience was attached to the order. The bishop of London who had so strenuously opposed Tyndale had his name on the title-page as one of the supporters of this new Bible. This was called the Great Bible. It is considered the first authorized English Bible. Beginning with the second edition which appeared in 1540, its title-page bore the statement: "This is the Byble apoynted to the use of the churches".

To escape Mary's cruel opposition many Protestants fled to Europe. The best scholars of this group met at Geneva, Switzerland, where a French translation was being made. Here they developed an English Bible that came to be known as the Geneva Bible. This was printed on much smaller sheets—only nine and a half by twelve inches. It divided the material into verses—the first time this had been done in English. Words supplied to make the meaning clearer were printed in italics. Explanations of difficult terms were given in footnotes; some of these showed a strong dislike of the Roman Church. For example, a marginal note on Rev. 9:3 explains that "the locusts" are "false teachers, heretics, worldly prelates, monks, friars, Cardinals, Patriarchs, Archbishops, Bishops". After Mary's death and the coronation of Elizabeth,

English Protestants returned from the Continent with their new translation of the Bible.

The bishops of the Church of England felt that every English translation of the Bible had been done outside the church. Therefore they made their own, known as the Bishops' Bible. It too was classed as an authorized English Bible. It was not well done and never became popular, although several improved editions were published. The Geneva Bible became "the Bible" of the English speaking people.

However there was not complete satisfaction. Every translation indicated prejudices and special emphases. The new king, James, was eager to get the good will of church people. He agreed to the suggestion that he finance the bringing together of the best Greek and Hebrew scholars in England for the purpose of making a universal translation of the Bible which should surpass all others. This was done. In 1611 a masterpiece was published. It was the third version of the English Bible to be "authorized" to be read in English churches. It is often referred to as the Authorized Version, but more commonly the King James Version. Nearly eighty per cent of the terms used in it were first used by Tyndale.

Before the end of 1611 a second edition of the King James Bible was published. This had 800 variations from the first edition. Private printers were allowed to print the Bible. This led to many more variations. In 1769 the Oxford Press published an edition that thoroughly modernized the spelling of the 1611 editions. Very little change has been made since.

The King James Bible thus did not immediately replace the Geneva Bible. Many people were very critical of it. A hundred editions of the Geneva Bible were published after James came to the throne. When the Pilgrim Fathers came to America in 1620 they refused to allow a copy of the King James Bible on the Mayflower.

The King James translators recognized more than their predecessors the importance of having accurate copies of the Hebrew Old Testament and Greek New Testament. But the best copies of each they had were not very old and were the result of many copyings by hand. Each time a book was copied some errors crept in. The next time most of these errors were kept and others added. These translators also realized that there were many points of

11

Hebrew and Greek grammar and idiom which they did not understand, at which they had to guess. When they examined Wycliffe's translation of 225 years earlier they realized that the English language is constantly changing. Therefore the King James translators made a lengthy preface in which they acknowledged that their work was not perfect and expressed a fervent hope that before long another committee would be formed to carry out a similar task but do it better.

The King James committee did a highly commendable piece of work. As it gradually became accepted, the King James Bible was considered so good that little was done toward making another translation for 250 years. Here and there individuals or small groups made translations which did not prove popular. By 1870 the need for a revision was recognized. Many changes had entered into the English language. Much earlier copies of the Greek Bible than the King James translators had had become available. At least 5,000 copyists' errors had been discovered in the Greek New Testament texts used by the King James committee. An understanding of the language of the Bible had greatly increased.

The grammar and vocabulary of Homer and other classical Greek writers was much different from that of the New Testament. Early translators decided that the New Testament had been written in a "Holy Ghost" type of Greek. However, the discovery of large numbers of business and family letters of the first two centuries A.D. pointed out that the Christian scriptures had been written in the language of "the man of the street" (called Koine Greek).

A British committee similar to that in King James' day was formed. An American committee was also named. Directions were given to keep the new version of the Bible as much like the King James version as could be reasonably done. As work progressed it was realized that British English and American English differed to such a degree that a translation satisfactory in England would not be well received in America. The American committee also felt that additional research should be carried out before a new version was published. Therefore it was agreed that an English Revised Version of the New Testament would be published in 1881 and an American Version some years later. An English

12

Revised Old Testament appeared in 1885 and the American Standard Version of the Old and New Testaments in 1901.

These Bibles were classed as revisions of the King James Bible rather than new translations. They were much more accurate and understandable than the earlier translation, but lacked much of the beauty of expression used by the King James men in the age of Shakespeare. Both English and American committees recognized that they had not had the final word as to the meaning of the Bible and looked forward to later revisions or translations. Under the auspices of the National Council of the Churches of Christ in the United States of America the "Revised Standard Version" was published. Its title-page calls attention to its being "the version set forth A.D. 1611, revised A.D. 1881 and A.D. 1901, compared with the most ancient authorities, and revised A.D. 1946." The Old Testament was published in 1952. After thirteen years of labor, British scholars published in March, 1961 The New English Bible New Testament. This is an entirely new translation unrelated to the King James.

Back in 1582 Roman Catholic scholars translated the Vulgate into English for the benefit of their priests. This is called the Reims New Testament. A bit later the Old Testament was published. The two are called the Reims-Douay Bible. In 1941 another translation of the New Testament from the Vulgate was made. A Roman Catholic translation from the Greek is planned.

More than two hundred translations of the New Testament have been made by individuals and small groups. The most popular have been those made by R. F. Weymouth, James Moffatt, Edgar J. Goodspeed, and J. B. Phillips. Other Greek manuscripts or early translations will doubtless be discovered. English will continue to change. Other translations will prove valuable. The Revised Standard Version is not to remain static. As changes prove advisable they will be made. In this New Testament we have a text that will remain alive. It is *the* New Testament of American Protestant churches. Therefore it is used throughout this survey of the New Testament.

Assignment

1. What two books had difficulty being accepted as a part of the Christian scriptures?

2. What two books not considered a part of the New Testament were the last ones to be dropped?

3. Identify the following dates in their relation to the Bible: 397, 407, 735, 1384, 1536, 1611, 1881, 1901, 1946.

4. Identify: Diatessaron, Marcion, canon, Vulgate, Jerome, Caedmon, Bede, Wycliffe, Tyndale, Coverdale, King James.

Supplementary Reading

1. *The Interpreter's Bible.* New York and Nashville: Abingdon Press; Vol. 1, 1952, pp. 63-105; Vol. 12, 1957, pp. 617-627.

2. *An Introduction to the Revised Standard Version of the New Testament.* New York: Division of Religious Education, National Council of the Churches of Christ in the United States of America, 1946.

3. Filson, Floyd V. *Which Books Belong in the Bible?* Philadelphia: The Westminster Press, 1957. Chapter V.

4. Goodspeed, Edgar J. *The Formation of the New Testament.* Chicago: University of Chicago Press, 1925.

6. Goodspeed, Edgar J. *Strange New Gospels.* Chicago: University of Chicago Press, 1931.

7. Price, Ira M. *The Ancestry of Our English Bible.* (Rev.) New York: Harper & Brothers, 1956.

8. Robertson, E. H. *The New Translations of the Bible.* Naperville, Ill.: Alec R. Allenson, Inc., 1959.

9. Sloan, W. W. *A Survey of the Old Testament.* New York and Nashville: Abingdon Press, 1957. Chapter 2.

14

Chapter 2

"Many Have Undertaken to Compile a Narrative"

Peter was dead. Who would now tell the stories about the origin of the Christian message to the new churches across southern Europe? Most of those who had walked the shores of Lake Galilee or the hills of Judea with the Master were no longer available to recount their experiences. Someone who knew well the stories of Jesus should write them down before they were forgotten. Recent persecution by the Roman emperor Nero made a written record essential. This could be copied, sent to distant Christian groups, or used by bands of Christians in hiding. Christians were convinced that they must continue to bear witness to what God had done through Christ. Jesus had commanded them to be witnesses. To do so a written record must be made.

Peter's younger friend and travelling companion, Mark, was the man to do this. For years he had gone from church to church with Peter. He had sat beside Peter as people looked with awe at the rough fisherman who had been so close to Jesus. People wanted to know what Jesus had said and done. They wanted the information directly from the man who knew. But Peter could speak ·very little Greek, the language of these new Christians. Peter and the others of Jesus' twelve disciples spoke Aramaic, a language much similar to the Hebrew in which the Jewish scriptures or Old Testament had been written. Mark was a member of a Jewish family who had lived outside of Palestine. As good Jews they used Aramaic in their home, but to talk with their neighbors in the island of Cyprus they had found it necessary to learn Greek. Mark could speak both languages with ease. He traveled with Peter and translated Peter's addresses and sermons into the Greek spoken throughout the Mediterranean world.

Who could do a better job of writing an account of Jesus for non-Jewish readers? Mark had translated for Peter so often that he could tell the stories without Peter. It is generally believed that in A.D. 70 or a bit later, Mark settled down in Rome and produced our first written story of Jesus of Nazareth, describing the beginning of the gospel, the good news. There is definite indication that the writer incorporated blocks of material compiled by someone else—possibly some of these blocks were sermons of Peter; some may have been sermons of other preachers. An early Christian leader, Papias, reported a generation or so later: "Mark, having become the interpreter of Peter, wrote down accurately everything that he remembered, without however recording in order what was either done or said by Christ." There is some repetition and haphazard arrangement in Mark's book. The comments of preachers seem to be added to some quotations of Jesus. Since quotation marks were unknown it is not always possible to distinguish between Jesus' statements and comments about them.

This account was written not chiefly that a record of Jesus might be preserved. Rather, it was a guide for Christian preachers, the message of salvation through Jesus Christ. Allegiance to Christ above all else, including government, is the theme of the entire New Testament. Mark has something of an anti-Jewish atmosphere. Because of this a few Bible scholars feel that the book could not have been written by Peter's translator. Mark or Marcus was a common name at that time.

Who was this man Mark, who is generally considered the book's author? His mother had a home in Jerusalem in which the earliest Christians met from time to time (Acts 12:12). Evidently she was a widow, for no mention is made of her husband. Mark knew the twelve disciples of Jesus. In the Mark material not copied elsewhere there is a story (Mark 14:51-52) about a "young man" who seems to be Mark himself. Just after Jesus was arrested in the Garden of Gethsemane this youth, who perhaps was taking a bath or had gone to bed, followed Jesus with only a linen cloth about his body. Those who were leading Jesus to the high priest grabbed for the young man but got only the cloth; he got away nude. There seems to be no religious value in this story. The other gospel writers did not bother telling it. Apparently Mark could not resist the temptation to include in his account this one incident in which he played a part, to say, "I was there". He could scarcely have got this item from Peter, for Peter was among those

16

of whom it had just been said, "They all forsook him and fled".

The next item we have about Mark is quite definite. Some years later Christianity had spread north of Palestine to the city of Antioch in Syria. The Christians there decided that they should share the knowledge of Jesus which had been brought to them. They appointed their two ablest men, Paul and Barnabas, as their representatives in spreading the Christian message. As these two planned to go to the island of Cyprus Barnabas suggested that they take the young man Mark along as a helper. Mark was a close relative of his, probably his nephew. Mark went to Cyprus with the older men, but, after the party went to Turkey, quit and returned to Jerusalem.

Paul and Barnabas eventually went back to Antioch and a bit later planned a second missionary journey. Again Barnabas suggested taking Mark along, but Paul vetoed the idea. "And there arose a sharp contention" with the result that Barnabas and Mark went to Cyprus while Paul took another associate and went to Turkey. Evidently Paul and Mark in time became reconciled. Some ten years later Paul was in prison in Rome. In two letters which he wrote there Paul lists friends who are visiting him in his imprisonment. In both lists he includes Mark.

After his travels with Peter and his recording of Peter's memoirs, we hear nothing more of Mark. However, tradition says Mark founded the church in Alexandria, Egypt. Venice, Italy, considers Mark its patron saint and claims to have his body in the great church there named for him.

Mark's gospel account is not only the first of our four to be written: it is also the shortest. It is vivid, vigorous, concise. It moves along quickly. It hurries from one episode to another. It does not give a great amount of Jesus' teaching. Mark, and the compilers of the later gospel accounts, did not attempt to write a complete biography of Jesus. Mark recorded details that Peter and other early Christians had found useful in winning people to faith in Jesus and instructing them in Christian living. Jesus must have expressed himself on numerous matters, but only those of religious significance are reported.

Mark wrote his book nearly forty years after the Crucifixion. Why had no account of the life of Jesus been written sooner? At that time books were scarce and expensive. There was no printing press; all books were hand-written. Very few biographies had been compiled, so a book about Jesus would not be expected. However, there was another reason that no one had recorded the events of Jesus' life. The early church was convinced that the Messiah, the Christ, would return soon. With Jesus back with them there would be no great value in having a written account.

However, Mark was not the only one to record something about Jesus. There was already in circulation a collection of his sayings. These may have been recorded by the disciple Matthew in the Aramaic language. Matthew had been a tax collector for the Roman government. He possibly knew shorthand and jotted down things he heard Jesus say. Apparently these sayings of Jesus, sometimes called the "Logia" were translated into Greek about A.D. 50. We must keep in mind that Jesus did not speak to his disciples in Greek, but Aramaic. No translation exactly represents the original. The translator is required to use his own understanding. We trust that the translation of the "Logia" was carefully, intelligently, done. Notes on activities of Jesus may have been added. Bible scholars call this document *Q,* from the German word *quelle,* source. It is possible that there were more than one small *Q.*

The message and concern of the earliest church was a proclamation. It was an expression of the conviction that Jesus of Nazareth was the expected Messiah, that by the power of God he had done many mighty works, that he had been crucified, was raised up by God and would come again for judgment. Mark's gospel is an expansion of this proclamation. Biblical scholars call the proclamation the *kerygma.* As the church got under way another factor came to be recognized as important. This, the teaching of Jesus, called by Biblical scholars the *didache,* came to have an increasing emphasis in the church. This is the major element in *Q.* The kerygma might be said to represent Christian faith, the didache Christian duty.

The question arose, Why not combine these *Q* sayings with Mark's account? Mark's writing was popular, but to many people it seemed inadequate. Then there was another lack in what Mark gave—there was nothing about the birth and childhood of Jesus and not much about events after the Resurrection. But stories about both of these were in circulation; they were a part of what

18

we call the oral gospel. Since many people could not read or write, the Hebrews from the time of Moses had developed the custom of memorizing unwritten records of teachings and activities of religious leaders. These were taught to the children of each generation. Why not also incorporate such material about Jesus with Mark's account?

Between A.D. 80 and 85 someone—possibly a committee—accepted this challenge. The writer's Jewish background caused him to note another inadequacy in the earliest gospel account—it did not have sufficient appeal to Jewish readers; it was written chiefly for non-Jewish people. There were many places where Mark could have pointed out the similarity of Jesus' teaching and actions with the teachings and hopes recorded in Jewish scripture.

These needs were well answered in a greatly expanded revision of Mark's account, possibly made in Antioch of Syria. Very little of what Mark had written ten to fifteen years earlier was omitted. But at five places generous sections of the Matthew sayings of Jesus are inserted. One of these sections is the fifth, sixth and seventh chapters of "The Gospel According to Matthew". Another such section is the thirteenth chapter. At the close of each of these sections the compiler says in these or similar words, "And when Jesus had finished these sayings", and then pushes on with the narrative.

To show that Jesus was the fulfillment of Old Testament hopes, the Matthew editor many times took care to point out parallels between Old Testament events and teachings and those connected with Jesus. Christianity was considered the consummation of God's purpose for his people as first given in the Old Testament.

Church problems toward the end of the first century are reflected in the Matthew emphasis. Many Bible scholars are convinced that some statements attributed to Jesus are really what the Matthew editor felt Jesus would have said relative to conditions existing when the gospel account was put into final form. To a lesser extent this is also true of Mark. For example, when Mark tells of Jesus' discussion about divorce, he includes the clause relative to a woman, "if she divorces her husband and marries another she commits adultery" (10:12). Jewish women could not get divorces. This was not a problem among Jesus' hearers, but it was a problem among non-Jewish Christians when Mark wrote his book. On the other hand, the gospel records deal with problems with which the church was no longer greatly concerned, such as fasting, Sabbath healing, and tribute to Rome.

Jews delighted in tracing their ancestry. Therefore the Matthew account opens by giving the ancestry of Jesus back to the first great Hebrew, Abraham. The compiler next tells of the birth of Jesus at Bethlehem, the visit of the wise men and the flight into Egypt. He then takes up the narrative of Mark, rearranging it somewhat but using 606 of Mark's 661 verses. Not only does he insert large sections of the sayings of Jesus from Q, but puts in other bits here and there from the oral gospel or possibly other written accounts which we no longer have. We presume that we do not have the original ending of Mark, but we can be quite sure that the Matthew writer included some post-resurrection events not given in the first account.

Two accepted writings dealing with the life of Jesus were now in circulation. The information in them was called the good news, the gospel. Therefore it was natural to refer to the earlier account as the gospel according to Mark. But what should the expanded account be called? The author was an anonymous Jew who had been converted to a world view of Christianity. Perhaps he did not want his name used. Possibly the church did not know who did the compiling. The bringing together or unifying of Mark, Q, and miscellaneous material may have been done by a group of men. To call this new book the gospel according to anonymous or according to a committee would not be satisfactory. Since the major new contribution to this account was the Matthew sayings the record came to be called the gospel according to Matthew.

Although most biblical scholars believe that the tax-collector disciple of Jesus never saw "the Gospel According to Matthew", it is not impossible that at the age of 70 or 80 Matthew saw the Mark record and felt it needed improvement. Using his earlier notes and his memory he could have produced the enlarged account. A greater boldness in rearranging details in Mark than shown by Luke, his interest in statistics, and a concern about astronomers hint at the editorship of the book-keeper disciple. His employment suggests that he knew Greek. It is quite possible that shortly before the destruction of Jerusalem he and other Christians fled to Antioch. There he would find opportunity to become at ease in the Greek language. About one seventh of the material in Matthew appears in no other gospel account. This special material is sometimes referred to as *M*.

The Matthew account was so Jewish; it so made Jewish readers feel at home that when Christian writings began to be put in the same volume with the Old Testament it seemed quite proper to put Matthew as the first book in the New Testament. It served as a bridge between the two Testaments.

By the time the Matthew account had been compiled, Christianity was appealing to more Gentiles than Jews. These Greek and Roman Gentiles needed a gospel account more complete than that of Mark. But the Matthew report would tend to antagonize Gentile readers because of its strongly Jewish flavor. Another expression of the gospel was needed.

Dr. Luke, the "beloved physician" (Col. 4:14) and apparently a Greek traveling companion of Paul, recognized this need. He had seen the church grow among non-Jewish people. He, therefore, set out to give a comprehensive account of its birth and growth. Such a complete account could not be put on one scroll. Consequently, he planned a two-volume book that would trace the Christian religion from the birth of Jesus until the establishment of Christianity in the center of the Mediterranean world, Rome. The two volumes were probably circulated together until the church developed the habit of considering the Mark, Matthew, and Luke accounts, and a fourth later account we call John, as a unit. This caused Luke's second volume to be handled separately. It came to be known as "The Acts of the Apostles." Luke's writing doubtless was done not later than A.D. 90.

Turn to Luke's preface, the first four verses of his gospel account. Note that he says that "Inasmuch as many have undertaken to compile a narrative of the things which have been accomplished among us" it seemed good to him also to write an account. Who are the "many"? The Mark and Matthew accounts were available, but can two be called "many"? Perhaps Luke thought of Q as a writing distinct from the Matthew compilation. He probably did not have access to "Matthew." Apparently there were other writings about Jesus which we have in part but which were rejected by the early church as of little value.

The letters of Luke's friend Paul had all been written before Mark. In time they had become popular and were circulated among the churches. Luke decided to put his account of Jesus and the early church into the form of letters. This may have helped their popularity. Who was the "most excellent Theophilus" to whom Luke addressed his letters? The "most excellent" suggests a Roman officer. "Theophilus" means "friend of God." Theophilus was possibly a Roman acquaintance of Luke who was becoming interested in Christianity. Or it could have been an imaginary name used by Luke to give his writing the atmosphere of letters. Definitely Luke did not intend his letters to be read by only one person.

The length of scrolls limited the size of books. Therefore Luke could tell very little more about the life and teachings of Jesus than was given in the Matthew account. However, he had found a large amount of valuable material not included in Matthew. He used an entirely different group of infancy stories and another list of ancestors of Jesus. The purely Lucan material is sometimes called *L*. Luke condensed Mark, slightly rearranged its order, and made some definite changes. He possibly omitted some of the *Q* materials used in Matthew. Instead of inserting *Q* in large sections he broke it up into small parts which he put in at the places he felt Jesus had said these things. For example, much of the Matthew Sermon on the Mount (chapters 5, 6, and 7) is found scattered through Luke. Luke used 320 of Mark's 661 verses. He did not agreed with the Matthew editor as to which bits' of Mark should be omitted. Of the 55 verses of Mark not used in Matthew, Luke used 31. Consequently there are but 24 verses in Mark not found in either Matthew or Luke.

Luke's account has been called "the most beautiful book in the world." At heart Luke was a poet and story-teller. In his two volumes he gives a number of songs. He condenses accounts here and there to make room for some of Jesus' longer parables. Only in Luke do we find the parables of the Good Samaritan, the Friend at Midnight, the Prodigal Son, and the Rich Man and Lazarus. Luke emphasizes Jesus' interest in Samaritans and other non-Jews. He begins by telling of "good news of a great joy, which will come to all the people" (1:10). He ends by saying that the disciples "returned to Jerusalem with great joy" (24:52). Luke is interested in the poor and hungry, the sick and the outcast. As a physician he is concerned with healings. He is interested in narratives and parables dealing with women.

Luke points out from time to time that Jesus' concern was not limited to Jews. Mark and Matthew had made use of lines from Isa. 40 to describe John the Baptist as beginning the gospel message. However, it is only Luke who includes the words, "and all flesh shall see the salvation of God" (3:4-6). Luke pictures Jesus as a universal savior. Luke adopted his Jewish material to Gentile ways of thought.

The relationship between the Mark, Matthew and Luke accounts can best be recognized by examining a "Harmony of the Gospels" in which the three gospel records are given in parallel columns. One can easily see what the other writers incorporated from Mark. Many times they repeat his exact words. What Matthew and Luke have in common apart from Mark can also be seen; these are the Q materials. The distinctive contributions of the second and third accounts can be recognized.

Bible scholars early recognized the similarity of these records. They invented a name to include all three. Collectively the three accounts are called *the synoptic gospels.* What words do you recall that begin with "syn"? The root means "together" or "like." We recognize the root, "optic," in such expressions as optic nerve, optician. It means "seeing." The term, synoptic gospels, means the gospel accounts that see Jesus from the same viewpoint. The good news from God emphasized in all these accounts is the coming of the Kingdom of God.

In contrast to the synoptic gospels is a fourth gospel account written much later, possibly as late as 110. The author is generally considered to be a Greek Christian named John. The Jews were not philosophers. The Greeks were. The theology of the Jews, especially the expectation of one anointed by God, the Messiah, did not appeal to the Greeks. The Greeks were not looking for a Messiah. However, they were wanting to understand God. They talked about the "Logos," understanding or knowledge, reason or science. We use this root extensively in English. We speak of monologue and dialogue, what one person says or what two people say. A catalogue is a summary of categories. Biology is the knowledge of bios or life. Psychology is the knowledge or science of the psyche, soul, or mind. To the Greeks Logos was an expression of a vaguely conceived Supreme Being. John presented Jesus to his fellow Greeks by saying that Jesus was the Logos made flesh or incarnated. Jesus was all things to all men, to the Jew the Messiah, to the Greek the Logos. The Greek term Logos is generally translated into English as "Word." John did not deny that Jesus was the Messiah. He uses the term, or more often its Greek equivalent, Christ, a number of times. In order not to antagonize Jewish readers he points out near the end of his book that he wants readers to believe that Jesus is the Christ (20:31).

Recent discoveries in the scrolls found in caves near the Dead Sea indicate that some outlooks we have considered purely Greek were also held by the Essenes. This suggests the possibility that John was an Essene Christian writing at a date considerably earlier than 100. This would explain why John uses a number of Hebrew expressions. It is also noted that John's contrast between light and darkness was used by the Essenes. However, if John were as Essene, a Jew, why would he speak of the opponents of Jesus as "the Jews"? What would he know about the Logos?

John took for granted that his readers had one or more of the synoptic gospels. He did not duplicate the earlier accounts but supplemented them. Only eight per cent of the contents of the fourth gospel coincides with material in the synoptics.

John's gospel account is an interpretation, an evaluation of Jesus. He does not attempt to give an event by event report of what Jesus did. Rather he shows the quality, the character of Jesus. Early in his account he notes the courage of Jesus by telling about his driving the money changers out of the temple. The synoptic writers place this in the last week of Jesus' earthly life. Did it occur twice? No; John was not trying to give an accurate time setting. John was more interested in theology than in biography. He gave fewer events than did earlier writers, but attempted to examine the inner meaning. Some sections of "the Gospel according to John" appear to be sermons which the writer had delivered.

To give insight into the personality and significance of Jesus, John employs many figures of speech. He calls Jesus the bread of life, the true vine, the good shepherd, the door. He quotes Jesus the Logos as saying, "I am the way, the truth and the life."

John never pictures Jesus as speaking in parables but in long mystical discourses. He has Jesus speaking with a sophisticated elegance much different from the homely but penetrating wisdom reported in the Synoptics.

The synoptic gospels are, with the exception of a few paragraphs, photographs of Jesus. The person who views these photographs is allowed to make his own interpretation. The Fourth Gospel is a portrait. It gets behind outward appearances, shows the mind, the personality of the man portrayed. John the philosopher adds a contribution not made by the synoptic writers. It is difficult in his gospel to distinguish between what the historical Jesus said and what the writer felt that the eternal Christ was telling him. John's style and that of the discourses he attributes to Jesus are the same.

For Class Discussion

Which is our most valuable gospel account?

Assignment

1. What does the Matthew account add to Mark? What does Luke add? John?

2. Explain the terms: synoptic, Logos, Messiah, kerygma, didache, Q, Theophilus.

3. To get a bird's-eye view of the life of Jesus read the entire book of Mark. Read it as if you had never heard of Jesus. Prepare to be examined on what Mark said about various things.

Supplementary Reading

1. *The Interpreter's Bible*. New York and Nashville: Abingdon Press, Vol. 7, 1951. Pages 3-38; 60-74; 231-249; 629-646; Vol. 8, 1952. Pages 3-26; 437-462.

2. Beech, Curtis. *The Gospel of Mark, Its Making and Meaning*. New York: Harper & Brothers, 1959.

3. Filson, Floyd V. *Opening the New Testament*. Philadelphia: The Westminster Press, 1952. Chapters 3, 4, and 5.

4. Guy, Harold A. *The Origin of the Gospel of Mark*. New York: Harper & Brothers, 1955.

5. Hunt, A. M. *Introducing the New Testament*. Philadelphia: The Westminster Press, Rev., 1957. Part Two.

6. Reece, E. H., and Beardslee, W. A. *Reading the Bible*. Englewood Cliffs, N. J.: Prentice-Hall, 1956. Chapter II.

7. Rowlingson, Donald T. *Introduction to New Testament Study*. New York: The Macmillan Company, 1956. Chapters III and IV.

CHAPTER 3

The Palestine of Jesus' Day

The little Jewish kingdom in Palestine lost its independence in 63 B.C. when Rome took control. Palestine was a small part of the Roman Empire during New Testament times.

Rome soon discovered that it had an ally. This was Antipater of Idumaea in southern Palestine. The Idumaeans were descendants of the Old Testament Edomites who had fled north of their original homes. As his father before him, Antipater was governor of Idumaea. Because of his cooperation and outstanding ability he was made procurator of Judea (or Palestine) by Julius Caesar. Shortly after Antipater was murdered in 43 B.C., his son, Herod, was appointed his successor and given the title of king. Herod met with resistance. Not until 37 B.C. was he able, with the help of Roman soldiers, to gain full rule over his little kingdom. Although Herod's grandfather had been forced to adopt Judaism, the family was looked upon by the Jews as foreigners. Herod determined to be as great a builder of palaces and temples as Solomon had been nine hundred years earlier. He built numerous temples honoring the emperor Augustus. He rebuilt the Old Testament city of Samaria, naming it Sebaste from the Greek form of the same emperor's name. On the coast northwest of Sebaste he built a great port city which he named Caesarea, again honoring his emperor. Herod's lavish display and his loyalty to Rome won the approval of the emperor, but the increased dislike of the Jews. To please them Herod in 20 B.C. commenced an elaborate rebuilding of the temple at Jerusalem. This was not completed until A.D. 64, long after his death. Only six years later the temple was destroyed by the Romans while putting down a Jewish rebellion. The temple was in the process of being rebuilt during the entire lifetime of Jesus.

Herod, who became known as Herod the Great, was still living when Jesus was born. Herod died in 4 B.C. He had murdered three of his own sons, but divided his kingdom among three others. Archelaus was given the territories of Idumaea, Judaea and Samaria. This was all of Palestine west of the Dead Sea and Jordan River nearly as far north as the Sea of Galilee. Antipas was given Galilee, the territory west of the Sea of Galilee. He also was given Perea east of the Jordan river and south of the Sea of Galilee. Philip was given a largely Gentile territory east and north-east of the Sea of Galilee. Rome refused the title of king to these sons of Herod the Great. However, their subjects often used the word in flattery. All three used the term Herod as prefixes to their names. The Herod mentioned in Mark is Herod Antipas. Between Perea and Philip's territory was a loose confederation of Greek cities known as the Decapolis and protected by the governor of Syria to the north. To some extent the governor of Syria kept an eye on all of Palestine.

Archelaus was only 18 years old when his father died. He had no understanding of the Jews and lacked the skills his father had, but imitated him in being cruel and oppressive. Complaints about him were lodged with Rome with the result that in A.D. 6 the emperor removed him and appointed a Roman governor or procurator in his stead. The fifth of these, Pontius Pilate, was procurator A.D. 26 to 36. It was he who sentenced Jesus to be crucified.

Although the Jews disliked Archelaus, many of them despised being ruled by a Roman. This group, known as Herodians, insisted that some descendant of Herod should be their ruler. They would have liked to have the rule of Antipas extended southward.

Violent opposition to Rome centered in a group of Jews known as the Zealots or Cananeans. They doubtless came into existence at the time Rome took control of Palestine. We find them organized when Rome in A.D. 6 tried to list the Palestinians for tax purposes. Their attempts at a reign of terror cost numerous Romans their lives. One of Jesus' twelve disciples was a Zealot.

A much more dignified opposition to Roman rule existed in the well known and highly respected vital religious political group called Pharisees. The word means separatist or separated. They attempted to avoid Greek influence and style. They wanted to have nothing to do with the Romans. They often called themselves neighbors. They felt that they were maintaining the religion

28

and tradition of the past, attempting to keep Judea for the Jews. At the time of Jesus about six thousand men classed themselves as Pharisees. These often quarrelled among themselves. We know of seven different types of Pharisees.

In theology the Pharisees had elements in common with Christianity. They believed in the existence of non-human spirits both good and bad, angels and demons. They believed that after death righteous people would experience resurrection, the wicked were left in Sheol suffering punishment. The Pharisees believed that God would "anoint" some leader, the Messiah, to free them from their enemies and usher in a better life.

The Pharisees made much of the laws and regulations of the Old Testament, especially the 365 negative and 248 positive laws of the Torah, the first five books of the Hebrew scriptures. Many of these were not detailed enough to satisfy them. They kept asking, How did the rabbis of the past interpret this rule? They set out detailed interpretations which they insisted must be exactly obeyed. These, they believed, were a part of the "Oral Torah," rules made by Moses but never reduced to writing. The command to "Remember the sabbath day to keep it holy" they felt needed to be implemented. They had a sense of social responsibility. They honestly sought to adapt old laws to new conditions. In Ex. 16:29 it was decreed, "Remain every man of you in his place, let no man go out of his place on the seventh day." Did this mean one's house? The Pharisees felt that they were liberalizing this by declaring that one might go a "sabbath day's journey" from home, two thousand cubits, three thousand feet or a little over a half mile. However, there were those among the Pharisees who did not want this restriction and found ways around it. They asked, What is home?, and gave their own answer, Where your food is. One who obeyed the letter of the law but did not hesitate to disobey its spirit could hide a little food a Sabbath day's journey from home, declare he was again home and go that much farther. By putting food at various places he could walk as far as he wished and still maintain that he had gone no farther from home than the law permitted.

If the Sabbath was to be the day of rest it was obvious that burdens should not be carried on that day. But what is a burden? Was a pin a burden? It might be necessary to fasten one's clothes.

But a needle was another matter; it was an instrument of work. To wear clothing with a needle in it was breaking the Sabbath. Should a mother pick up a child and carry it on the Sabbath? What if the child had a stone in its hand? No blame was put on the child, but some of the Pharisees felt that the mother was guilty. Others were more charitable. Should one eat an egg laid on the Sabbath? is another question about which the Pharisees argued. Should fruit which had fallen on the Sabbath be eaten?

Cleanliness and purity, were important elements in the Jewish religion. This led the Pharisees to draw up a set of regulations about ceremonial washings. Tithing, giving a tenth to religious causes, was required. This again led to detailed regulations. Many Pharisees were always fearful that they were disobeying one of the many rules that had been made. This led to a degree of unhappiness. God was considered the lawgiver to be obeyed through fear. Love for God was not absent from the teachings of the Pharisees but fear had a more prominent place.

Jesus felt that this was an unhealthy condition. He criticized the petty regulations that the Pharisees tended to feel very important. They had gone so far as to say that if a regulation made by the Pharisees was found in conflict with a rule given in the Old Testament, the regulation of the Pharisees was the one that must be observed. Because of this we often give the Pharisees less respect than they deserve.

Jewish opposition to the Pharisees headed up in a smaller but aristocratic group called the Sadducees. The Pharisees were respected by the common people in Palestine, but these same people disliked the Sadducees, perhaps jealous of their learning and wealth. The word Sadducee probably means "righteous one," although it is possible that the name was derived from that of Zadok, a prominent priest in the time of David and Solomon. The Sadducees felt that they were the real conservatives. They denied the existence of angels and evil spirits and the resurrection into a future life. They claimed these to be modernistic ideas since they are not discussed in the Torah, the earlier and basic part of the Old Testament.

The Sadducees believed that the laws found in the Torah should be observed, but they would have nothing to do with the

"Oral Torah." They felt that individuals should be allowed to make their own detailed interpretations.

The Sadducees did not like the Romans but insisted upon being realistic. The Romans were there; the Jews might as well cooperate with them. Thus the Sadducees became the appeasement party. They were rewarded for their stand. After Rome took over Palestine it determined who should be the chief Jewish official, the high priest in charge of the temple. Rome vetoed the nomination of any one who was not a Sadducee. This enabled the Sadducees to get large incomes from temple dues. Because of this, by the time of Jesus the Pharisees had lost some of their interest in the temple; consequently they put more emphasis upon the synagogues. The Pharisees claimed that the Sadducees put politics ahead of religion.

There was still another group of Jews, not named in the Bible, the Essenes. Jesus is never reported to have criticized them. He probably had little contact with them. We are learning much about the Essenes as we investigate some of their libraries found recently in caves near the Dead Sea.

With the exception of one group, the Essenes did not marry. They lived a semi-monastic, communal life, rejecting luxuries such as meat, which they ate only at certain ceremonial feasts. They had a rigid organization and were subject to numerous rules they developed for themselves. They had great respect for physical labor, had their own gardens, and worked as masons, carpenters, potters. Their earnings were put into a common treasury. Much time was spent reading and copying the scriptures and other sacred writings. Possibly part of their living expenses were financed by copying and selling books. Regular worship, communal meals, and frequent washings were emphasized. They believed in immortality and laid stress on Sabbath observance. Elements of Greek thought and oriental mysticism are found in the religion of this group.

The Essenes held many doctrines similar to those of the Pharisees, but had their own priests whom they considered righteous and pure descendants of Zadok. Teaching and interpreting the Law were considered the duties of the priest. The Essenes had been forced to flee from Jewish centers. Some seem to have gone to Damascus and Syria. Probably some settled in other places, but the leading group developed its center at Khirbet Qumran in the wilderness just west of the north end of the Dead Sea. There they came to the conviction that they were carrying out the command of Isa. 40:3, "In the wilderness prepare the way of the LORD." They felt they were preparing for the coming of the Messiah, or possibly two Messiahs.

The Essenes had withdrawn from association with other Jewish leaders. They did not participate in warfare, but looked forward to one great Holy War, in which the Messiah would purify Israel and then conquer the world. They called this "The War of the Sons of Light Against the Sons of Darkness." They would have nothing to do with the temple, for they felt that the Sadducee priesthood was corrupt. However, they looked forward to having a part in temple worship after its perfection in the Messianic Age.

Like Jesus, the Essenes insisted that oaths must not be used to assert the truth of statements. However, upon joining the order each Essene took an Oath of the Covenant which he renewed each year in an elaborate ceremony based upon the directions given in the latter part of Deut. 27.

The majority of Jews were not Pharisees, Sadducees or Essenes. Nor were they Herodians or Zealots. However, in conflicts among these groups individual Jews tended to take sides.

In New Testament times there were institutions and professional groups we should know. The temple has been mentioned. It was the center of Jewish worship. The original temple built by Solomon about 950 B.C. had been destroyed in 586 B.C. Later Zerubbabel's temple was built on the same site. It was completed in 516 B.C. This was the temple that Herod the Great had gradually rebuilt in an elaborate fashion. People did not want the old temple destroyed but were glad to have it improved. By the time this was completed little of the old building was left.

Animal sacrifices were made daily under the supervision of priests. As far as the temple was concerned the Sabbath was practically the same as any other day. The Jews had five feasts each year. When these celebrations were held great crowds of Jews came from all Palestine and smaller groups from abroad. Every day people came to the temple to have sacrifices made. They hoped thus to secure God's blessing upon personal or family enterprises, or to show appreciation to God for blessings, regained health, a successful venture. Coming to the temple brought people under the domination of the priests, a conservative group who tended to oppose all progress or change.

During the time, more than five hundred years before Jesus, when the Jews were in Babylonian captivity and had no temple they developed the synagogue. The synagogue was a local gathering of people for prayer, reading the scriptures and discussing religion. Much the same group came each Sabbath. Members of these groups got to know one another. The synagogue became a social center and in time a school. When the Jews returned to Palestine and built their new temple they had come to like the synagogue so much that they kept it too. In time every Jewish town had a synagogue. The cities had several.

The men of a local synagogue elected a council of elders who organized the finances and directed the services. This council was a local court of justice or Sanhedrin. One member was elected ruler of the synagogue.

Most synagogues had one or more rabbis or teachers. The word rabbi was a term of respect. It originally meant "my great one." Rabbis commonly conducted schools in which boys learned to read and write. Portions of the Hebrew scripture were their textbooks. Rabbis were expected to know the Torah thoroughly and to instruct the people of their communities in its finer details. They might preach in the synagogue services but that was not always done. A rabbinical training school existed in Jerusalem but many people were called rabbis who did not attend it. Jesus was frequently addressed as rabbi.

Another term we often find is scribe. Scribes were originally men who wrote letters for the illiterate or made copies of older writings. Portions of the Hebrew scriptures were the writings most copied. Therefore the scribes came to be called both scribes and rabbis. There was no sharp distinction between the two titles. The word rabbi may have been an honorary title given to some scribes. The Hebrew laws were the scriptures or were derived from the scriptures. Therefore the scribes of Jesus' day were considered lawyers.

Long before the Romans took control of Palestine the Jews

33

had a chief judicial council which came to be called the Great Sanhedrin, sometimes the Council. It had legislative, governing and judicial functions. It met in impressive chambers of hewn stone in the temple area. It had 70 members plus the high priest who presided at its meetings. Religiously it had power over Jews everywhere, but after the death of Herod the Great the Romans limited its judicial power to Judea. It had been accustomed to sentencing criminals to death and executing them, but Rome changed this. It allowed executions to take place only when approved and ordered by the representative of the Roman government. The Sanhedrin had its own police.

In Judea the Sanhedrin had charge of collecting taxes for Rome. It sold this privilege to local speculators or publicans who were allowed to keep all they collected above what they had paid for the office. These tax collectors were considered to be serving the enemy, Rome. Many times they made demands upon tax payers which were unfair, unethical. Therefore, tax collectors were commonly hated. The Pharisees criticized them severely. Jesus chose one of them to be a member of his inner circle of twelve disciples. To the Pharisees this was not respectable; it laid Jesus' movement open to suspicion.

Assignment

1. Make a map of Palestine indicating the territories assigned to Archelaus, Antipas, and Philip.
2. Identify the following: Antipater, Herod the Great, Archelaus, Antipas, Philip; procurator; Herodians, Zealots, Cananaeans, Pharisees, Sadducees, Essenes; temple, synagogue; priest, rabbi, scribe, publican, sanhedrin.

Supplementary Reading

1. *The Interpreter's Bible.* New York and Nashville: Abingdon Press, Vol. 7, 1951. Pages 75-113.
2. Johnson, Sherman E. *Jesus in His Homeland.* New York: Charles Scribner's Sons, 1957. Chapters I-V.

3. Kee, H. C., and Young, T. W. *Understanding the New Testament*. Englewood Cliffs, N. J.: Prentice-Hall, 1957. Pages 39-45.

4. Miller, Madeleine S., and Miller, J. Lane. *Harper's Bible Dictionary*. New York: Harper & Brothers, 1952. Articles dealing with the topics suggested for identification above.

5. Perowne, Stewart. *The Later Herods*. New York and Nashville: Abingdon Press, 1959.

6. Perowne, Stewart. *The Life and Times of Herod the Great*. New York and Nashville: Abingdon Press, 1959.

7. Rece, E. H., and Beardslee, W. A. *Reading the Bible*. Englewood Cliffs, N. J.: Prentice-Hall, 1956. Chapter 10.

8. Sloan, W. W. *A Survey of the Old Testament*. New York and Nashville: Abingdon Press, 1957. Chapter 35.

9. Snaith, Norman H. *The Jews from Cyprus to Herod*. New York and Nashville: Abingdon Press, 1958.

10. Wright, G. E., and Filson, Floyd V. *The Westminster Historical Atlas to the Bible*. Philadelphia: The Westminster Press, Rev., 1956. Pages 81-83.

CHAPTER 4

Mark's Gospel Account

Read carefully the Gospel according to Mark. Be able to tell what Mark gives about each of the following. Note Mark's vocabulary and method of expression. Do not confuse the Mark account with any other.

1. John the baptizer
2. Sea of Galilee
3. "Follow me and I will make you become fishers of men."
4. Zebedee
5. Capernaum
6. Levi
7. Unshrunk cloth
8. Grainfields one sabbath
9. An eternal sin
10. "Who are my mother and my brothers?"
11. "A sower went forth to sow."
12. A lamp
13. A grain of mustard seed
14. The country of the Gerasenes
15. "Is not this the carpenter?"
16. "A prophet is not without honor."
17. Nothing for their journey except a staff
18. King Herod
19. Herodias
20. Some of his disciples ate with hands defiled
21. Corban
22. No sign
23. "Who do you say that I am?"
24. "Get behind me, Satan."
25. "Whoever loses his life for my sake and the gospel's".
26. A child

27. A cup of water
28. A great millstone
29. Children
30. "Go, sell all that you have."
31. The eye of a needle
32. "We want you to do for us whatever we ask."
33. "Whoever would be great."
34. A colt
35. Hosanna
36. Tables of the money-changers
37. A den of robbers
38. "Is it lawful to pay taxes to Caesar?"
39. "Which commandment is the first of all?"
40. "The second (commandment) is this."
41. A poor widow came
42. An alabaster jar
43. A man carrying a jar of water
44. "Take; this is my body."
45. "Before the cock crows twice."
46. Gethsemane
47. He came and found them sleeping
48. "The one that I shall kiss."
49. A linen cloth about his body
50. The high priest
51. One of the maids of the high priest
52. Pilate
53. Barabbas
54. A crown of thorns
55. Simon of Cyrene
56. Golgotha
57. Two robbers
58. "Truly this man was a son of God."
59. Mary Magdalene
60. Joseph of Arimathea

Be able also to answer the following questions:

1. How did the man generally considered the author of this account secure much of his material?

2. Where, in what language, and about what year was the book of Mark written?
3. What do we know about the man Mark?
4. For what purpose did Mark write his book?
5. Why had no account of the life of Jesus been written earlier?
6. Why does the Revised Standard Version put Mark 16:9-20 as a foot-note?

CHAPTER 5

"Unto Us a Child Is Born"

Read Matt. 1 and 2; Lu. 1, 2, and 3:23-38.

All that we have concerning the first thirty years of Jesus' life is recorded in the first two chapters of Matthew and Luke. Some of the other "gospels" rejected by the early church contain unacceptable stories. Some of these are reports of healings or other miracles secured by touching the clothing or bath water of the baby. The Gospel of Thomas reports that Jesus, at the age of five made twelve clay sparrows. He was reprimanded by Joseph for doing this on the Sabbath. Jesus clapped his hands and told the sparrows to go. They flew away chirping.

Only Luke tells of the birth of John, later known as John the Baptizer or Baptist. His parents were Zechariah and Elizabeth. The King James Version of the Bible calls the father Zecharias. Most Greek names end in "s". Hebrew names seemed less strange to Greek readers if put into Greek form. We generally speak of the last German kaiser as William rather than by his German name Wilhelm. In a similar way Old Testament characters Isaiah, Elijah, and Elisha are called in the Greek New Testament Esaias, Elias, and Eliseus. The King James translation put these Greek spellings over into English. The Revised Standard Version editors have restored the Hebrew form of these names. They made an exception of the Hebrew Joshua, which in Greek is Jesus. Zechariah is a familiar Old Testament name—there are twenty nine Zechariahs in the Old Testament. It seems better to continue the familiar spelling Zechariah than to use the Greek Zecharias.

Zechariah and his wife faced the problem found so often in the Old Testament. They had no children "and both were advanced in age." There would be no one to look after the old folks when they could no longer earn their living. There would be no one to care for their graves or carry on family traditions. Various solutions were found in the Old Testament. Like the parents of Samson, Samuel, and others in Hebrew history, Zechariah had been praying for a son. While at his semi-annual term of service at the temple he became convinced that his prayer was being answered affirmatively. This knowledge struck him dumb.

Although the Matthew account says that it is Joseph who is told of the prospective birth of Jesus, Luke tells of the promise to Mary. Mary is Luke's heroine. As Protestants we probably have not made enough of Mary. The one who gave Jesus his first religious education deserves great admiration. We tend to accuse Roman Catholics of going to the extreme of worshipping Mary. The raising of Mary to almost deity serves a psychological need. With no singular personal pronoun that does not designate sex we use masculine pronouns in referring to God. This is in accord with a tendency through history for men to be considered the stronger sex. God is neither masculine nor feminine. He has the desirable qualities of each. Therefore to speak of God as either is incomplete. Buddhists came to think of Buddha as representing God, but many Buddhist temples in China and Japan place beside statues of Buddha statues of the goddess of mercy to complete the representation of God. Similarly the church which calls itself Christian Scientist often refers to God as the father-mother God. With this in mind we can understand what is behind so-called Mariolatry.

In both Matthew and Luke it is pointed out that the child is to be called Joshua or its Greek equivalent Jesus. This is a fairly common name. There were four Joshuas in the Old Testament. The name Jesus appears more than a dozen times in the Apocrypha referring to various people. Lu. 3:29 lists a Jesus as an ancestor of Jesus of Nazareth. A Jesus called Justus and a Bar-Jesus also appear in the New Testament. Hebrew names have definite meanings as do many of our names today, but doubtless many people paid little attention to the meaning of their names. Joshua or Jesus means Yahweh (the Hebrew name most often given to God) saves, or Yahweh is healing or salvation. This proved to be a very appropriate name for the man whose birth the Matthew and Luke accounts record. The stories through the

40

gospel records are given to emphasize that by Jesus salvation came to men, that God made Jesus the savior of the world, that it was he who "will save his people from their sins."

Those who speak English have come to hold the name Jesus in such high respect that to name any boy Jesus seems to be irreverent. Spanish speaking people and Arabic people take a different outlook. They feel that to name a child for him is to show great respect for Jesus.

Luke, the poet at heart, notes quotations which have become songs still in use. Elizabeth's greeting to Mary, "Blessed are you among women" in 1:42 became so much used by the church that it was inserted in the angel's greeting of 1:28 in medieval copies of the Bible. These words do not appear in 1:28 in the earliest copies of the New Testament we now have. The enlarged twenty-eighth verse is used as the prayer of the Roman Catholics and song of all Christians, the Ave Maria.

Mary's song in Lu. 1:46-55 is often used, called the Magnificat for the first word in Latin. It is an imitation of the song of another woman who rejoiced that she was to become a mother, Hannah the mother of Samuel (1 Sam. 2:1-10). Zechariah's song, called the Benedictus from the first word in the Latin Vulgate, is composed of a chain of Old Testament phrases.

Matthew gives no details of the birth of Jesus. It is Luke who reports that Mary and Joseph were in Bethlehem because they had come from Nazareth in Galilee to fulfill the requirements to register for a Roman census. If one were to read Matthew alone he would get the impression that Bethlehem was the home of Joseph. Luke emphasizes the humble origin of Jesus by saying that there was no room for the family in a Bethlehem inn and the child was therefore born in a stable.

One problem concerning the birth of Jesus is that of the time. Herod the Great was king, but he died in 4 B.C. We do not know what year Jesus was born—some time between four and seven B.C. "B.C." means "before Christ." Why this inconsistency? Each nation had its own method of counting years. It was common to record events as occurring in a certain year of the reign of a definite king. Kings did not conveniently die at the end of a year. The last year of one king would overlap the first year of his successor. Counting back over a series of reigns was difficult.

41

International correspondence was also confused by this method.

When Rome conquered most of the Mediterranean world she set up her own system of dating from the supposed year of the founding of the city of Rome. However, when groups broke away from Rome they did not want to honor their oppressor by continuing that system of dating. Some five hundred years after the birth of Jesus this matter of recording dates became a problem. A Christian monk suggested that the birth of Jesus was the beginning of a new epoch, an event all might well honor. He began dating events from what he thought was the year in which Jesus was born. Gradually this system was adopted. Each year was dated "anno domini," the "year of our Lord." Therefore our term "A.D." Long later it was discovered that the monk was in error a few years. Too many historical dates had been recorded in accordance with his report, too many corner-stones and tombstones cut, to correct the figure, even if we had known just when Jesus was born.

Even today many Orientals keep no record of birth dates. More than three hundred years after the birth of Jesus Christian groups felt that it was appropriate to set aside a day in special recognition of Jesus. This came to be called the Mass of Christ or Christmas. Various dates were observed by different groups. Individuals in the Orient today often celebrate certain days as their "Feast Days" without any necessary connection with the anniversary of their birth. So did the Christians in relation to Jesus. Even today the British Empire celebrates the birthday of its king or queen early in June regardless of when the ruler was born. Romans had a heathen festival on the shortest day of the year. Sixteen hundred years ago this was the twenty-fifth of December. Christians found that the best way to do away with undesirable elements of this festival was to substitute something good. Therefore December 25 came to be considered the Feast Day of Jesus or Christ-mas. In time this came to be considered the birthday of Jesus.

In what month was Jesus born? Luke tells us that shepherds were with their flocks during the night. The only time that Palestinian shepherds ordinarily do this is during the lambing season in March or April.

Note that Luke gives another song, the Gloria in Excelsis, the angelic message to the shepherds with its emphasis upon peace and good will.

Luke reports the naming or circumcision of the child which according to Jewish law took place eight days after his birth. Luke then goes on to tell of the ceremony of the purification of the parents which in the case of a boy took place thirty-three days after circumcision, of a girl sixty-six days after a preliminary two-week period (Lev. 12:2-5). According to the Old Testament law (Lev. 12:6-8) a lamb and a bird were to be offered as sacrifices, unless the family was poor, in which case two birds might be offered. According to Luke two birds were brought. Nothing is said about a lamb. Since Bethlehem is within six miles of Jerusalem this took place at the temple. The Simeon and Anna met in the temple are mentioned nowhere else. Simeon's psalm, the Nunc Dimittis, contains a number of phrases from Second Isaiah.

Luke next says that Joseph and his family returned to Nazareth. Luke pays no attention to the Matthew story of the visit of the wise men and the flight into Egypt.

While Luke tells of humble local shepherds paying homage to Jesus, Matthew reports wise men or magi coming from Persia or Mesopotamia many hundred miles away. These people probably were Zoroastrian priests, astronomers who often confused astrology with astronomy. There is little value in trying to identify the "star" although Jupiter and Saturn were in close conjunction three times in 7 B.C.

The Matthew account says that the magi consulted with Herod, whose advisers reminded him of a verse in Micah (5:2) which indicated that the hope of Israel would come from Bethlehem. This probably meant that a descendant of David, who was Bethlehem's favorite son, would be the great ruler or Messiah. It was suggested that the magi investigate Bethlehem.

The child Jesus was found in a house. Does this conflict with the pictures so often seen portraying the wise men in front of a manger? Their coming would have been considerably after the birth of the child. Better accommodations than a stable would soon have been found for the family. On the other hand, the stable or place for animals was often a part of a family's house. It was not unusual for a baby to be kept in a manger during the day.

The magi were not kings, despite our song, "We three kings of Orient are." Nor do we know that there were three magi. Church tradition has varied from three to twelve. The mention of three gifts suggests three, but these gifts may have come from a common treasury. So popular has the number three become that names have been given the visitors, Gaspar, Melchior, and Balthasar.

Joseph was afraid of Herod the Great. Herod had killed his wife, his mother-in-law, two brothers-in-law and his three oldest sons. Matthew tells us that Joseph took Mary and the child to Egypt. This may have been just south of the border into the Sinai peninsula which at that time was a part of Egypt.

After Herod the Great's death Joseph decided to return to Palestine. However the reputation of Archelaus who ruled Judea was no better than that of his father. Joseph went north of the territory of Archelaus to that of Archelaus' brother, Antipas, and settled in Nazareth. If Nazareth was his home why would Joseph give any consideration to living in Bethlehem? Again we get a hint that the Matthew compiler thought Joseph was a Bethlehemite. With his tendency to tie into the Old Testament as much as possible, the Matthew writer seems to play on a statement made about Samson in Judges 13:5, "The boy shall be a Nazarite," which meant that he should be set aside to the service of God.

Matthew tells nothing more about the infancy of Jesus. Luke bridged the gap between John's infancy and adulthood by saying (1:80), "The child grew and became strong in spirit, and he was in the wilderness till the day of his manifestation to Israel." He does the same thing with Jesus twice. In 2:30 he says "The child grew and became strong, filled with wisdom; and the favor of God was upon him." In the last verse of the same chapter Luke records, "Jesus increased in wisdom and in stature, and in favor with God and man," pointing out Jesus' four-square development.

Between these two statements Luke gives the one story we have of Jesus' boyhood. The Gospel of Thomas tells some wild stories of Jesus as an exhibitionist and boy wonder, but the church universally rejected these.

The Jews had three major and two minor festival occasions centering about the temple at Jerusalem. Great crowds of men

44

and some women came to these feasts, especially the first three. Of these the spring festival called the Passover was the most important. Between his twelfth and thirteenth birthdays a boy was accepted as one of the men, at what was called the Bar Mitzvah ceremony. Something similar to this is done in many other groups around the world. Most Protestants accept young people into church membership about this period. When his parents went to Jerusalem to the Passover after Jesus had reached the age of twelve the boy went along.

This is probably the first time Jesus really saw Jerusalem. He had heard much of the holy city and its temple. Now he could investigate it for himself. He had considerable freedom and doubtless gave his boyish curiosity full play during the seven days of festivity. When the group which Joseph and Mary had joined started back toward Nazareth Jesus failed to go with them. Men stayed quite a bit to themselves and women would be busy telling each other of their experiences in the city. Doubtless each parent thought Jesus was with the other. It was evening before they discovered otherwise. This necessitated a trip back and a search for the boy.

Eventually the parents "found him in the temple, sitting among the teachers, listening to them and asking them questions." Of course this was not within the temple proper which was entered only by priests, but in one of the outer corridors or porches. The title often given to a famous painting of this scene, "The Boy Jesus Teaching in the Temple" is somewhat misleading.

Jesus seemed to be a bit surprised at the concern of his parents. He answered, "Didn't you know that I must be about the things of my Father?" The word, "things" did not seem definite enough to the King James translators. They therefore rendered the sentence, "Wist ye not that I must be about my Father's business?" Since the problem in Mary's mind was where Jesus was, the translation, "Did you not know that I must be in my Father's house?" seems more likely correct.

Jesus' use of the word Father in referring to God is quoted by some people as a recognition upon the part of Jesus at this early age that he was in a peculiar sense *the* son of God. This is something like wishful thinking. "Father" was a highly respectful title given to God. It was used only six or seven times in the Old Testament, but in other Jewish writings shortly before the time of Jesus it was quite commonly employed. Jesus was using the vocabulary of his time, doubtless that of the teachers to whom he was listening.

Most lists of names in the Bible are commonly by-passed, but they have values to those who study them carefully. Both the Matthew editor and Luke found lists of the ancestors of Jesus. Both writers were setting forth their conviction that Jesus was the hoped for Messiah. Since the Messiah was expected to be "great David's greater son" it was generally expected that he would be a blood descendant of David. Both genealogies emphasize the same thing Paul emphasized in Rom. 1:3 that Jesus was "descended from David." Although the Matthew account was made for Jewish readers, the first four verses of Matthew's genealogy contain the names of three foreign women, not descendants of Abraham. It also contains the name of another woman whose first husband had been a foreigner. Was this to tie Jesus in with non-Jews? Perhaps Luke emphasizes the same thing by carrying his list back before Abraham to the origin of the human race. It might also be noted that two of the women in Matthew were prostitutes, professional or otherwise. Bible writers do not try to cover up unpleasant bits of history.

The Matthew and Luke genealogies do not agree. Matthew has twenty-seven names between David and Jesus; Luke forty-two. Matthew traces Jesus' descent from David through Solomon and a group of kings. Luke traces it through David's little known son Nathan and other less outstanding individuals. When confronted with the two genealogies some people have suggested that one is a list of ancestors of Mary. However, records of women were never kept—when a woman married she became part of her husband's family. Both accounts definitely say they are lists of the ancestors of Joseph.

Sometimes the beauty and significance of the accounts of the birth and early childhood of Jesus are lost to Christians today because of differences of opinion about details. Our Bible contains much of poetry and figure of speech. We cannot agree where to draw the line between such poetic expression and fact. The importance to the human race of the man whose birth is sung in these chapters grows through the centuries with the increase of human knowledge.

We know almost nothing of Jesus' youth and young adulthood. It would seem quite evident that Joseph died not long after Jesus childhood visit to the temple. Thus the widow Mary was left with five boys and at least two girls. We have the names of the boys. In addition to Jesus there were James, Joseph (or Joses), Simon and Judas. Names of the girls are not given. They are simply mentioned in the plural. There may have been more than two.

Who were these brothers and sisters of Jesus? We commonly consider them children of Joseph and Mary, younger than Jesus. Some Christian groups in the Middle East say that they were children of Joseph by an earlier marriage. Roman Catholics insist that they were not brothers and sisters, but cousins.

It would appear that Jesus as the oldest brother was responsible for the family after the death of Joseph, that he followed Joseph in the carpenter business and found it necessary to remain at home until the other members of the family had grown up, the boys had jobs and the girls husbands. Jesus learned to read and write in the synagogue school. The Hebrew scriptures were his text book. He came to know them thoroughly. His study of them caused him to be dissatisfied with the religion about him. He saw many instances where current religious practice was contrary to what he was convinced was the will of God. The emphasis upon form and rule, upon the offering of sacrifices, was distasteful to him. Jesus doubtless longed to be able to spend less time in the carpenter shop, visit other communities, and share some of his understanding of God.

Assignment

1. What differences do you find between the Matthew and Luke accounts of the birth and infancy of Jesus?
2. Identify (a) Simeon, (b) Anna.

Supplementary Reading

1. Laymon, Charles W. *The Life and Teachings of Jesus*. New York and Nashville: Abingdon Press, 1955. Chapter 5.

CHAPTER 6

"The Devil Tempted Him"

Read Mk. 1:1-20; Matt. 3:4; Lu. 3:1-22; 4:1-30; John 1:19-42

Was John the Baptizer an Essene? The more the Dead Sea scrolls reveal about this group the more we are inclined to think that John may have lived at the great Qumran settlement of Essenes near the northern end of the Dead Sea. Tradition says that John was born about four miles west of Jerusalem. We have nothing of John's youth and early manhood. Luke concludes the story of his birth by stating: "And the child grew and became strong in spirit, and he was in the wilderness till the day of his manifestation to Israel" (1:80). John must have belonged to some monastic group. Luke returns to the story of John by saying that "the word of God came to John the son of Zechariah in the wilderness; and he went into all the region about the Jordan preaching" (3:2-3). If John was an Essene he deserted the monastic life to share his ideas with the crowds he could attract.

So novel and startling was this new preacher along the lower Jordan river that Mark says, "There went out to him all the country of Judea, and all the people of Jerusalem" (1:5). Instead of criticizing Mark for exaggerating, the Matthew writer adds, "and all the region about the Jordan" (3:5).

Like other writings, there is much in our Bible that cannot be taken literally. We might ask, in all that region was there no one sick in bed, no one in jail? In America we brag that we call a spade a spade, but even here we are told that everybody is going to the fair or to a sale. We do not call the announcer or the advertiser a liar. The Oriental uses many more figures of speech than does the Westerner. The new preacher, John, did not hesitate to use such terms. Both Matthew and Luke report him to have called his audience, "You brood of vipers." He said that one who would come after him would baptize with fire, "his winnowing fork is

48

in his hand . . . the chaff he will burn with unquenchable fire."
We must learn to search for the truths behind these figurative
expressions found throughout our Bible.

John, the son of Zechariah and Elizabeth, had developed into
a rough, vigorous outdoor man. He was disgusted with the artificial niceties of the religion of both the Pharisees and the Sadducees. In startling terminology he was demanding reform. He
insisted that the Hebrew religion of his time must be rethought.
People must get a new mind relative to religious matters. That
is the meaning of *repent*. How often religious terms have come to
be stereotyped, their original meaning forgotten! We need to
examine the root meaning of our religious vocabulary, tear words
apart, and discover of what they are made. *Re* is a familiar root.
We have it in such words as re-enter, re-read, re-emphasize, It
means *again*. The root *pent* or *pens* is found in our word *pensive*,
thoughtful, and the French verb, *penser*, to think. In Spanish,
Italian, Portuguese the verb to think is quite similar. Repent, then
means to re-think, re-evaluate—not to be sad or cry. The latter may
be the result of repenting, but happiness may also be the result.

John was convinced that Yahweh was greatly displeased at the
religious expression of the Jews, that the Day of the Lord long
expected by the Hebrew people was about to be realized. He believed with some of the Old Testament prophets that this day
would be one of justice, even more—of vengeance. He was sure
that those whose religion was one of form, of feeling safe because
they were descendants of Abraham and therefore God's pets, were
about to experience "the wrath to come." Those whose religion
had not made them helpful to less fortunate people around them
would be destroyed. "Even now the ax is laid to the root of the
trees; every tree therefore that does not bear good fruit is cut
down and thrown into the fire" (Lu. 3:9) .

Those who wished to accept his ideas and follow his directions
John recognized by a symbolic washing. Baptism had been used
by various religions. Jews used it with their Gentile converts.
Doubtless some of John's audience resented his use of baptism,
saying that they were already Jews and had no need to be baptized. John probably felt that they had deserted the real Israel
and needed to be converted, brought back into the religion as
Gentiles were. The symbolism was that of washing away the past,

49

getting a clean start. John used it as an initiation into his band of followers. The Essenes made frequent use of such washings. Washings were also used as a part of certain temple ceremonies.

We do not know what mode of baptism John used. Possibly his converts stood knee-deep in the shallow Jordan while he poured a gourd or handful of water over each of them. He may have put his initiates completely under the water to symbolize the cleansing of the entire personality. The person baptized may have dipped himself under the water in the presence of witnesses. However, the majority of Christians, taking over this method of initiation from John, have used the simple form of sprinkling. As a narrow wedding ring is just as much a symbol of marriage as a wide ring, so a small amount of water can symbolize spiritual cleansing just as much as can a large amount of water.

Baptism came to symbolize a separation from the heathen world. Early in church history Christians felt that there should be a symbol to indicate that their children did not belong to the heathen community. Therefore infant baptism was instituted. With this the parents vow before God and a group of people to rear the child in Christian teaching. The child is expected to confirm this pledge at an age of responsibility, that is, to make his own statement of a desire to be Christian.

Word of John's reform movement reached Nazareth. In Jesus' carpenter shop there doubtless were heated discussions about John's heresies. (While we take for granted that Jesus supported his family by work as a carpenter until he was about thirty, it is possible that he too spent some time in a monastery. Celibacy was not practiced in Jewish villages. His being classed as a teacher and his extensive knowledge of the Hebrew scriptures suggest a schooling much as one might receive in a monastic community. He used ideas which the Dead Sea scrolls now reveal were already held by the Essenes. This strengthens the suggestion.) Jesus became interested in the positive active religion of John. It was much as he thought religion should be. Therefore he went to the lower Jordan to hear John. The message appealed to him and he decided to become one of John's followers, to be initiated into the fellowship. Jesus therefore was baptized by John.

The synoptic gospels all report that Jesus had a spiritual experience of special significance in connection with his baptism. Luke says that he was in prayer. All say that he felt the spirit of God upon him and that God was calling him his beloved son with whom he was well pleased. Is this the first time that Jesus felt a special relationship with God? This experience does not prove that Jesus then felt that he was the Messiah. The varying gospel accounts make it difficult to determine just when Jesus came to consider himself the Messiah.

Jesus took his religion seriously, although he was not one of the professional religious people. He must have asked many questions about John: Was he going far enough? Was he too harsh? Did he put too much emphasis on fear? To what degree did he understand the will of God? Jesus decided that he must think through his own program, determine whether to follow John or make a different approach. He therefore went off by himself for six weeks of solitary prayer and planning—we find him doing this for shorter periods a number of times during his ministry. Mark explains, "The Spirit immediately drove him out into the wilderness" (1:12). Evidently Q gave more detail than Mark. Both Matthew and Luke tell of the type of problems Jesus faced. In vivid figurative language they record this in the form of three temptations. The order of the temptations is not the same in the two accounts. Doubtless they were involved, all present at the same time. These temptations kept coming back to Jesus during his entire ministry. The three described here were not the only ones Jesus faced. A late New Testament writer refers to Jesus as "one who in every respect has been tempted as we are" (Heb. 4:15).

Temptations were pictured as coming from the devil. One of the last writings in the New Testament proclaims, "Let no one say when he is tempted, 'I am tempted by God'; for God cannot be tempted with evil and he himself tempts no one" (Jas. 1:13).

With the scarcity of food in the wilderness Jesus' mind would be called to the need of many people for food. He had noted hunger all about him. Why not push an agricultural program? Why not dedicate his life to raising the economic standards of his people? Hebrew prophets had often dreamed of the time when there would be plenty of food for all. Could not Jesus fulfill the hopes of these men of God? Although he would later teach his disciples to pray, "Give us this day our daily bread," he knew that loaves and fishes were not the most important thing in life. "Man shall not live by bread alone, but by every word that proceeds from the mouth of God." (Matt. 4:4). There is something more important than economic goods.

If Jesus was to give people this word of God he must get their attention. Why not go to the heart of the Jewish religon, the temple, and do something spectacular, like jumping off the top of the Roman watch-tower or off the temple wall? He would have a guardian angel. He recalled the 91st Psalm in which it was asserted that "He who dwells in the shelter of the Most High" will be protected. Many people find their greatest satisfaction in getting into the public eye. Why should he not do so in a good cause? But Jesus knew his scripture well. Another verse came to his mind as if it were an answer to the verse from the Psalms. This answer was Deut. 6:16, "You shall not tempt the Lord your God," ask God to cancel his laws for you, make you his special pet.

Perhaps Jesus' approach should be through politics, government. That would be popular. The Jews despised being controlled by a foreign power, Rome. In imagination Jesus could see all the kingdoms of the world and the glory of them. Perhaps all that the people needed was a leader to overcome the oppressor, as was the case when the Midianites were driven out by a small group inspired by Gideon (Judges 7), or when the Ammonites were driven back because Jephthah had been willing to lead his countrymen to battle (Judges 11). There were millions of Jews throughout the Roman world. These people would come under his leadership. The dream many Jews had of turning the tables, of making Romans their servants, could be fulfilled. Perhaps he could be a great emperor and get his people the good things they lacked. Would this be serving God or would it be glorifying himself? Might not this be serving mammon? As if in answer to these questions there came to his mind another verse from the sixth chapter of Deuteronomy, the 13th, "You shall worship the Lord your God and him only shall you serve." No, political power was a temptation that must be resisted. Jesus would not become a tool for the nationalist ambitions of his fellow Jews.

Service to his fellowmen, helping people understand the word and will of God, must be Jesus' program. He was to tell his friends

52

at a later time, "He who is greatest among you shall be your servant" (Matt. 23:11).

If this was to be Jesus' life work he must lose no time. The Mark and Matthew accounts point out that John's preaching was brought to a halt by his being arrested by Herod Antipas. The early church thought of Christianity as a continuation and expansion of John's program. Jesus was later to say, "Among those born of women there has risen no one greater than John the Baptist" (Matt. 11:11). To become a successor to John was to court the same fate. Jesus courageously took up the work of John with a somewhat different emphasis and in a different setting. He went back to his home region and began sharing his ideas with whoever would listen to him. Synagogues offered him a chance to talk with religiously minded Jews. Consequently he visited various Galilean synagogues. At Capernaum he found four sympathetic young fishermen who accepted his invitation to become his associates: Simon Peter, Andrew his brother, James and his brother John. Most of those who became closely associated with Jesus were young people.

At this point Luke inserts a lengthy narrative about Jesus' experience in his home town, Nazareth. He was accustomed to worshipping at the synagogue on the Sabbath. As usual he went to the local synagogue. The shema was recited. Prayers were chanted by the cantor. The prescribed portion of the Torah was read and translated from the ancient Hebrew to Aramaic. Then Jesus was invited to read any portion he chose from the prophets and to address the congregation.

Jesus asked for the Isaiah scroll. All three Isaiah writings were copied on one scroll. He unrolled it to near the end, the 61st chapter. From this he read a little more than a verse. It is interesting that he broke off his reading just before the reference to the "vengeance of our God". Did he not believe in a vengeful God? Was this one point where he differed from John?

In his study of the scriptures Jesus had found here five planks for his platform, five phases of life with which he felt religion must deal. The first plank is "Good news to the poor." This is not "pie in the sky when you die." To the poor, good news is economic help now. Had not Jesus just rejected the economic as his life program? At no point does Jesus attack money or economic good as such. He insists that they must be kept in their proper place, not made the whole of life. An interpreter of Jesus was to say later, "The *love* of money is the root of all evils" (1 Tim. 6:10).

Jesus' five planks may well be compared to the five fingers of the hand. If any one is missing the hand is inefficient. If one should grow two or three times as long as the others, the hand would be very cumbersome. All five fingers or elements in the program of religion must be developed in much the same proportions.

"Release to the captives" would suggest to Jesus' listeners an interest in government, for they all were acquainted with political captives, people who had raised their voices against Roman oppression. When Jesus was a boy of ten or twelve in Nazareth, a Galilean named Judas had led a revolt against Rome. Many of Jesus' neighbors had been executed as a result; others had been imprisoned. Jesus was concerned with freedom of expression, political freedom.

"Recovering of sight to the blind" symbolized Jesus' great interest in physical health. He spent much time helping those who were physically and mentally ill. "To set at liberty those who are oppressed" referred to the great psychological needs of mankind, those conditions which lead to unhappiness, divorce, suicide, murder. "The acceptable year of the Lord" is sometimes interpreted (possibly imaginatively) as social, being acceptable, getting along with other people, a need all of us have.

These five planks of Jesus' platform, however we interpret them, constitute the spiritual program to which Jesus had dedicated his life. He had gone beyond the program of John. This was Jesus' answer to the temptations that came to him during his six weeks in the wilderness. To what degree is the church today concerned with these five factors?

With his universal interest Luke points out that Jesus told his congregation that his program was for all people, that God has no pets. He went on to illustrate his contention by giving two illustrations with which his hearers should be familiar. One was that of Elijah's helping a Phoenician woman as told in 1 Kings 17:8-24. The other was that of Elisha's helping the Syrian general Naaman as told in 2 Kings 5:1-14. Jesus was not praising or soothing his audience. His was not an orthodox sermon. His neighbors were angry that their local carpenter should think them no better than these foreigners. Therefore they attempted to lynch him, but Jesus escaped from them.

Mark and Matthew tell of another time when Jesus visited his own country and preached in the synagogue. Again the people were critical of preaching by a carpenter, the son of a carpenter. "And he did not do many mighty works there, because of their unbelief" (Matt. 13:58). It is possible that these two stories are two understandings of the same event.

For Class Discussion

1. Why did Jesus have John baptize him?
2. What is the devil?

Assignment

1. Make a list of hyperboles or figures of speech, used by your friends.
2. List the religious ideas of John the Baptist; the social ideas.
3. What three types of temptation is Jesus reported to have met in the wilderness? How is each discussed in the Q account?
4. List the five planks of Jesus' platform and with each of these give an illustration of what the church is doing now to further these aims.

Supplementary Reading

1. Kraeling, Emil G. *Rand McNally Bible Atlas.* New York: Rand McNally & Co., 1956. Pages 367-384.
2. Laymon, Charles M. *The Life and Teachings of Jesus.* New York and Nashville: Abingdon Press, 1955. Chapters 7, 8, 9.

CHAPTER 7

"You Have Heard That It Was Said"

Read Mt. 5 and Lu. 6:17-36

The Matthew compiler brought together the gist of the teaching of Jesus in the three chapters we call the Sermon on the Mount. Luke handles this material in Q in a different way. He has a short sermon, part of one chapter, but much of the remainder of the Matthew sermon is scattered through Luke's account. Luke put these teachings of Jesus where he felt they had been given. Matthew put them into his account as a summary of Christianity, the cornerstone of our religion. Although we speak of the Sermon on the Mount in superlative terms, we must remember that it does not contain every teaching of Jesus. With his Jewish emphasis the compiler of Matthew may have thought of Jesus as a new Moses giving a new law for a new Israel.

The Matthew account opens with a collection of nine statements we call the Beatitudes. This term comes from the Latin word with which each statement is introduced and which in English we call "Blessed." What does blessed mean? Synonyms are happy, contented, satisfied, fortunate. This does not refer to a frothy, "hip, hip, hooray" kind of happiness, but a deeper, more lasting joy. As used here and in other places in the Bible it might be paraphrased, "I congratulate you."

The poor in spirit are congratulated. This first beatitude could quite properly be translated, "The poor in spirit are blessed because the kingdom of heaven is theirs." These are the people who recognize their spiritual needs. Is this a spiritualized version of the beatitude in Luke, "Blessed are you poor, for yours is the kingdom of God?" Or, was the Matthew statement the original one, which Luke, in his interest in the under-dog, changed? That Luke's is the original statement is suggested by the woes which

56

Luke reports, "Woe to you that are rich, for you have received your consolation" (6:24). Jesus doubtless knew many poor people in Nazareth whom he admired. He felt that they had satisfactions in life that no financial riches could buy.

"Blessed are the meek, for they shall inherit the earth" is practically a quotation from Ps. 37:11. It parallels the first beatitude. The terms, "poor in spirit" and "meek" may easiest be explained by giving their opposites. The poor in spirit are the opposite of the proud in spirit, boastful, arrogant. The meek are the opposite of the aggressive, domineering. Jesus had observed that these latter people often ended up with very little other than failure. Jesus did not make rules. He recognized the way human relations work, the laws of the universe, and put them into words. Gravity existed long before the day of Newton. Newton did not make the law of gravity. He analyzed it, put it into a mathematical formula. In a similar way Jesus put God's laws regarding human relations into simple statements.

Long before the time of Jesus there were dinosaurs in the world. There were also ants. The dinosaurs were aggressive, noncooperative. Ants learned to cooperate. The dinosaur is no longer. The ants have inherited the earth. At one time there were probably as many lions in the world as sheep. The aggressive, dominating lion now has very little of the earth. The sheep has more than held his own. So with human dictators. How much of the earth did any one of them control for any great length of time?

The Matthew beatitude, "Blessed are those who mourn, for they shall be comforted," has its parallel in Luke, "Blessed are you that weep now, for you shall laugh." This beatitude sounds like a contradiction. How can one who mourns be happy? Yet it contains several truths. We do not know which one or ones Jesus had in mind. One who mourns the death of a dear one turns his mind to the good qualities of the departed and finds a satisfaction in recalling them. Jesus may have been referring to one who shares the sadness of another, who does what Paul advocated when later he taught "Bear one another's burdens" (Gal. 6:2). Satisfaction comes to one who realizes that he is helping another bear his burden. Jesus could have been referring to those who mourn for their sins or the sins of the group to which they belong. Recognizing one's sin is the first step in overcoming it. Jesus may well

57

have had in mind the advice of Joel 2:12-13, "Return to me . . . with mourning, and rend your hearts and not your garments."

Luke reports Jesus as saying, "Blessed are you that hunger now, for you shall be satisfied." In Matthew the term "hunger" has become "hunger and thirst for righteousness." The Matthew analogy is easily understood. One who is hungry enjoys food more than one who has no appetite. The person who really wants to live right will find blessing or satisfaction in achieving his aim. Jesus' listeners may have recalled Ps. 42:2, "My soul thirsts for God."

"Blessed are the merciful, for they shall obtain mercy," may well be compared with Jesus' statement in Lu. 6:38, "The measure you give will be the measure you get back." Later in Matthew we find Jesus criticizing the Pharisees for neglecting mercy (23:23). Mercy was despised by the Romans and little used by Greeks. Jesus was making a needed emphasis in religion. In the sixth beatitude Jesus noted that it is the impurities of life that draw a screen between us and God. Jesus found the Pharisees laying great importance upon ceremonial purity. His insistence was on inner purity. Perhaps he was reminding the Pharisees that Ps. 24:4-5 puts much more emphasis on a pure heart than on clean hands.

Luke's concern for peace is reflected in the angelic song at the birth of Jesus (2:14). It appears again in the seventh beatitude. As God wants peace among men, those who bring about peace will be called sons of God. Has everyone who has tried to bring peace between two people who were fighting always been commended? If not, was Jesus wrong? Or are his beatitudes statements of averages, the way situations generally work out? This is likewise true of our laws of nature. Not every atom acts the same way as all other atoms.

One wonders how near the end of his life Jesus gave the last two beatitudes. How much had he been persecuted? Those who are persecuted for their Christian living and witness will be in a noble tradition. The Luke account recommends "Rejoice in that day, and leap for joy" (6:23).

In the next section of the Sermon on the Mount, are the references to light and salt related? In telling his listeners that they are the salt of the earth does Jesus mean that they give zest or tang to life? A small boy is reported to have defined salt as "That which makes potatoes taste bad without." Salt had another very important value in the Palestine of Jesus' day, that of preserving food. Fish taken from the Sea of Galilee to Jerusalem in the summer would have spoiled had they not been salted. Could Jesus have meant that people should be a preserving power, conserving that which was good in the past? Light has value in seeing ahead, showing the way. Could Jesus have meant, You must save the best of the old and keep looking forward for better things, be both conservative and progressive? Do people who brag about their conservatism or "fundamentalism" miss as much of complete Christianity as those who, seeing no value in the past, constantly emphasize their progressiveness or "modernism"? John makes several references to Jesus' being the light of the world. In one of them he reports Jesus as saying, "As long as I am in the world I am the light of the world" (9:5). Does this imply that his followers must carry on this lightgiving?

Jesus demonstrated conserving and pushing forward at the same time in the following section of the Sermon. He insisted that his purpose was not to destroy the law and the prophets, the common term for the Hebrew scriptures. He not only would keep them but do more; fulfill, fill full, round out, complete them. He recognized that the Hebrew religion was good, but not good enough. He must fill in the empty places, take care of the inadequacies. God's demands are more than legalistic. They are ethical, moral, and must never be watered down. Could we say that Jesus meant he had come to improve the teachings of the Old Testament?

In the next few paragraphs Jesus deals with Old Testament laws. Moses had been considered the great lawgiver, getting his instructions while on Mount Sinai. Could the Matthew compiler have seen a fitting analogy here and put together Jesus' new laws as part of a sermon delivered on another mountain? Jesus was not dogmatic, but he spoke authoritatively. His was not a secondhand religion. He was patient, but he knew definitely what he meant.

Matthew gives six instances of inadequacies of the Old Testament. The first two mentioned are from the Ten Commandments: "You shall not kill" and "You shall not commit adultery." Jesus does not feel that these commands are wrong. Like a good physician he believes that the cause of the trouble should be discovered and eradicated. Murder is the result of anger, hate. Adultery is the result of lust. If these causes are eliminated murder and adultery will be abolished. Jesus emphasizes the importance of getting rid of causes with two vivid analogies, saying that if an eye or a hand is the source of trouble, get rid of it. People have been known to cut off a hand that participated in theft. Does Jesus teach that one should literally destroy his hand? How about a case of gangrene? Jesus uses a similar analogy in Matt. 18:8-9.

Jesus recognizes that sin is more than acts. There are sins of the mind and spirit. Sin is what a man *is*. Regardless of how they live, Christians in general give lip service to the teachings of Jesus with the possible exception of his statements regarding divorce. We are not sure just what Jesus taught. Both here and in Matt. 19:3-9 Jesus is reported to have said that there must be no divorce except in cases of unchastity. However, in Mk. 10:2-12 and Lu. 16:18 Jesus makes no exception whatever. Did the Matthew writers feel this was too rigid and add the qualifying phrase? A man could get a divorce "for any cause" such as deciding that he wanted a younger or prettier wife. A woman could not get a divorce, although under certain limited conditions she could force her husband to divorce her. Did Jesus feel that men and women should have equal rights and therefore prohibit divorce? Before any gospel account was written Paul quotes Jesus as making no exception. However, Paul was bothered about heathens who wanted to separate from Christian husbands or wives (1 Cor. 7:10-16).

Old Testament characters frequently took oaths. Although these people often had objectionable qualities, we must admire their insistence upon keeping their oaths. Ps. 15:4 commends one "who swears to his own hurt and does not change." The rabbis of Jesus' time discussed at length whether or not swearing was to be permitted. Jesus took a definite stand. He felt that swearing indicated that lying had become a habit. He insisted that the Christian should develop such a reputation that men knew his "yes" was "yes," his "no" was "no." Today we might raise the question as to whether Jesus' teaching applies to profanity or to oaths in court. Why do we have oaths in court? Is it not that otherwise some people might lie, that calling God to witness may convince others that the statement is true? Why profanity? Is it not, in a crude form, largely for the same reason?

What is profanity? Is not superstition, putting a black cat or a four-leaf clover in the place of God, more blasphemous than the misuse of divine names? How many people recognize their own profane vocabulary? What is the origin of such terms as Lordy, Gosh, Zounds, Gee?

Jesus took issue with the statement in the Book of the Covenant that one should retaliate "an eye for an eye and a tooth for a tooth" (Ex. 21:24). This had been an improvement over the philosophy of Lamech (Gen. 4:23, 24), but itself had been softened to some extent by the setting up of cities of refuge (Joshua 20). The element of forgiveness was suggested by the prophets but only meagerly developed as contrasted with Jesus' teaching that one should forgive seventy times seven (Matt. 18: 22). Jesus insisted that an evil person should not be resisted. The King James translators blundered here, making Jesus say that evil should not be resisted. God loves the sinner but not sin. Jesus felt that evil should be retaliated with love. Jesus' teaching was expressed by Paul later, "Do not be overcome by evil, but overcome evil with good" (Rom. 12:21). Like Elisha and some of the writing prophets, Jesus knew that the best way to destroy an enemy was to make him a friend. According to Roman law a soldier of the empire could force an individual to carry the soldier's load for him. Rome felt it was very just in limiting this to one mile. Jesus suggested that instead of resenting such conscription one might well surprise the one making the demand by going twice as far as required. Those who have followed the recommendation of Jesus have found great satisfaction in doing so. M. K. Gandhi of India, the "Mahatma," based his non-violent resistance program on this teaching of Jesus. When others use this method, should it be called the Gandhian method or the method of Jesus?

The sixth point at which Jesus went beyond the Old Testament is in the same vein. One must love even his enemy. God has no pets, makes no distinctions. We should be God-like, not choose the object of our love, but love the unlovable.

Assignment

1. Define the term "blessed."
2. What did Jesus mean by (a) the salt of the earth? (b) the light of the world?
3. What is meant by "the Law and the Prophets"? What was Jesus' attitude toward them?
4. List the six points at which Jesus went beyond the Old Testament and tell in each instance his teaching.

Supplementary Reading

1. *The Interpreter's Bible*. New York and Nashville: Abingdon Press, Vol. 7, 1951. Pages 155-164, 278-304.
2. Bowman, John Wick, and Tapp, Roland W. *The Gospel from the Mount*. Philadelphia: The Westminster Press, 1957. Pages 11-105.

CHAPTER 8

"Piety Before Men"

Read Matt. 6, 7 and Lu. 6:37-49; 11:1-14

Alms-giving, prayer, and fasting were considered by the Pharisees to be the three pillars of Judaism. These did not require the temple but could be practiced by Jews anywhere. Jesus had no objection to giving and praying, probably none to fasting. But Jesus did object to doing these things in such a way as to squeeze praise from other people. Jesus disdained religious artificiality. Giving, praying, fasting must be done with all sincerity before God. Each of these acts must be a private relation between the individual and God. Some early scribe and the King James translators missed the point by stating in the 4th, 6th and 18th verses that God would openly reward those who gave, prayed or fasted. The earliest copies of our scriptures do not have the word "openly" in any of these verses. Note the type of figure of speech Jesus often employed when he said, "Do not let your left hand know what your right hand is doing."

Jesus' teaching about prayer will be discussed in Chapter 14. In connection with the Lord's Prayer given here in Matthew two points may well be noted. The first is Matt. 6:12, "Forgive us our debts, as we also have forgiven our debtors." Why do many Christian people say, "Forgive us our trespasses?" No English translation of the Bible in common use today has the word trespasses at this point. However, Tyndale used the word. His translation was used in making the prayer book of the Church of England. This wording carried over into the American Protestant Episcopal Church and the Methodist churches and has influenced some local churches of other denominations. Jesus was not limiting his thoughts to financial obligations or to getting on some one else's real estate. "Sins" (as given in Lu. 11:4), "offences", "faults," "failings," or "shortcomings" have been used in other translations. Possibly these represent what Jesus had in mind better than either "debts" or "trespasses." However, sin was thought of by the Jews as unfilled obligation or debt owed to God.

What has become of the concluding doxology, "For thine is the kingdom and the power and the glory, forever, Amen"? The footnote in the Revised Standard Version explains this. Evidently it was not in the prayer as originally given by Jesus. Some early Christians felt the prayer was incomplete. Therefore, they loosely borrowed a phrase from a prayer of David given in 1 Chro. 29:11 and added it.

Fasting is depriving the body of its normal satisfactions in order to maintain the supremacy of the spirit over the body. Fasting is common to many religions, early Judaism, Hinduism, Islam. Jesus is referred to as fasting during his wilderness temptation experience. If he fasted after that he followed his own advice to do it in secret. At one time he and his disciples were criticized for not fasting as John's disciples and the Pharisees did. Jesus answered, "Can the wedding guests fast while the bridegroom is with them? As long as they have the bridegroom with them they cannot fast. The days will come, when the bridegroom is taken away from them, and then they will fast in that day" (Mk. 2:19-20). Did Jesus expect Christians eventually to fast? To a degree some Christians fast in Lent or on Fridays.

Through the remainder of the sixth chapter Jesus demanded that men give complete devotion to the right god. Secondary things have their place, but must be kept secondary. As a keen psychologist Jesus recognized that a man's interest or concern follows his investments. If we invest in things of the spirit, educational institutions, hospitals, churches, we shall become interested in these things.

In a proverb about the eye Jesus pointed out that insight is needed, that if the spirit which guides one is selfish his whole personality becomes selfish. The importance of light rather than darkness was emphasized not only by Jesus and his followers, but also by the Essenes. One of the writings of the latter found among the Dead Sea scrolls is entitled, "The War of the Sons of Light and the Sons of Darkness." Jesus noted that one cannot serve the selfish interests of property or "mammon" and the outreaching interests of God at the same time.

Mark reports Jesus as saying, "The cares of the world, and the delight in riches, and the desire for other things, enter in and choke the word" (4:19). Jesus is saying the same thing in the Sermon on the Mount, warning not to be distracted by cares. He does not say that one should have no insurance, no social security, no provision for a "rainy day" or old age. The person who has provided for emergencies and the future, tends to be less anxious than the man who has made no such provision.

In the seventh chapter we again find Jesus attacking religious artificiality. Doubtless Jesus' disciples were prone to criticize others. He showed his broad humor by his illustration of one offering to take a speck or splinter from another's eye when he had a log or building timber in his own eye. Jesus did not mean that one should make no decisions or choices. Rather, one should avoid critical faultfinding.

The sixth verse has bothered some people. Would Jesus refer to people as dogs or swine? Paul did (Phil. 3:2), but that is contrary to the spirit of Jesus. Dogs were not man's friends but were considered along with pigs as filthy, the lowest of creation. Does not Jesus say, If you think of people as dogs or swine there is no use doing anything for them? Looking down on people will never build Christian brotherhood.

The teaching of Matt. 7:7-12 is given in Luke after the Lord's prayer. It emphasizes the importance of persistence in prayer, as well as the goodness of God. Matthew adds to this the Golden Rule. Rabbis and other religious leaders, Buddha and Confucius, emphasized the Silver Rule, Do not do anything to anyone you would not want him to do to you. Jesus went far beyond this negative approach. There are many people who are good, but good for nothing. Jesus insisted that one must be good for something, active. This is one of the most significant points at which Jesus went beyond the Old Testament. Avoiding evil is not enough. Jesus was positive. He demanded action.

The next paragraph notes the same thing. After his experience with the rich young ruler Jesus commented, "How hard it is to enter the kingdom of God" (Mk. 10:24) Here he is saying the same thing. His teaching is not limited to the future life. The good things of life do not come by sitting around. The things we want, good grades, a college degree, an important position, a good home are not found along a wide, easy road, but on the road of hard work. Few people make the most of their opportunities in life.

The remainder of the Sermon on the Mount deals with Jesus' emphasis upon the importance of action. Only as one achieves, bears fruit, can he be considered a member of the Kingdom. Form, ritual, subscribing to a creed are of no value if one does not do "the will of my Father who is in heaven."

Note that in Jesus' parable of the two houses the person who does the things Jesus taught is not guaranteed protection, safety. He can experience rain, floods, winds, but his character will be such that he will be able to survive hardships; he will not fall.

Matthew concludes by pointing out that Jesus' difference from the scribes astonished his hearers. Scribes universally quoted earlier writers or commentators to back up their ideas, making someone else responsible. Jesus almost completely avoided this. He was convinced that he was right regardless of how many differed from him: "You have heard that it was said . . . but I say." There was no "probably" or "I think so" with Jesus. His message rang out with God-given assurance. All four gospel accounts, in various connections, bear witness to the uniqueness and impressiveness of Jesus as a teacher. "All . . . wondered at the gracious words which proceeded out of his mouth" (Lu. 4:22). "They were astonished at his teaching" (Mk. 1:22). "Some . . . said, 'This is really the prophet'" (John 7:40).

For Class Discussion

Do Matt. 5:16 and Matt. 6:1-18 contradict each other?

Assignment

1. Write in your own language an outline of the Matthew Sermon on the Mount, using headings, sub-heads, and sub-sub-heads.
2. Write a short paper on the question: What do you find Jesus' own religion to be? This should not be from the standpoint of what he taught others to think and do. It should deal with the religion

Jesus had for himself. Present this under three topics: his attitude toward God, his attitude toward other people, his attitude toward himself.

Supplementary Reading

1. *The Interpreter's Bible*. New York and Nashville: Abingdon Press, Vol. 7, 1951. Pages 155-164, 278-336.
2. Bowman, John Wick, and Tapp, Roland W. *The Gospel from the Mount*. Philadelphia: The Westminster Press, 1957. Pages 107-167.
3. Braden, Charles S. *Jesus Compared*. Englewood Cliffs, N. J.: Prentice-Hall, 1957. Chapter 1.

Chapter 9

"Nothing Without a Parable"

Read: Matt. 13; 25:1-13; Lu. 11:5-8; 16:19-31

As a preacher Jesus was down to earth. The synoptic gospels
give no philosophical dissertations, no abstract regulations. To
Jesus God was very near, friendly like a father, but not soft, easy-
going. To him religion dealt with everyday affairs. Jesus saw religion in the work of the housewife, the carpenter, the farmer,
the fisherman. In his preaching Jesus was careful to use illustrations his audience understood. As in his Nazareth sermon, he at
times referred to well-known stories from the Hebrew scriptures.
He saw God working through events of the Old Testament. More
often Jesus illustrated his teachings by means of experiences he
had had in his home, experiences similar to those of his hearers.
In his teachings we see Jesus' home life: two women grinding at
the mill, the oven being heated for the baking, the working of
leaven in the dough. We hear children asking for bread, eggs,
fish, and shouting at their games. We note clothes being patched.
We see little dark houses being swept and an olive oil lamp being
used to find a lost coin. We have references to baskets and beds,
chickens and goats, moths and rust, yokes and plows.

As a youth Jesus had doubtless entertained his younger brothers
and sisters with stories. He learned that he could get across a
point by using such illustrations. He had heard rabbis in the
synagogue use stories or parables to illustrate a teaching. He had
found such stories in the scriptures. Men could not forget Nathan's
parable of the ewe lamb (2 Sam. 12:1-9). Now Jesus was a teacher.
Why not use the same method? With his supremely keen intellect
Jesus became the master teacher.

Jesus used numerous figures of speech. He employed analogies
and allegories. He spoke in pictures. However, his most common
instrument came to be the parable. A parable is a teaching story

from one phase of life running parallel to the phase of life being illustrated. If a teacher wishes to emphasize the need for the pupil to store up knowledge for the future and tells of one who failed to do so, he does not have a parable but an illustration. However, if the teacher tells of squirrels storing up nuts for the future he has a parable. A parable must also be distinguished from a fable. A parable is a story that could take place. A fable is also a story paralleling some teaching, but the fable has impossible elements in it, gives human characteristics to non-human objects. Jotham's story of trees selecting a king (Judges 9:7-15) is such a fable. A parable is not a complete allegory. It is told to illustrate only one point. The parable of the Friend at Midnight and that of the Unjust Judge are told to illustrate the importance of persistence in prayer. They do not show the character of God.

Something like thirty parables of Jesus are recorded in the synoptic accounts. Jesus doubtless told many more. The Matthew compiler inserted into his Mark sources a group of parables about the Kingdom, most of which he found in *Q*. This has become the 13th chapter of Matthew. In the 34th verse the writer makes an exaggerated statement that indicates his great respect for the parables of Jesus. He says, "All this Jesus said to the crowds in parables; indeed he said nothing to them without a parable." Within a short space the writer has Jesus using other teaching methods as well as parables. Nearly half of what Luke reports Jesus as saying is in the form of parables.

Through parables Jesus opened windows that men might see the face of God. Jesus discovered that people could remember his stories, sometimes their applications, much better than they could remember abstract reasoning. The characters and objects of Jesus' stories were familiar to all; they were immediate, not far away. They were real, not imaginary. As he sat in a fisherman's boat Jesus told the parable of the dragnet. In the royal city of Jerusalem he told of the wedding of the king's son. Jesus adapted his teaching to his hearers, used words and illustrations they understood.

Old Testament parables dealt with immediate problems which turned out to be temporary. The parables of Jesus dealt with permanent truths with which we are still concerned. They were so vivid that they could not be forgotten. Life shown in his parables is not as strange to Americans as at first thought it might seem. Some people are not so fortunate. The Eskimo has difficulty understanding references to sheep and goats. The man along the equator does not know what snow and frost are, what is meant by winter and summer. Customs our grandfathers understood are becoming less common today. With sanforized cloth Jesus' reference to sewing a new patch on an old garment may not be understood. Probably even some housewives today do not understand Jesus' reference to leaven or yeast, certainly not to new wine in old wineskins. However, some of Jesus' parables are more easily understood as we investigate the social customs, the life of Palestine of his day. Details regarding the teachings of these parables will be discussed in later chapters.

The parable of the Soils or of the Sower is the one given first in Mark. Jesus noted that "A sower went out to sow." Going out might mean going a considerable distance. As in much of the world today, the farmer in Palestine lived in a village, not on his land. He kept his farm animals in the village with him, often under the same roof. Fences were little known. Those found were stone piles formed chiefly to get rid of some of the stones with which the land was covered. Paths were often formed across the farmer's little field. Some of the grain broadcast by hand fell on these paths where it was easily spotted by birds. Often large stones were and are still left in the field to give some shade and hold a little moisture in the ground around. Palestine is very hilly. Most fields are on hillsides. To hold back some water and keep the soil from washing away the hills are terraced. The back of the terrace has very little soil over the bed-rock. The stone reflects heat, causing grain to spring up quickly, but when the roots strike stone they wither and die.

Jesus mentioned other grain falling among thorns. Thorns and thistles entwine their roots among the stones and easily choke out the young shoots of wheat. At harvest the thorns are not wasted. They are ground on the threshing floor for cattle feed, or are bound in bundles, dried, and used as fuel in baking ovens.

Jesus concluded his parable with an interesting demand: "He who has ears to hear, let him hear." His audience had heard this cry many times before. When a government order was proclaimed

70

the crier preceded it by repeating this call three times. Jesus thus emphasized the importance of his teaching.

The Matthew account follows this teaching with another parable about the sowing of grain. In this case an enemy sowed weeds in the farmer's wheat field after the good seed had been sown. Such revenge seems to have been frequent. The tare or darnel is a very obnoxious weed. The plant so resembles wheat in its early stage that the two can scarcely be distinguished. When the plants are far enough along to be recognized the roots are so entangled that it is impossible to pull out the tares without pulling out the wheat. Even at harvest time it is difficult to tell which is which. The grain of the tare is the same shape and size as wheat, but slate-gray in color. After the wheat has been thrashed the grain is spread in large pans. Women are employed to pick out the darnel.

Darnel makes satisfactory chicken feed, but animals and people are nauseated by eating it. People still sometimes suffer from having darnel in grain or flour they buy. Such people may be heard to curse the merchant: "May he spend the price of what he sold us at the funerals of his children! May God destroy his home!"

The Matthew list gives a third parable of a man sowing. This one is relative to the yellow-flowering black mustard. It grows to a height of twelve feet, but we should scarcely call it a tree.

To emphasize the idea of the Kingdom growing from very small beginnings, Jesus gave another parable, one from the home. His listeners all had observed the process of bread-making. Leaven or yeast was considered a symbol of growth or fecundity. A bride was given a lump of leaven to symbolize the hope that she would have many children. She would paste this lump over the door before entering the house of her husband.

A lump of sour dough, the "starter," was saved from each baking and preserved in dry flour. At bread-making time water was added to the flour and the whole mixed in a wooden trough. Moisture and heat caused the yeast to form gas. This penetrated all the flour, making it expand or rise. The dough was then made into small, round, flat loaves. The family oven, or probably more often a community oven, was heated by burning tares, straw, or

71

other refuse in it, after which the ashes were drawn out and the loaves put into the oven for baking.

Some of Jesus' closest friends were fishermen. From the practice of fishermen Jesus drew an analogy regarding the Kingdom. Various kinds of nets were employed, but the one referred to in Matt. 13 is the dragnet used in catching fish that swim in shoals or schools. The nets are long and narrow, having floats at the top and weights at the bottom. Sometimes such nets are used from the shore as they were in the time of Jesus. More often they are cast from fishing boats, one boat at each end of a net. Sometimes bait is thrown into the water between the net and the shore. As the net is dragged it becomes a wall. The ends are hauled together forming a mesh prison which is pulled to shore.

Sitting on the ground, the fishermen separate the fish into three groups. One group is composed of "clean" fish having fins and scales (Lev. 11:9-12) to be sold to Jewish customers. Another is fish that others would eat. The third is fish no one would eat. These are thrown away or used as fertilizer.

Only Matthew has the parable of the Ten Maidens (25:1-13). Weddings are the greatest events in oriental family life. They are celebrations of much eating and drinking, singing and dancing. They are community festivities. Much of the feasting and celebrating takes place at night. Some of the festivities are participated in only by men; others by the women alone.

A practice found yet today in a variety of forms is indicated by Jesus' parable. While the groom is celebrating at the home of friends, the bride is taken by her companions to her future home. There she is dressed in her wedding finery while there is much eating and chatter. Toward midnight the groom is brought to his home in a torch-light procession which can be heard and seen quite a distance away. The young women then come out with their lamps to receive the men. One without a burning lamp would be disgraced. Those who had failed to provide extra oil would have a difficult time awakening a merchant from whom to buy more oil. Even if they succeeded they might find the wedding feast going on without them, the door shut to any late comers.

Another midnight event is reported in one of the parables recorded by Luke, that of the Friend at Midnight. Before the use of modern transportation the cool of the evening was the time often chosen for a summer journey, as the sun was too hot during the day. Sometimes these journeys lasted well into the night. A man wishing to visit a friend could not conveniently send word that he was coming. Therefore the unexpected appearance at midnight.

Water for washing hands, face and feet, and a space for sleeping were always provided. Oriental courtesy would generally require the host to furnish food. If there should be no bread on hand the hostess would recall which neighbor had baked that day and send her husband to borrow some bread while she made other preparations for a meal.

Jesus suggested that the neighbor's husband might be unwilling to disturb his family to secure the requested food. "My children are with me in bed." Most houses had but one room. All members of the family slept on mats on the floor. During the day the mats were rolled up and put away. At night the father would sleep nearest the door in the position of a guard. To get to the shelf where the bread was kept might waken the baby or others. The three loaves requested would furnish a hearty meal for the average adult.

The 15th chapter of Luke reports three parables given by Jesus to point out how important to God the individual is, God's love for the lost. The first, that of the Lost Sheep, is also given in Matthew. The Jews' greatest heroes had been shepherds, Abraham, Moses, and David. Jews never tired of stories of shepherds. Sheep and goats were and still are among the most important products of Palestine. They are able to find a living on land so steep and rocky as to make agriculture impossible.

A shepherd looked after not more than a hundred sheep. Often he had an assistant shepherd. The sheep were his own, those of his employer, or more often his own and those of some of his neighbors. He must find water and pasture. Sometimes this meant traveling considerable distance from home. If he was able to bring his sheep home at night they were kept in a fold or corral. Often this was a community enclosure used by several shepherds.

At the close of the day and several times during the day, the shepherd would count his sheep to see if any had got caught in a thicket or by a wild animal, had otherwise been injured, or had strayed away. If a sheep was missing the faithful shepherd would retrace his steps in search of it, listening for its bleating for its mates.

The shepherd was held responsible for every sheep that was not his own. He must prove that he had not stolen it or sold it. If a sheep was killed he would, if possible, bring back the carcass as evidence. A lost sheep would be a financial loss to its owner. The employed shepherd would be penalized, might be discharged. The shepherd would be greatly concerned over the loss of a sheep and much relieved when the sheep was found. This might well be an occasion for celebrating with neighbors, at least a subject for conversation and bragging, for the shepherd liked to be with other people after a day alone with his sheep.

Luke follows the parable of the Lost Sheep with that of the Lost Coin. The two stories have the same teaching. Coins were first minted a little after 700 B.C. By the time of Jesus various types of coins were in circulation. This coin of his parable was the Greek silver drachma. The footnote in our Bible saying that it was worth sixteen cents does not help us much. It was the average daily wage. To lose a drachma meant much more than to lose sixteen cents would today.

Women were the bankers. If the family got a few coins ahead or the wife had received some coins as a dowry, she sewed them to her head-piece or attached them to a chain around her neck. This is still done, although much "money" so seen is imitation, artificial. If a coin was lost in the house, the woman had a task something like "finding a needle in a haystack."

The earthen floor of many Palestinian houses was often strewn with rushes to absorb moisture and keep the floor from becoming muddy. These were not frequently changed. To find a lost coin, not only would cushions, sheepskin rugs, and any furniture have to be moved, but all the rushes gathered up and shaken. Houses had but one door and small windows, if any at all. To search for a coin it would be necessary to light a lamp. This was a small earthenware saucer with a protruding lip curled up at one point in the rim where the wick would be. Olive oil was the fuel used.

Jesus noted that a successful search would result in the woman's calling together her friends. The Greek word is feminine. She would call in some of the neighboring women to celebrate her escape from a beating by her husband.

Luke made room for some of Jesus' longer parables. One of these we call the Prodigal Son. Luke places it along with the stories of the lost sheep and the lost coin as an illustration of God's rejoicing over the finding of one who was lost. In it we see reflections of a number of social customs of Palestine at the time of Jesus.

In accordance with the law of Deut. 21:17 a man's oldest son received twice as much of his father's property as did any other son. This birth-right compensated the oldest son for the obligations that were his. He was not allowed to establish himself away from his father's home. It was necessary for him to take over many of the responsibilities of the father as the latter reached old age. The oldest son represented the family at clan meetings. He took care of his parents when they became old. He looked after the family graves and carried on family traditions.

Commonly the younger sons stayed on with their older brother. Sometimes it seemed much wiser for them, or at least some of them, to leave home and set up enterprises of their own. If the father wished, he could aid these ventures by dividing his property before his death, giving the younger sons capital with which to start on their own. This was the case in Jesus' parable.

Jesus pictured the younger son's sinking as low as possible. After he had spent all his money in loose living in a foreign country he got work tending pigs. No job was considered by Jews to be lower. He became so desperate he envied the pigs the pods of the carob tree they were fed. These are something like the pods of locust trees but wider. While considered good animal feed, they were not eaten by people except in cases of dire need.

When the son realized how foolish he had been he recalled that his father's hired servants ate better than he did. There were three types of servants at the time. The lowest group were slaves, who were fairly well fed to maintain their strength. There was an upper group of poor relatives for which custom required the well-to-do man to make some provision. Between the two groups were hired servants, paid as little as they would accept. If they became sickly others could be employed in their place. Consequently they often had little to eat. The son felt he was even worse off than they.

When the son returned he was kissed by his father. Kissing is still a common greeting among men in the Middle East.

The ring was a symbol of authority. Servants could not afford to wear shoes. The father not only gave the son clean clothes, but "the best robe" reserved for distinguished guests. This was in addition to other indications of rank and authority. The fatted calf was kept in reserve for important celebrations. Its killing betokened a blood covenant between guest and host.

It was typical that the older son would be working in a field away from the village, possibly a mile or two. He would not know of his brother's return until sunset. At the end of his work day, as he neared the house, he heard the unexpected sounds of music and dancing.

Luke also preserves the parable of the Rich Man and Lazarus. This is the only parable of Jesus we have in which a character is named. We often give the rich man a name too—Dives. This is the Latin word used in the Vulgate for rich man.

The rich man not only ate well. He had the most costly clothing, inner garments of Egyptian flax and outer garments dyed the costly purple originally afforded only by royalty. Beggars were plentiful in Palestine. They often had open sores covered with flies. Dogs were frequently in the same condition. Dogs were seldom pets. They were a torment to beggars, often stealing the food tossed to these unfortunate men. Frequently they irritated the beggar's sores by licking them. Beggars were found in front of synagogues and Greek places of worship, appealing to the religious feeling of those who came there. They were also found in front of the homes of wealthy people who threw bones and scraps of food over the wall as they ate. Thus Lazarus lay at the gate of the rich man.

The rich man died and was buried. There would be an elaborate funeral with hired mourners and noisy lamentations. The poor beggar also died but nothing is said about burial. Bodies of beggars were commonly thrown on a garbage dump south of the city of Jerusalem in the valley of Hinnom or "Gehenna". Bodies of criminals were also put in this place of smoldering fires and worms. The Old Testament writer of the last verse of Isaiah noted that the bodies thus treated "shall be an abhorrence to all flesh." It was Jesus who pointed out in his parable that that did not determine the happiness of one's future life.

For Class Discussion

If Jesus had lived in a different climate, among different conditions how much different would his religion have been?

Assignment

Write a parable of your own. Be sure the story parallels the phase of life you wish to illustrate.

Supplementary Reading

1. *The Interpreter's Bible.* New York and Nashville: Abingdon Press, Vol. 7, 1951. Pages 165-175.

2. Bailey, Albert E. *Daily Life in Bible Times.* New York: Charles Scribner's Sons, 1943.

3. Bouquet, A. C. *Everyday Life in New Testament Times.* New York: Charles Scribner's Sons, 1953.

4. Miller, Madeleine S. and Miller, J. Lane. *Encyclopedia of Bible Life.* New York: Harper & Brothers, (Rev.), 1955.

CHAPTER 10

"Thy Kingdom Come"

Read Matthew 13 and other references to the Kingdom you find. Recall what you noted in Mark about the Kingdom.

Jesus spoke more often about the Kingdom of God than any other subject. The gospel accounts record 144 references to the Kingdom. In his concept of the Kingdom, Jesus had a new message of God's purpose. It became Jesus' master thought, his watchword. Mark reports that the theme of Jesus' first sermon was "The Kingdom of God is at hand" (1:15). Luke says that the theme of Jesus' discourses with his disciples after the Resurrection was the Kingdom of God (Acts 1:3).

Throughout the Old Testament the Hebrew people thought in nationalistic terms. After the division into two small nations following the death of Solomon, they dreamed of a united kingdom equal to that of David. Many times they dreamed of a kingdom greater than David's. During the Babylonian captivity they looked forward to a re-established kingdom. When they returned to their homeland they were but a part of the Persian empire. Following this, they were ruled by Alexander as a part of his Greek empire; later by Egypt, and then by Syria. The Maccabean rebellion brought about a Jewish kingdom but it was small and uncertain. Before long Rome took over. During the time of Jesus Rome was in control, but the idea of a Jewish kingdom held a prominent place in the minds of most Jews. Their great hope was that a leader would rise up and drive out the Romans. Some even dreamed of conquering Rome and ruling the known world.

When Jesus talked of the Kingdom of God this hope naturally came to the minds of his hearers. Some people believe that Judas saw in Jesus this desired leader and joined his inner circle in order to secure for himself a prominent place in the kingdom, or at least to have a part in bringing it about. Could other disciples have joined for the same reason? The mother of James and John doubtless had this in mind when she requested Jesus to "command that these two sons of mine may sit, one at your right hand and one at your left, in your kingdom" (Matt. 20:21). With his many analogies about the Kingdom, Jesus failed to get across to even his closest followers just what he meant by the Kingdom of God. We are told in Acts that the last time the disciples as a group definitely experienced the presence of Christ they asked him, "Lord, will you at this time restore the kingdom to Israel?" (1:6). They still expected a physical throne and crown, a political government with an army.

Likewise many Christians today fail to understand what Jesus meant by the Kingdom. However, the mistake they make is not the one the disciples made. They do not think of it as a political state but as an existence beyond the grave. The Matthew compiler is responsible for this. He (or the Matthew committee) was very Jewish in outlook. At one period during the development of the Hebrew religion the name for God, "Yahweh," came to be considered so sacred that the good Jew would not pronounce it. For this he substituted the common word for God, "El" or "Elohim" which originally meant any god. By New Testament times even this word had become so sacred that orthodox Jews thought it blasphemous to use it. Again they sought substitutes. "Heaven" was also used to mean God. It is interesting that a parallel use of "Heaven" developed in China, but for a different reason. Some Chinese believed in many gods; others in but one. To avoid controversy the Chinese said "Heaven" desires this and that. They built altars to Heaven.

Whereas the other gospel accounts refer to the Kingdom of God, which is doubtless the wording Jesus used, Matthew generally refers to the Kingdom of Heaven. This term appears nowhere else in the Bible. It is Matthew's special term for the Kingdom. The expression, Kingdom of God, appears four times in Matthew. Could these appearances be errors made in copying earlier manuscripts?

What did Jesus mean by the Kingdom? He taught people to pray, "Thy Kingdom come . . . on earth." He told the Pharisees that "the kingdom of God is in the midst of you" or, according to the footnote, "within you" (Lu. 17:21). He told a scribe, "You are not far from the kingdom of God" (Mk. 12:34). These references scarcely suggest that the Kingdom is limited to a condition beyond death.

A kingdom implies a king. In the kingdom of God, God is king. Some people prefer to translate Jesus' term as the "Kingly Rule of God." In ancient kingdoms, the king was the law-maker. People were required to obey his laws. One is in the Kingdom of God when he recognizes the kingship of God, and strives to discover and obey the laws of God. Jesus was speaking for the king when he said, "I came that they may have life, and have it abundantly" (John 10:10). God has set up a set of laws by which people can have an enjoyable, abundant, eternal life. To attempt to go contrary to these rules reduces the abundance of life. This applies to physical life. If we eat wrong foods, in wrong quantities or at wrong times we cannot expect healthy digestion. One of the laws is that two physical objects cannot be in the same place at the same time. If I try to put my head where a brick wall is, I do not break the law, but attempting to do so may break my head. Jesus was much more concerned with the laws relative to getting along with people. To attempt to break them also brings unpleasant results. The loyal subject of God will try to learn what God's laws are and to live in accordance with them.

Being a member of God's Kingdom does not make one less loyal to his own nation. Being a good American does not make one a poorer citizen of his state or community.

Jesus wanted everyone to be able to say with him, "I seek not my own will but the will of him who sent me" (John 5:30). He believed that some could already say this, that for some people the Kingdom was then present. He looked forward to the time when everybody would understand and do God's will. He was convinced that this would eventually come about, that the Kingdom would grow from a small beginning as mustard grows from very small seed or as a large pan of flour is leavened from a small lump of yeast. "Men will come from east and west, and from north and south, and sit at table in the kingdom of God" (Lu. 13:29). To Jesus nothing else was so important. As one gives up all other possessions to become the owner of hidden treasure, or as a pearl merchant sells all his pearls in order to buy the one pearl of outstanding value, so men must "seek first his kingdom and his righteousness" (Matt. 6:33).

Being a part of the Kingdom does not cease at death. Those who find a desirable future life are those already members of the Kingdom. In the next life they continue obeying God—"Thy kingdom come . . . on earth as in heaven."

Jesus described the Kingdom as growing. He also told the Pharisees, "The kingdom of God is not coming with signs to be observed; nor will they say, 'Lo, here it is!' or 'There!'" (Lu. 17:21). However, there are references that suggest a sudden appearance of the Kingdom. These are what we call apocalyptic expressions, figurative language dealing with the future. Jews and early Christians made much use of this form of speech. We know of about a hundred books written in this form. Daniel in the Old Testament and the Revelation to John in the New are the best known. People were familiar with this type of expression. Jesus used it at times, or possibly it was the gospel writers who expressed Jesus' thoughts in such terms occasionally.

In apocalyptic writings of the last two centuries B.C. there was the dream of the time when the heavens would open up and God or his representatives would come to earth very dramatically and take over. Certainly this would be the establishment of a kingdom of God. Mark 13 and parallel passages in Matthew and Luke, along with other scattered verses, attribute such a concept to Jesus. Probably the greatest value in these chapters is Jesus' recognition that the progress of the Kingdom would not be "smooth sailing"—"they will deliver you up to councils; and you will be beaten in synagogues; and you will stand before governors and kings for my sake, to bear testimony before them" (Mk. 13:9).

Before the gospel accounts were written Christians had experienced these very things. No wonder any hint that Jesus expected this was emphasized and possibly expanded by the writers. Some references to the Kingdom attributed to Jesus can be understood only in light of the experiences of the early church.

Early Old Testament religion dealt entirely with God's relation to society, to the nation; God was not pictured as concerned with individuals. Near the end of the Old Testament period religion swung toward an emphasis upon the personal. Jesus emphasized God's interest in individual men, women and children. Many

Christian people today seem to feel that God is concerned only with the individual, that the Christian approach should be entirely upon changing, converting, saving individuals. Two approaches are necessary: that of changing the individual and that of changing the environment in which the individual lives. Jesus came to save that which was lost, to save society as well as individuals.

The Kingdom has not yet reached its fulfillment. We might well ask in what ways society must yet be changed. Can the Kingdom of God be completely achieved as long as we have war? Do poverty and disease interfere with the growth of the Kingdom? Do racial conflicts and misunderstandings fit into the Kingdom? Are the satisfactions of the Kingdom enjoyed by those who cannot read or write? What other social changes must be brought about before Jesus' vision of the Kingdom is fulfilled?

For Class Discussion

1. Which is the more erroneous, the disciples' idea that the Kingdom meant an anti-Roman political organization, or the idea that the Kingdom refers only to life beyond the grave?

2. Into what difficulties do apocalyptic writings in the Bible get people today?

3. Has the Kingdom been slower developing than Jesus expected?

Assignment

1. Describe what Jesus meant by the Kingdom?

2. Make a list of at least ten social changes that must be achieved before the Kingdom has reached its fulfillment. Do not include individual change such as more forgiveness, prayer or church attendance.

Supplementary Reading

1. *The Interpreter's Bible.* New York and Nashville: Abingdon Press, Vol. 7, 1951. Pages 145-154.

2. Bright, John. *The Kingdom of God.* New York and Nashville: Abingdon Press, 1953.

3. Filson, Floyd V. *Jesus Christ the Risen Lord.* New York and Nashville: Abingdon Press, 1956. Chapter V.

4. Tilden, Elwyn E., Jr. *Toward Understanding Jesus.* Englewood Cliffs, N. J.: Prentice-Hall, 1956. Chapter 16.

CHAPTER 11

"Who Is the Greatest?"

Read: Matt. 6:18; 7:3-5 and 15-23; 9:10-13; 12:31-32; 18;
      20:20-28; 21:28-32; 22:37-39; 23:1-33; 25:41-46.
      Mk. 1:14-15; 6:7-12; 12:38-40.
      Lu. 6:46; 12:47-48; 13:1-5; 18:9-14; 22:24-27.
      John 8:32; 13:1-17; 14:16-17; 16:12-13.

Jesus not only expanded the Old Testament concept of the
Kingdom of God. He also developed the emphasis found in late
Hebrew religion that God expects certain things of the individual.
Moral values of honesty, truthfulness, fair play were expected.
Kindness, friendliness, generosity were demanded. Obedience
and faithfulness to God and communion with him through prayer
were more definitely religious demands.

In the Sermon on the Mount we found two points on which
Jesus put much more emphasis than is found in the Old Testament. One of these was that of using intelligence—repent, love
God with all the mind, ask, seek, knock. Jesus insisted that his
followers use their intelligence. His second emphasis was that
of action—"Not every one who says to me, 'Lord, Lord' shall enter
the kingdom of heaven, but he who does the will of my Father"
(Matt. 7:21).

Jesus was bothered by people's seeking recognition. In the
parable of the Marriage Feast he instructed, "Do not sit down
in a place of honor . . . every one who exalts himself will be
humbled, and he who humbles himself will be exalted" (Lu.
14:7-11). James and John, or their mother, wanted the highest
positions in his glory. The disciples wanted to know, "Who is the
greatest in the kingdom of heaven?" (Matt. 18:1), and even at
the Last Supper when Jesus was completing his ministry among
them, they disputed "which of them was to be regarded as the
greatest" (Lu. 22:24). Jesus told them, much as he had said on

other occasions, "Whoever would be first among you must be slave of all" (Mk. 10:44). John reports that Jesus demonstrated this by washing and wiping the disciples' feet (13:5). Service to other people was the chief way to carry out the will of God. "Whoever would be great among you must be your servant" (Matt. 20:26).

To the question, "Who is greatest in the kingdom of heaven?" Jesus replied, "Unless you turn and become like children, you will never enter the kingdom of heaven. Whoever humbles himself like this child, he is the greatest in the kingdom of heaven" (Matt. 18:3-4).

Did Paul agree with this when he said, "When I became a man, I gave up childish ways" (1 Cor. 13:11)? Are childlike and childish the same thing? Does not childlike mean having the desirable qualities of a child? Does not childish mean being immature, being less developed than one should be?

What are the childlike qualities Jesus found desirable? Humility seems to be the quality emphasized here. Might not teachableness be a better term? The child recognizes that there are many things he does not know. He realizes that older people know much more than he does.

But the normal child is more than willing to learn. He is inquisitive, investigative, wanting to see "what makes the wheels go 'round." This curiosity is something Jesus commended. He wanted people to ask, seek, knock. How essential is this element to scientists, engineers, explorers?

A third quality in children commended itself to Jesus. That is forgiveness. A child can become very angry, but then his anger is gone. A youngster wanted to have a party. "Whom do you want to invite?" inquired the mother. "I want to invite Mary." "But you said you never wanted to speak to Mary again." "Aw, Mother, that was yesterday." Jesus insisted upon forgiveness— seventy times seven.

With his keen power of observation Jesus noted these qualities in children. He insisted every adult must have them. What other childlike qualities may Jesus have had in mind when he said, "Unless you turn and become like little children"?

Love was Jesus' highest requirement. Matthew quotes him

twice as emphasizing, "Love your neighbor as you love yourself" (19:19), and again, "You have heard that it was said, 'You shall love your neighbor' . . . But I say to you, Love your enemies and pray for those who persecute you" (5:43-44). Jesus could not help loving people. It was his life. God is love, and Jesus expected the true disciple to be God-like: "You therefore, must be perfect, as your heavenly Father is perfect" (Matt. 5:45). This is the adventure of Christianity. The Christian continually attempts the impossible. He is never contented, satisfied. His cannot be a popular religion. Jesus pointed out bluntly that "the gate is narrow and the way is hard" (Matt. 7:14). It is not easy to love one's enemies, to forgive seventy times seven. No halfway measures are allowed. True discipleship is an affair for heroes.

Although Jesus went apart for periods of prayer and meditation, he did not believe in separating himself from the world. No monastery or monk's cell for him. He lived with people and for people. He constantly utilized opportunities to be of service to his fellowmen. Here, as well as in his attitude toward his enemies, Jesus differed from the Essenes, with whom he had some points in common. The true disciple of Jesus must be more than an Essene.

What are our standards for greatness, for importance today? Are beauty, wealth, position, the test? What are history's criteria? Make a list of the ten greatest people in American history. When the list is completed ask why you put each name on your list. Is it because the person was beautiful? Is it because he was a millionaire? Is it because he was once president of the United States? List your reasons and then compare them with Jesus' criteria: service, humility, inquisitiveness, forgiveness. Does this comparison again suggest that Jesus was much more than a theorist, that he was a realist?

Old Testament prophets had attacked artificiality, insincerity in the Hebrew religion. Amos had pictured God as saying:

> I hate, I despise your feasts
> . . . .
> Even though you offer me your burnt offerings

85

and cereal offerings,
I will not accept them.
. . . .

But let justice roll down like waters,
and righteousness like an ever-flowing stream (5:21-24).

Jesus took up the attack upon religious artificiality. In our study of the Sermon on the Mount we noted his criticism of the artificial use of giving alms, praying, and fasting. In the same sermon he scolded those who offered to take a speck out of another's eye while having logs in their own eyes. Jesus demanded absolute sincerity. Strong emphasis on ceremonial washing, Sabbath observance, tithing, brought forth Jesus' condemnation. Jesus was not opposed to cleanliness, Sabbath observances, or tithing, but he noted how the real value in these matters could be lost. They might be merely a means of securing the praise of other people. They might encourage the picture of God as a great book-keeper, rewarding people in accordance with how accurately they had observed the letter of regulations. Jesus felt that a God-like spirit or attitude was far more important.

Words, promises, are of no value unless accompanied by action. In the parable of Matt. 21:28-31 Jesus pointed out that what counts with God is actual conduct. Confessions of faith, creeds, pious statements are valueless unless supported by deeds. "Not every one who says to me, 'Lord, Lord,' shall enter the kingdom of heaven, but he who does the will of my Father" (Matt. 7:21).

Jesus' story of the last judgement (Matt. 25:32-46) makes the division between the saved and the lost not upon a basis of piety or professions but upon that of action: "I was hungry and you gave me food." Results depended entirely upon what had been done "to one of the least of these my brethren." In Lu. 6:46 Jesus is reported to have asked, "Why do you call me, 'Lord, Lord' and not do what I tell you?"

There were many good things about the religion of the Pharisees, but their strict demands upon the observance of detailed regulations disgusted Jesus. "Practice and observe whatever they tell you, but not what they do; for they preach, but do not practice" (Matt. 23:3). He disapproved of those who enlarged their religious symbols in order to draw attention, and sought for themselves places of honor. To a lawyer he declared, "Woe to you lawyers! for you take away the key to knowledge; you did not enter yourselves, and you hindered those who were entering" (Lu. 11:52). Was it only Pharisees he accused of being such as "outwardly appear righteous to men, but within . . . are full of hypocrisy and iniquity" (Matt. 23:28)? Such "sins of the saints" were to Jesus extremely offensive. To try to help such people seemed to Jesus almost hopeless. Sarcastically he said, "those who are well have no need of a physician . . . I came not to call the righteous, but sinners" (Matt. 9:12-13).

The use of intelligence in religion received major emphasis from Jesus. Several times he insisted that men should repent, rethink, get a new outlook. He had his disciples preach the same thing. When Jesus was asked to give the most important law he quoted Deut. 6:5, "You shall love the LORD your God with all your heart, and with all your soul, and with all your strength." To this he added "and with all your mind" (Mk. 12:30). The word used in Deuteronomy which we translate heart may have included what we call mind, but Jesus was not satisfied that this be only implied. He pointed out the importance of using our minds in religion, applying our thought and understanding. When Jesus insisted that one must use the abilities, the talents, God has given him, he included all one's intellectual skill. Jesus knew that truth would stand up under the most thorough investigation. He wanted people to seek the truth. Finding truth would bring release from traditions, rules, restrictions. One should be much more concerned with finding truth than with impressing his neighbors. "You will know the truth, and the truth will make you free" (John 8:32).

According to John, Jesus felt that truth was a part of God, the spirit of God himself. Many people were incapable of receiving the truth, but those who really followed Jesus would find the truth: "the Father will give you another Counselor, to be with you for ever, even the Spirit of truth" (14:16-17). "When the Spirit of truth comes, he will guide you into all the truth" (16:13).

As Micah had insisted that the Lord desires "the knowledge of God, rather than burnt offerings" (6:6), so Jesus insisted that knowledge, understanding, are of utmost importance. Ignorance and superstition have no place in well-developed religion. Taken out of its context this might seem contradicted by Jesus' prayer, "I thank thee . . . that thou hast hidden these things from the wise and understanding and revealed them to babes" (Matt. 11:25 or Lu. 10:21). Jesus had been expressing his disgust with the leaders of certain cities who thought they were wise and mighty. They did not understand or accept him. He was glad he was, at least to some extent, understood by his disciples, simple unassuming folks, probably looked down upon by the city aristocrats as babes.

Those who have ability, intelligence, and do not apply it to religion will be punished for their failure. To them will come much greater regrets, remorse, for their misdeeds than to those who are incapable of understanding, or doing better. "That servant who knew his master's will, but did not make ready or act according to his will, shall receive a severe beating. But he who did not know, and did what deserved a beating, shall receive a light beating" (Lu. 12:45-47). Is this not the same conviction expressed later in Jas. 4:17, "Whoever knows what is right to do and fails to do it, for him it is sin"? Intelligence carries with it very definite responsibility.

For Class Discussion

What other phases of religious artificiality do we find today? What about rewards or pins for Sunday school attendance? Religious mottos or pictures on our walls? Wearing crosses or religious "medals"?

Assignment

1. In addition to other references at the beginning of this chapter read Lu. 11-18. Make a list of ten characteristics or qualities of a follower of Jesus. Tell in what book, chapter, and verse each of these is found.
2. Compile a list of the ten greatest people in the world who have lived in the 20th century. After each name note the quality or qualities that caused you to put the name on your list.
3. Sum up Jesus' attitude toward artificiality in religion.

4. What was Jesus' attitude toward intelligence and ignorance in religion?

5. How would Jesus have answered the question, "What do you think about superstition?"

Supplementary Reading

Anonymous: *By An Unknown Disciple*. New York: Harper & Brothers. 1919.

CHAPTER 12

"This Day Our Daily Bread'

Read: Matt. 4:4; 6:19-21, Mk. 10:17-31, Lu. 5:20 and 24;
7:18-22; 12:13-21; 16:1-31; 19:1-27.

Money, things, economic goods, did not miss Jesus' attention.
He had much to say on this subject. A number of his parables
dealt with the problems of wealth. Jesus was a realist. He knew
that the question of money gets mixed up with the lives of ordinary men.

In his wilderness experience Jesus rejected the temptation to
be an economic saviour. In his sermon at Nazareth he included
good news to the poor. When John the Baptist sent two of his
disciples to Jesus to inquire, "Are you he who is to come, or
shall we look for another?" Jesus replied, "Go and tell John . . .
the poor have good news preached to them" (Lu. 7:18-23). Luke
quoted Jesus as saying, "Blessed are you poor" (6:20). Jesus was
definitely concerned about the poor, but found no automatic
virtue in poverty.

The best things in life cannot be bought or sold. "A man's life
does not consist in the abundance of his possessions" (Lu. 12:15).
Love, friendship, cannot be bought. The care of God cannot be
purchased.

Did Jesus despise the rich? Luke quoted him as saying, "Woe
to you that are rich" (6:24). On another occasion he said, "You
cannot serve God and mammon" (16:13). At no time is Jesus
reported to have said that money or possessions are bad. One of
Jesus' early interpreters is often quoted as claiming that money
itself is bad, but the quotation is "The *love* of money is the root
of all evils" (Tim. 6:10). Again it is often claimed that Jesus
said that a rich man could not get to heaven. Note the quotation,
which is exactly the same in all three synoptic gospels: "It is easier

for a camel to go through the eye of a needle than for a rich man to enter the kingdom of God" (Mk. 10:25; Matt. 19:24; Lu. 18:25). It is interesting that even Matthew, as we now have it, uses the term "kingdom of God" in this instance. Did the Matthew compiler fear people might misquote the statement?

What Jesus meant here is that a rich man tends to be so concerned with taking care of his possessions that he does not make time to serve his fellowmen or to develop an inquisitive, investigative attitude. Such a person is not likely to be humble and possibly not even forgiving. Although a camel can never go through the eye of a needle Jesus did not imply that a rich man can never have a part in God's kingdom. It was a figure of speech similar to the one in which he told Pharisees that they swallow camels.

Jesus was able to live with poor and rich alike. He accepted dinner invitations from the rich and seemed to be at home with them. He was interested in persons, not in economic classes. In Jericho he welcomed the rich Zacchaeus as heartily as he welcomed Bartimaeus the beggar. The seamless robe Jesus wore was not a garment of the very poor. He did not object to expensive ointment being poured on his head or feet.

Jesus felt that all possessions originally came from God, even the rain and sunshine (Matt. 5:45). He would have agreed that "the cattle on a thousand hills" are God's (Ps. 50:10). Possessions are a sacred obligation. Men are their stewards. They carry with them an obligation. To misuse wealth is to secure God's severest condemnation: "Depart from me . . . I was hungry and you gave me no food . . . naked and you did not clothe me" (Matt. 25: 41-43).

Jesus did point out that riches can be a terrible temptation, or handicap. They can interfere with making the most of one's life. The rich ruler, whose inquiry brought about the reference to the needle's eye, wanted to inherit eternal life. To him that seemed the most important thing. However, Jesus recognized that the young man was more interested in his money. When Jesus told him that to have the kind of life he wanted he must get rid of his handicap, money, he was unwilling to do so; he put his possessions first. When Nicodemus came to Jesus (John 3:1-15) he was

91

not told to dispose of his wealth, but to get a new understanding of the problems with which Jesus was dealing. Jesus is not reported to have told any one else to give up his possessions.

Jesus seems to have noticed that wealth can become a barrier between a man and his fellowmen. Instead of increasing social sympathies, possessions may make him selfish and unsocial. They may break down the sense of dependence which binds men to one another. In Jesus' story of the rich man and Lazarus (Lu. 16:19-31) the rich man evidently had been made haughty and arrogant by his riches. They built a partition between him and Lazarus. To Jesus a life given to sumptuous living and indifference to the want and misery of one at his doorstep was definitely immoral and sinful.

In the parable of the Rich Fool (Lu. 12:16-21) riches seem to have come between the man and God. There is no gratitude for his wealth. He communes with himself rather than with God. "So is he who lays up treasure for himself, and is not rich toward God."

Treasure can give a false sense of security. Jesus noted that "moth and rust consume and . . . thieves break in and steal" (Matt. 6:19). Wealth must be kept in its proper perspective. Spiritual things must take preeminence. "Where your treasure is, there will your heart be also" (Matt. 6:21). If physical possessions are the most important things we have, that is where we put our concern, our "heart."

Is there a Christian attitude toward getting money? Does it matter how we secure our income? We would doubtless agree with the Old Testament, "You shall not steal" (Ex. 20:15), but what after that? Is it Christian to make one's living as a bar-tender, selling intoxicating drinks? Is it Christian to be employed by a distillery manufacturing alcoholic beverages? How about increasing one's income by having stock in such a firm or renting property to it?

Property is indispensable to personal freedom. Is there a Christian attitude toward spending money? Jesus doubtless felt like asking with the second Isaiah, "Why do you spend your money for that which is not bread, and your labor for that which does not satisfy?" (Isa. 55:2). John reports Jesus as saying, "Do not labor for the food which perishes, but for the food which endures to eternal life" (6:27). Earlier in the same chapter, in connection with the feeding of the five thousand, we learn that Jesus commanded, "Gather up the fragments left over, that nothing may be lost" (6:12). Jesus agreed that "The earth is the LORD's and the fulness thereof" (Ps. 24:1). Nothing belonging to God is to be wasted. We are stewards of God's property. It must be used wisely for him.

Is there a Christian attitude toward saving? Did not Jesus teach, "Do not be anxious, saying, 'What shall we eat?' or 'What shall we drink?' or 'What shall we wear?'" (Matt. 6:31). Is not the man who has savings, insurance, a pension, less anxious than one who has no provision for an emergency or old age? Jesus set up no standards of how much one should save. Do the teachings of Jesus have any bearing on how savings should be invested?

How about giving? Jesus definitely encouraged this, although he warned that giving should not be attempting to buy glory for one's self. The Hebrews had insisted upon giving a tenth of their incomes to that which represented God. What was Jesus' attitude? He felt that the Pharisees were wasting time in carefully weighing minute amounts of garden herbs in order to determine a tenth of them. This time might much better have been used in activities of justice, mercy, and faith. The matter of tithing "you ought to have done, without neglecting the others" (Matt. 23:23).

For Class Discussion

1. What is graft? What is wrong with it?
2. What is gambling? What is wrong with it?
3. Was Jesus' teaching on wealth ascetic? Was it socialistic?
4. What is the distinction between property for use and property for power?
5. Is it Christian to be employed in the manufacture of munitions of war?
6. What standards should determine where a Christian buys?
7. On what things do we tend to spend too much money?
8. What are the values of a budget?
9. Discuss the thesis: One should save ten per cent of his income and give ten per cent, living on the eighty per cent.
10. If one tithes, what items should be included in the tithe? Should the tithe be a tenth of one's listed salary or of his "take home" pay?

93

Assignment

What was Jesus' attitude about money? What dangers did Jesus see involved in possessions? How did he feel they should be used?

Supplementary Reading

1. Laymon, Charles M. *The Life and Teachings of Jesus.* New York and Nashville: Abingdon Press, 1955. Chapter 15.
2. Mathews, Shailer. *Jesus on Social Institutions.* New York: The Macmillan Company, 1928. Chapter VI.
3. Stewart, James S. *The Life and Teaching of Jesus Christ.* New York and Nashville: Abingdon Press, 1957. Chapter XV.

CHAPTER 13

"Show Us the Father"

Read: Matt. 5:34-35 and 43-45; 7:7-11; 20:1-16; 22:36-37;
Lu. 4:25-27; 12:22-31; 15:3-32; John 5:17.

Practically all mankind has recognized that behind the universe there is power greater than man. This power is intelligent. Regardless of how often one throws pieces of metal and glass into the air, they will not come down as a watch or radio. A bushel of type may be thrown into the air an indefinite number of times, but will not come down arranged as a psalm. For the watch there must be an intelligent watch-maker. To have a psalm there must have been a poet. The universe must have had an intelligent creator (or, some have said, creators). The Hebrew concept of God grew throughout the Old Testament. As we first meet these, our religious ancestors, the Hebrews had just grown out of animism, thinking of gods of stones, streams, trees, and other objects. They had developed a form of polytheism, thinking of each group of people as having its own god or gods, about equally strong. From a loyalty to their god, Yahweh, came a conviction that he was stronger than other gods: "O give thanks to the God of gods" (Ps. 136:2). The first Old Testament writer to go definitely beyond this henotheistic attitude was Second Isaiah, who about 540 B.C. quoted God as saying, "I am the LORD, and there is no other" (45:5). This monotheistic understanding was universally accepted by the Jews at the time of Jesus.

In their developing concept of God the Hebrews kept asking, what is our god like? Although they had thought of God as walking with Adam, eating with Abraham, wrestling with Jacob, they were afraid of God. They believed that for any ordinary person to see God would result in death. They told Moses, "You speak to us, and we will hear; but let not God speak to us, lest we die" (Ex. 20:19). To the Hebrews, God was the great power responsible for anything they could not understand. When, in obedience to God's command, Moses returned to Egypt he became "deathly" sick. This was explained by the statement that, "the LORD met him and sought to kill him" (Ex. 4:24). It was thought that vengeance belonged to God and he did not hesitate to use it, although at times he seems to have been believed to be kind and considerate. It was felt that God might act one way one day and another the next. Although Moses thought in one instance that he persuaded God to change his mind, he found in God law and order and system. But Moses does not seem to have known of God's love. A bit later the Hebrews concluded that God loved Israel when the nation was good. However, they believed that God turned his back on them when they failed to do his will. It was the prophet Hosea who, out of experience with a sinful wife whom he continued to love, concluded that God loved Israel when it was sinful. He even spoke of God's being willing to suffer for his people. He used the term "Father" in referring to God.

That God was just, dependable, and even to some extent a loving Father to the Hebrew people was believed by the Jews of Jesus' day. In their concept of one god, intelligent goodness, the Jewish people were far ahead of their time. Greece contributed to the world an appreciation of art and beauty. Rome contributed an understanding of law. The Jews gave to the world an understanding of God.

Jesus took the existence of God for granted. He never attempted to prove God by logic. Like his Hebrew ancestors, Jesus did not think in philosophical terms. He experienced God. He had a joyous idea of God. He brought God very near to men. One's religion is to a large extent determined by his picture of God. Although Jesus used different terms for God, his most common description was Father—your Father, our Father, my Father. This name appears 150 times in our gospel accounts. In Jesus' first recorded words he asked, "Did you not know that I must be in my Father's house" (Lu. 2:49)? Luke says that his last words on the cross were, "Father, into thy hands I commit my spirit" (23:46).

To Jesus, God was no little Jewish deity. In the first sermon of Jesus we have recorded he pointed out that God was also interested in the Syrians and the Phoenicians. His own interest in

Samaritans, Romans, Greeks reflected God's concern for people of all nations and races. Since God is Father, all men are brothers. The family of God includes all nationalities, all races.

The prophet Jeremiah seems to have been the first person to preach that God is interested in individual men, women, and children. Jesus put strong emphasis on this concept. He noted that God cares for us. He knows what we need (Lu. 12:30). He knows our hearts (Lu. 16:15) and sees in secret (Matt. 6:4). God knows individuals so well that Jesus in his figurative language said, "Even the hairs of your head are all numbered" (Matt. 10:30). His interest in people is a loving concern: "Your Father who is in heaven give [s] good things to those who ask him" (Matt. 7:11). God is generous as was the householder in Jesus' parable of the Vineyard Laborers (Matt. 20:1-16).

God's love is not limited to those who obey him: "He makes his sun rise on the evil and on the good, and sends rain on the just and on the unjust" (Matt. 5:45). Jesus pictured God as interested in every phase of man's activity, even his food and clothing. He created mankind and ordained marriage (Matt. 19:4). Death does not end God's concern for man. Jesus knew that even then God looked after him: "Into thy hands I commit my spirit" (Lu. 23:46). Jesus believed that God has as much concern for every other individual.

Jesus described God's love as boundless, as always forgiving. In his parable of the Prodigal Son (Lu. 15:11-32) Jesus portrays God as the father. When the son "was yet at a distance, his father saw him and had compassion, and ran, and embraced him." Jesus never pictured God as becoming angry. However, God does not say, "Oh, just forget it." People suffer the consequences of wrongdoing. If they attempt to go contrary to the rules of God's universe they find themselves in difficulty. Jesus pictured this as a most unpleasant hell. In his justice God is not soft, easy-going. God has no pets. He does not set aside his rules for anyone. In his realization of this Paul later wrote that God "did not spare his own son" (Rom. 8:32). But God toils with men to mend their past. He searches for men. To make sure that people would understand this quality of God, Jesus told two other parables, that of the Lost Sheep and that of the Lost Coin (Lu. 15:3-16).

Jesus pictured God as interested not only in his highest crea-

97

tion, man, but in all that he had created. He is concerned with a sparrow that falls to the ground (Matt. 10:29). God is interested in grass, flowers, colors (Matt. 6:28-30). Jesus went on to point out how much God is concerned with people. All things were made for mankind, "and behold, everything is clean for you" (Lu. 11:41).

Jesus portrayed God by his deeds as well as by his words. God is like Jesus. So much is this true that many people find trouble distinguishing between God and Jesus. We agree with the statement John attributes to Jesus, "He who has seen me has seen the Father" (14:9). God and Jesus were in agreement, at one, with one another. Again John reports Jesus' praying that his disciples "may be one, even as we are one" (17:11). Jesus lived as the son of God. He expected others to do the same. He expected people to have the same love that God has, even for one's enemies: "Love your enemies and pray for those who persecute you, so that you may be sons of your Father who is in heaven" (Matt. 5:45). God's concern for good will and peace should be reflected: "Blessed are the peacemakers, for they shall be called sons of God" (Matt. 5:9).

God is man's great companion, to be found in nature, in history, in other people. He is friend of all. However, he is not to be treated as a pal, an equal. God is to be reverenced, respected. He is our spiritual Father, but we do not call him Dad. He is a king upon a throne, in comparison to which the earth is but a footstool (Matt. 5:35). In contrast to the Hebrews' concept of God as to some extent limited, Jesus proclaimed that, "with God all things are possible" (Matt. 19:26).

People are expected to search for God's will and do it. Those who enter the kingdom are those who "do the will of my Father who is in heaven" (Matt. 7:21). It is thus that one loves God. Matthew twice tells of Jesus' quoting with approval Hos. 6:6, "I desire mercy, and not sacrifice" (9:13 and 12:7). In both instances Jesus was being criticized for acting contrary to the traditions of the Pharisees. On another occasion he scolded the Pharisees: "You leave the commandment of God, and hold fast the tradition of men" (Mk. 7:8). The commandment is to love God with all one has.

God not only continues his interest in all that he created, God remains active: "My Father is working still" (John 5:17). It is God who causes the sun to shine, the rain to fall. It is he who feeds the ravens and clothes the grass of the field. It is God who hears and answers the prayers of his children.

For Class Discussion

To what extent is God like a human being?

Assignment

1. What characteristics did Jesus attribute to God?
2. What did Jesus teach that men's attitude toward God should be?

Supplementary Reading

1. Craig, C. T. *The Beginning of Christianity*. New York and Nashville: Abingdon Press, 1943. Chapter VII.
2. Denny, W. B. *The Career and Significance of Jesus*. New York: Thomas Nelson & Sons, 1933. Chapter XXXII.
3. Filson, Floyd V. *Jesus Christ the Risen Lord*. New York and Nashville: Abingdon Press, 1956. Chapter VII.
4. Glover, T. R. *The Jesus of History*. New York: Harper & Bros. Rev. 1950. Chapter V.

CHAPTER 14

"*Lord, Teach Us to Pray*"

Read: Matt, 6:5-15; 7:7-11; 14:22-23; 18:19; Mk. 1:35;
Lu. 6:12-13; 11:1-13; 22:39-46; John 17.

Prayer is a universal practice. Practically every religion teaches men to pray. Through the Old Testament we can trace the growth of the use of prayer. In early Hebrew religion it was thought that prayer was appropriate only for priests and extremely important men. Hannah, the mother of Samuel, broke down the taboo against women's praying. Toward the end of the Old Testament we find such laymen as Nehemiah and Daniel praying regularly. The quality of prayer also improved as the Hebrew religion came to a clearer understanding of God and his will.

Prayer appears to be a law of nature which men can learn to utilize. To pray is not an obligation; it is an opportunity. It brings people close to God, develops a fellowship with God. Jesus made extensive use of prayer. It enriched his life. He wanted others to find the same satisfaction and help in prayer that he found. Mark's statement, "In the morning, a great while before day, he rose and went out to a lonely place, and there he prayed" (1:35), is doubtless descriptive of Jesus' regular practice. Luke took particular care to point out that when Jesus had important decisions to make or deeds to perform he spent time praying about them. It has already been noted that only Luke told of Jesus' praying at the time of his baptism. Again only Luke reports that before naming his twelve disciples Jesus "went into the hills to pray; and all night he continued in prayer" (6:12). Although all the synoptic accounts tell of the Transfiguration, only Luke tells of Jesus' praying in this connection (9:28). We are familiar with his praying in Gethsemane and on the cross. After the feeding of the five thousand when "they were about to come and take him by force to make him king" (John 6:15)

Jesus went off by himself apparently to pray through his decision.

Jesus did not approve all the praying he observed. To him prayer was not something to be done as an exhibition seeking for the praise of men. Prayer was a private conversation between the individual and God. When he instructed "Go into your room and shut the door and pray to your Father" (Matt. 6:6), he was not prohibiting leading others in prayer, expressing prayer in the presence of other people. The seventeenth chapter of John portrays Jesus as praying aloud with an audience.

Jesus found people using set prayers which often they did not understand, in a language or vocabulary beyond their comprehension. Jesus was very distrustful of such "empty phrases." To Jesus prayer should be simple, in terms which the individual understands. To illustrate, Jesus gave "the Lord's Prayer." Has "repeating the Lord's Prayer" put it into the category of vain repetitions? A number of prayers of Jesus are preserved in the gospel records. With the exception of the one given in John 17, they are all shorter than the Lord's Prayer. Close spiritual union with God made the use of many words unnecessary.

This does not mean that Jesus would object to the use of prayers written ahead of time or by some one else. Prayer can be planned, organized in advance as one might plan what he would say in a conference with the president of the United States. If one is to lead the praying of a group of people or even pray with an individual it would be well to think ahead of time what the needs of that group or individual are. If a prayer formed by someone else is forbidden we must refrain from using the Lord's Prayer.

Doubtless Jesus' nights in prayer were to a large extent experiences of fellowship with God with very few actual petitions definitely worded. Is it such communion as this that Jesus meant when he recommended that one "ought always to pray and not lose heart" (Lu. 18:1)?

Prayer seemed to be so helpful to Jesus that his disciples wanted to know his secret. They asked that he give them some lessons in prayer (Lu. 11:1). Jesus taught prayer not only by example but by admonition. In the parables of the Unjust Judge (Lu. 18:1-7) and the Friend at Midnight (Lu. 11:5-13) he insisted that one should never become discouraged in praying, should continue his search for God's direction until he finds it. With Jesus, prayer was persistent and strenuous. Sixty years after the crucifixion a Christian writer said, "In the days of his flesh, Jesus offered up prayers and supplications with loud cries and tears" (Heb. 5:7).

When Jesus taught, "Ask, and it will be given you; seek and you will find; knock, and it will be opened to you" (Matt. 7:7), did he mean that by prayer one would always get what he thought he wanted? Does he not answer this in the same paragraph when we find him saying, "How much more will your Father who is in Heaven give good things to those who ask him" (7:11)? Not every thing we ask for is in the long run a good gift. Are not many prayers answered negatively? The small child who prays for a sharp knife may learn in time that "No" was the kindest answer. This understanding should be applied to Jesus' statement in Matt. 18:19: "If two of you agree on earth about anything they ask, it will be done for them by my Father in heaven." Many times we do not recognize the answer to our prayer. It comes so naturally, so quietly. God seldom does things in a spectacular, flamboyant way.

Jesus himself did not make blind demands of God in prayer. He sought the direction of God. In his prayer in the Garden of Gethsemane Jesus definitely did not want to die at his age. He noted this in his prayer but insisted, "Father, if thou art willing, remove this cup from me; nevertheless not my will, but thine be done" (Lu. 22:42). He instructed all to pray, "Thy will be done." Prayer does not change God. God is perfect and cannot be reformed. Prayer does change us. Sincere prayer brings one into accord with God. In close association with God we become Godlike.

In recognizing how much Jesus is like his Heavenly Father, the author of the Fourth Gospel pictures Jesus as saying, "Whatever you ask in my name I will do it" (14:13). This does not mean that there is any magic in ending a prayer, "In Jesus' name" or "For Jesus' sake." Rather it emphasizes that if one's prayer is the type Jesus would offer, if the prayer is in the attitude of Jesus, it is a good prayer.

Jesus did not attempt to analyze the "how" of prayer. With our interest in psychology today we like to raise such a question.

102

was not always successful. Relative to his home community "he did not do many mighty works there, because of their unbelief" (Matt. 13:58). Faith seems to have been essential upon the part of those who were to be healed: "Daughter, your faith has made you well" (Mk. 5:34); "According to your faith be it done to you" (Matt. 9:29). This faith, that through Jesus one could become well, functioned when Jesus was not physically present. Peter induced such faith in a man at the temple: "In the name of Jesus Christ of Nazareth, walk" (Acts. 3:6). Peter also had faith that he could generate such confidence in his patient.

Faith was also necessary upon the part of those who wanted to perform miracles. The disciples experimented with healings without success. Jesus told them their failure was because they lacked conviction: "Because of your little faith" (Matt. 17:20). Sometimes the faith mentioned is that of friends of people needing help: friends of a paralytic (Mk. 2:1-12), a mother (Mk. 7:24-30), or a centurion whose servant was paralyzed (Matt. 8:5-10). However, in some instances no reference is made to faith. Lu. 13:11-13 tells of a woman who had an infirmity eighteen years: "When Jesus saw her, he called her, and said to her, 'Woman, you are freed from your infirmity'." The Fourth Gospel emphasizes that belief in Jesus was a result of his miracles, which John calls "signs": "This, the first of his signs, Jesus did at Cana in Galilee and manifested his glory, and his disciples believed in him" (2:11); "he himself believed, and all his household" (4:53); "many of the Jews therefore who had come with Mary and had seen what he did believed in him" (11:45).

The more we understand Jesus the more we appreciate his experiences which we call miraculous. How much he understood his own power we do not know. There were many things he did not attempt to explain. It is possible that this is one thing he had in mind when he told his disciples, "I have yet many things to say to you, but you cannot bear them now" (John 16:12). He was convinced that what he did was the will of the Father, that each deed was the power of God in action. He believed that others who lived by the same spirit by which he lived could do the same things: "He who believes in me will also do the works that I do; and greater works than these will he do" (John 14:12).

People are bound by their lack of understanding. However, those who follow him will overcome this; "You will know the truth, and the truth will make you free." (John 8:32).

To what extent are we able to do the works that Jesus did? Probably many of his mental healings, called then casting out evil spirits, can be duplicated today. Possibly some of his physical healings are also being duplicated—we do not have the details of methods, materials and length of time Jesus employed. Physicians today are giving more recognition to the large part played in healings by confidence. Evidence their use of placebos and suggestion. The mind has a much greater part in physical health than has previously been recognized. A leading psychologist has said, "No twentieth century psychologist knows as much about the human mind as did Jesus of Nazareth."

We can scarcely think about Jesus' ministry of healing without asking questions regarding faith healing today. Doubtless the greatest need many sick people have is a conviction that they can get well. Physicians, friends, ministers often help people develop such faith. "Faith healers" whether Roman Catholics, Christian Scientists or others utilize this. However, there is the danger that the knowledge and intelligence God has given physicians fail to be used. An increasing number of Christians are finding confirmation of the statement of 1 Peter 5:15 "the prayer of faith will save the sick man." Jesus himself spoke respectfully of physicians, did not discredit them. Luke, the physician, would not do away with the value of medical service.

Some modern reports of faith healing are quite evidently false. Others are of a very temporary nature, easily understood. A basket-ball player with an injured leg that required him to use crutches dropped his crutches, at the permission of his coach, and rushed into the game at a crucial last minute. He won the game for his team and then fell in a faint. He had to use crutches for another month. He reports that during that minute of play he felt no pain. The emotion was greater than the pain. Does this not explain some temporary healings? May not this be dangerous and sometimes induce death? However, in the third place there are people who do not revert to their previous unhappy condition.

For Class Discussion

Do the stories of Jesus' miracles prove the greatness of Jesus, or does the recognition of the supreme genius, intelligence, and kindness of Jesus make the miracle stories easier to accept?

Supplementary Reading

1. McCasland, S. Vernon. *By the Finger of God*. New York: The Macmillan Company, 1951.
2. Laymon, Charles M. *The Life and Teachings of Jesus*. New York and Nashville: Abingdon Press, 1955. Chapter 12.
3. Brown, Robert McAfee. *The Bible Speaks to You*. Philadelphia: The Westminster Press, 1955. Pages 84-86.
4. Stewart, James S. *The Life and Teaching of Jesus Christ*. New York and Nashville: Abingdon Press, 1957. Chapter XI.

CHAPTER 19

'Though He Die, Yet Shall He Live"

Read: Matt. 10:28; 16:25-26; 25:31-46; Mk. 10:29-31; 12:18-
27; Lu. 16:19-31; 23:43; John 3:16; 11:25-26; 14:1-19.

The idea that existence does not end at the grave is universal.
It is found in all nations and races throughout human history.
Very few individuals reject this concept. Jesus' religious ancestors,
the Hebrews in general, took the idea for granted. It was not considered an issue in early Hebrew religion. Religion was not
thought of as dealing with this. To the Hebrews religion was
concerned with pleasing God so that he would prosper their
nation, protect them from other nations and from disease, famine
and drought. The basic scripture, the Torah, makes no mention
of immortality. One can read through his Bible to the 28th
chapter of 1 Samuel before he comes to a reference to future life.
The reference there is incidental. King Saul was desperate and
wished he could get advice from Samuel who was dead. He made
an attempt to talk with Samuel through a medium. We shall
not consider here whether or not he was successful. The value
to us at this point is that Saul believed that people live on after
death.

The few references in our Old Testament to the future life
give us a picture of changing ideas about the state of the dead.
The dead were considered as shades or shadows existing in Sheol
beneath the earth. One writer went so far as to say of this condition "there is no work or thought or knowledge or wisdom"
(Eccl. 9:10). There was nothing in such existence to fear, but
certainly nothing to enjoy, to get excited about.

As the Hebrew prophets helped their people develop a picture
of God they came to feel that God is just. Some people do not get
justice in this life. Some good people experience much suffering.
Others "get by with murder." Since neither group finds justice

in this experience there must be reward and punishment in the life to come. With this conviction the Hebrews developed two extreme pictures of the future life, states we have come to call heaven and hell.

Just south of the city wall of Jerusalem was the valley of Hinnom, which came to be called Ge-henna. Here a refuse or garbage pile was constantly burning. On this were thrown the bodies of dogs, of criminals, and of beggars. It was felt that some people deserved such a fate where "their worm shall not die, their fire shall not be quenched" (Isa. 66:24).

For people often attacked by enemies the desirable life was in a walled city where they would be safe. Jerusalem was the Hebrews' best such city. Therefore the ideal future life was considered to be a new Jerusalem. This would not have appealed to American Indians who thought of their ideal future life as a happy hunting ground. The Indian was looking for adventure; the Hebrew for protection. Are stone walls or bows and arrows essential for either? Both were thinking quite naturally in physical terms. Physical things are not needed for spiritual existence or happiness.

Most Jews in the time of Jesus held to the idea of heaven and hell. However, the Sadducees did not; since a future life is not mentioned in the Torah, they considered this idea as "modernistic," unorthodox, unsound. The Pharisees, with their emphasis upon God as the law-giver and judge, taught the existence of life beyond the grave. At this point Jesus agreed with the Pharisees but said very little about it. It was not his big emphasis. Our records do not tell of his preaching about it. He made some incidental references to the future life and answered questions that were asked him. His emphasis was "Thy kingdom come, thy will be done, on earth as it is in heaven." He did not believe that a loving heavenly father would allow the life of his son or daughter to be snuffed out like the light of a candle. Jesus' one argument for immortality was that God was quoted in Ex. 3:6 as saying that God *is* the God of Abraham, Isaac, and Jacob—not *was*. Therefore, explained Jesus, since God is not the god of the dead these worthies must have survived death.

It is not the physical body that continues in the next life. The Apostle Paul later said, "What you sow is not the body which is

131

to be" (1 Cor. 15:37). It is a transformed existence. Jesus noted that we should have much less fear of the person who might kill the body than one who might degenerate or destroy one's personality, the soul. It is the quality of one's living that counts. In the well-known verse, John 3:16, it is pointed out that belief in Jesus Christ, living by the standards given by Jesus, brings about eternal life. The same author quotes Jesus as saying, "I am the resurrection and the life; he who believes in me, though he die, yet shall he live" (11:25). He quotes Jesus at another time as saying, "Let not your hearts be troubled; believe in God, believe also in me" (14:1).

The Sadducees drew from Jesus one element relative to the future life not found earlier in our Bible. They told of a woman who in accord with the law of the levirate had had seven husbands, one at a time. To make the idea of life beyond death ridiculous, they wanted to know whose wife she would be then. Jesus replied that in the next life there will be no marriage. People will be like angels, sexless. Sex is largly physical, for procreation. With no death in the spiritual life, having babies will be unnecessary. Jesus did not say that people will be angels, but at this point like angels. That does not mean that husbands and wives will not know one another. Shall we not be able to have many friends, some ex-male, some ex-female?

Jesus emphasized that the quality of one's living in this life determines the quality of the next life. In his picture of the judgment the great division was made not on the basis of theology, church membership, baptism. It was based entirely upon how the earthly life had been used. Those who had ministered to others, had helped "the least" in their time of need, for example had provided food, drink, clothing, medical care, friendliness, would find life good beyond the grave. Those who had been selfish, stingy, disinterested in the welfare of others would find no enjoyment. In Jesus' parable of the Rich Man and Lazarus and again in his parable of the Rich Fool, he emphasized the importance of making proper use of one's possessions. Do not the parable of the Pounds and the parable of the Talents point out the same thing? One must be servant of all, put others above self if he is to have the rewarding future life. "Whoever seeks to

132

gain his life will lose it, but whoever loses his life will preserve it" (Lu. 17:33).

It is difficult to give a biblical description of the next life. There is so little in our scriptures about this. Writers in the Bible who mention it are not in total agreement. The following description should help us in our present understanding.

We do not have souls. We are souls and have bodies. The physical body does not continue. It is the soul that lives on. We might well ask what we take into the next life. This question might be answered in two words: character and memory. These are the two elements that cause us to continue being what we are in this life. Few, if any, physical cells live more than seven years but we are much the same people we were seven years ago. If we were mean, narrow, selfish, suspicious seven years ago, we are probably much the same today. If we were cooperative, generous, friendly, kind seven years ago, we are very likely the same today. Character can change. Sometimes it does. The older we get the less likely we are to change; we are in a groove, whether good or bad. Regardless of change in character, memory remains. We carry with us for ten years, fifty years, a thousand years our memories, good and bad. Death does not change character or memory. We are the same kind of people after we die as before. We have only got rid of our physical bodies.

However, satisfactions or dissatisfactions will be sharper. We steal something. The memory of the deed besets us, but we have the article stolen, which makes some compensation. In the next life the memory is still with us but not the article. We risk our lives in order to help someone but become physically crippled as a result. Our memory is pleasant but the pleasure may be diminished by physical pain. In the next life we have the satisfying memory but not the physical pain.

Might we not diagram our future life in the form of two letters "H", one large and one small? One represents heaven and one hell. Which is which? That depends upon what we have done with our lives. The worst of us will have some small pleasant memory which will come back from time to time in the future, in this life and in the next. No one of us has so many pleasant memories but that among them is some memory we regret, some-

133

thing we always wish we had done differently. No one in the Bible uses this description of the future life. However, does not Jesus suggest degrees of punishment in Lu. 12:47-48? Paul in 2 Cor. 12:2 speaks of degrees of heaven, a third heaven. By his example and teaching Jesus showed men how to make the most of their opportunities of this life, how to develop good memories, how to achieve noble character. The matter of atonement is discussed in Chapter 22 of this survey.

We learn of the unknown only in terms of the known. It is very difficult to think of the future life other than in physical terms. People talk of "going to heaven," but "go" is a physical term. Paul pointed out that one's body is sown a physical body, it is raised a spiritual body (1 Cor. 15:44). There is existence that is not physical. Men have often noted that love and hate exist but they cannot be located physically. They may be expressed by the caressing hand or the fist, but they are not located there. It is much easier for us to think of non-physical existence than it was a hundred years ago. A person can cup his hand and be sure he has radio or television waves in it. Yet he cannot feel them; they have no weight. He cannot see them; they have no color. They have no taste or smell. In his hand they make no sound. Nevertheless we know such waves exist. We are not waves, but the illustration helps us understand that things exist which cannot be perceived by our ordinary senses. This gives us some understanding of the soul and the future life.

This may also help us understand that heaven and hell cannot be located geographically. That does not do away with heaven and hell. They exist much more intensely than many of our ancestors thought. Both states are experienced before death. They continue to be experienced more vividly after death.

Death might be likened to a man taking off his coat. He is the same man after removing his coat as he was before. Death might be likened to a door. One is the same person, has the same character and memory after he passes through the door as before. Did not Jesus use the same analogy? John 14:2 reports his saying, "In my Father's house are many rooms." We live in one room. At death we pass to another, probably a much greater, room. Nor is there a time lapse, although there are "soul-sleepers" who believe otherwise. To one of the criminals on a cross beside him

Jesus said, "Truly, I say to you, today you will be with me in Paradise" (Lu. 23:43).

How eternal is hell? Memory, pleasant and unpleasant, will not be destroyed. It is eternal. Character can change in this life. Can it in the next? God has as much control of the next life as of this. As the good shepherd seeks every lost sheep, God will not give up his search for lost men. Punishment is for the reformation of the guilty, making a wrongdoer into a rightdoer. If one is permanently in the condition we call hell, then hell has no value and God's aim, his search, is defeated. Will God be permanently defeated, or will his life and direction eventually win?

For Class Discussion

1. Why did the picture of desirable future life held by American Indians differ from that held by the Hebrews?
2. Why do most people think that the next life is physical?
3. Just what is heaven? hell?

Supplementary Reading

1. Finigan, Jack. *Beginnings in Theology.* New York: Association Press, 1956. Chapters 16 and 17.
2. Kee, H. C., and Young, F. W. *Understanding the New Testament.* Englewood Cliffs, N. J.: Prentice-Hall, 1957. Pages 176-184.
3. Powers, Thomas E. *First Questions on the Life of the Spirit.* New York: Harper & Brothers, 1959. Part III.

CHAPTER 20

'Even the Spirit of Truth"

Read: Matt. 28:19-20; Lu. 12:10-12; John 14:15-17; 15:26; 16:7-15; 20:22.

Jesus' great commission as given in Matthew not only refers to the Father and the Son, but also to the Holy Spirit. The first two factors of this trinity have been discussed. What is the "third person of the trinity?" What do we mean by "the trinity?" The term is never used in the Bible. This concluding statement in Matthew is the nearest we come to it in scripture, other than the benediction given by Paul in 2 Cor. 13:14. It is true that in the King James Version we read in 1 John 5:7 "For there are three that bear record in heaven, the Father, the Word, and the Holy Ghost: and these three are one." However, this statement is found in no early copy of the Bible, and therefore is not even in a footnote of the English and American Revised Versions or the Revised Standard Version. This verse evidently was inserted by some late scribe to back up the theory of the trinity developed by the church.

The term trinity first appeared about A.D. 200. The whole idea grew out of the tremendous respect the church had for Jesus. Surely he was more than man. What other man, much of the church asked, could have handled his opponents so wisely as Jesus did when he answered questions about taxes, stoning an adulteress, or the greatest command? What other man had such power as was expressed in his miracles? The Greeks could have solved the problem by saying that Jesus was a god, but the Christians were definitely monotheists. If Jesus were all of God come to earth, to whom did he pray, what did he mean by "My father?" The church nearly split in two over the question as to whether Christ was "the same as the Father" or "like the Father." Jesus represented God. Both Paul and John found great difficulty distinguishing between the two. John quoted Jesus as saying, "He who has seen me has seen the Father. . . . Do you not believe that I am in the Father and the Father in me? The words that I say to you I do not speak on my own authority; but the Father who dwells in me does his works" (14:9-10). In this connection it is well to remember that John also quotes Jesus as praying that his followers "may all be one; even as thou, Father, art in me, and I in thee" (17:21).

There was also the problem of the Holy Spirit—Holy Ghost is the older English term found in the King James Version. Old Testament writers had spoken of the holy spirit of God as synonymous to God. The records of the earlier part of Jesus' ministry present the same concept: at Jesus' baptism the Spirit descended upon him like a dove; the Spirit drove him into the wilderness; by the Spirit of God he cast out demons. However at his last supper, Jesus said that the Holy Spirit would live in his followers. It would be sent by God. It seemed to be a separate entity. In some way it represented God. Paul seemed to confuse the Holy Spirit with both the Father and Jesus. In 2 Cor. 3:17 he wrote "Now the Lord is the Spirit."

Christians saw three expressions of God: the creative, sustaining force called the Father; God seen in human personality—particularly in Jesus; and God in reality about us—what Jesus called the spirit of truth. These were certainly not three gods, but three expressions of God as three sides of a triangle. We find many phases of life that have a variety of expression. His students think of the author of this New Testament survey as a teacher; those to whom he preaches on Sunday think of him as a minister; others may think of him as a writer. That does not mean three individuals, but three expressions of one individual. Early Christians recognized that they were seeing God in three ways. To express this trinitarian outlook they borrowed a term from the stage. Actors in Greek dramas played several characters. Costumes and setting were simple. An actor wore a mask to identify himself as one character. When he took another part in the play he wore a different mask. For a third character he wore a third mask or "persona." The word "persona" originally meant "that through which the sound comes." Thus God came to be thought of as expressing himself through three different masks or persons.

Jesus had said, "I will pray to the Father, and he will give you another Counselor, to be with you forever, even the Spirit of truth" (John 14:16-17). Jesus is also reported to have spoken of the Spirit "whom I shall send you from the Father" (John 15:26). This statement, in time, raised a great controversy in the church: Did the Holy Spirit come from the Father, or from the Father *and* the Son?

Jesus is reported three times to have called the Spirit the spirit of truth. Wherever one finds truth he finds an expression of God. Such truth may be found in the telescope, the microscope, the test tube, history, psychology or wherever people are searching for reality. Paul told his friends at Corinth, "The Spirit searches everything, even the depths of God" (1 Cor. 2:10).

In addition to calling the Holy Spirit the Spirit of truth, Jesus called it a Counselor. The Greek word, paraclete, is one called to one's side; this could mean either one who gives advice or one who gives comfort. He would be a teacher bearing witness to Jesus and guiding Christians into the truth. Beginning with Paul and continuing until today, people have applied a wide variety of qualities to the Holy Spirit. Probably the chief of these considers the Holy Spirit that which inspires people, leads them into a better life. Many times the Holy Spirit is referred to as "he" rather than "it," a personal reality.

The emphasis on the trinity has caused many people outside of Christianity to accuse Christians of believing that there are three gods. Some Christians have been confused at this point. One effort to deal with this problem at its height about the beginning of the nineteenth century was the developing of Unitarianism, an emphasis upon the unity and oneness of God.

An understanding of Jesus' definition of the Holy Spirit gives solution to a problem that bothers many people—that of the unpardonable or unforgivable sin, "Every one who speaks a word against the Son of man will be forgiven; but he who blasphemes against the Holy Spirit will not be forgiven" (Lu. 12:10). Some have suggested that suicide is the unforgivable sin, basing the claim upon the idea that after suicide there is no time when one may be forgiven. Others think of profanity as the unforgivable sin because of Jesus' use of the word blaspheme. Note that the blasphemy is against the Holy Spirit, the Spirit of truth. One who denies the truth, closes his mind to truth, has put himself into a situation where he cannot receive the forgiveness of God. The person who "likes to think of it this way" without making inquiry, without making an honest effort to discover the truth, has made repentance, re-thinking the situation impossible. If one repents he recognizes or receives the forgiveness which God is always willing to give. Such a person is following Jesus' admonition to seek, knock, ask.

For Class Discussion

1. Why is Holy Spirit a better term than Holy Ghost?
2. Why is the Holy Spirit called "He"?
3. Could God be thought of as four or five "persons" rather than three? If so, what?

Supplementary Reading

1. Bowie, Walter Russell. *Jesus and the Trinity*. New York and Nashville: Abingdon Press, 1960.
2. Miller, Madeline S., and Miller, J. Lane. *Harper's Bible Dictionary*. New York: Harper & Brothers, 1952. Articles: Holy Spirit, Trinity, Unpardonable sin.

CHAPTER 21

'The Son of Man Must Be Killed'

Read: Mk. 8:27-37; 9:30-31; 10:23-34; 14:32-42; Isa. 52:13-53:12.

Three times Mark gives what are called passion announcements, statements by Jesus that he expected to suffer at the hands of religious authorities and be killed. In each case Jesus is reported to have added that after three days he would rise again. Was this simple logic, common sense, upon the part of Jesus, a recognition that his program was leading to such a sharp conflict with religious leaders that it would result in his death? Or, was there some additional reason for his expectation?

An answer quickly given is that this was all predicted in the 52nd and 53rd chapters of Isaiah, that Jesus knew that it had all been planned long ahead of time by God. This answer raises a series of questions: Did the writer of the suffering servant passages have Jesus in mind? Was he predicting Jesus? Is God a cruel deity who would plan the suffering and death of an individual?

Christians through history have thought of Jesus as the Messiah, the God-anointed king whom the Jews expected would deliver them from their enemies. This hope was prominent in the minds of Jewish people. Not only Old Testament writers, but many other Jewish authorities, had made much of this expectation. The Dead Sea or Qumran scrolls indicate that for nearly two centuries after 100 B.C. the Jewish people were aquiver with the Messianic hope. Several different kinds of Messiah were expected. Numerous men were proclaimed to be the Messiah. Some were considered priestly; some political. However, in no instance was the suffering servant idea applied to the Messiah. A suffering, crucified Messiah was completely contrary to their dreams.

Did Jesus consider himself the Messiah or Christ? Some Bible scholars think he did not. However, there is much to suggest that some time during his ministry he decided that he was. He never went out of his way to claim to be the Messiah, but when the title was attributed to him he did not deny it (Mk. 8:29-30; 14:61-62). In the Matthew account of Peter's conviction that Jesus was the Messiah, Jesus is reported to have said that God had revealed this to Peter (16:17). In both Mark and Luke Jesus is reported to have asked his disciples to tell no one that he was the Messiah. Why was he keeping it secret? Jesus obviously had no intention of being the kind of Messiah most Jews expected, a political king who would drive the Romans out of Palestine. John differs from the synoptic writers at many points. When the Samaritan woman at Jacob's well mentioned the Messiah, John pictured Jesus as saying, "I who speak to you am he" (4:26).

When did Jesus conclude that he was the Messiah? Was it at his baptism? Was it during his wilderness temptation experience? Was it in connection with the transfiguration experience? The difficulty in believing that this last was the time is that in all synoptic accounts Peter's conviction is given before the transfiguration. Some suggest that the transfiguration experience was a divine confirmation of Peter's conviction.

In what way was Jesus the suffering servant? Nathaniel Hawthorne tells the story of "The Great Stone Face." A rock formation in the New England mountains looks like a human face. In the valley below the face there was a tradition that some day a man would come who looked like the face. A boy born in the valley kept asking questions about the great stone face man. He continued this questioning and thinking into adult life. Then one day his neighbors came to realize that he looked like the stone face. His thinking had made him such. Did not Jesus become the suffering servant in much the same way?

The passages of the second Isaiah refer to the Hebrew people as "the servant of God" who would need to suffer to teach the world about God. Jesus took upon himself this task. To serve God one must serve the children of God. Jesus recognized the importance of serving others. "Whoever would be great among you must be your servant" (Mk. 10:43). John reports that Jesus

141

demonstrated this by washing the feet of his disciples (13:3-5). It is interesting to note that in all of Paul's writings he never connects the suffering servant passage with Jesus.

Other terms describe Jesus beside those of Messiah and suffering servant. Many saw in him a similarity to the Old Testament prophets, courageous men who challenged the leadership and ritual of their day. He knew that the prophets had suffered much for their teachings. There was a tradition that every prophet had been put to death. Jesus recognized that he would be no exception. John the Baptist had been beheaded. Jesus was convinced that others would suffer for their stand. "Blessed are you when men revile you and persecute you and utter all kinds of evil against you falsely on my account. Rejoice and be glad, for your reward is great in heaven, for so men persecuted the prophets who were before you" (Matt. 5:11-12). Life was cheap. Many people had been killed. So would he be. Jesus was not only challenging the teachings of the Pharisees. He was challenging the priests, men who had considerable authority and had learned how to get their way with Roman officials.

In each of these passion announcements and at numerous other times Jesus called himself the Son of man. At no time is he called this by others except in John 12:34 and in Acts 7:56 and possibly some comments added to sayings of Jesus. What did this term mean? He seems to have used it as a substitute for "I" or "me," but it must have had some deeper meaning. Quite often in the Old Testament the expression is used simply to mean man. Ezekiel used it nearly a hundred times to refer to himself. Students are interested in another use of the term which appears only once in the Hebrew scriptures. In Dan. 7:13-14 the writer tells of a vision in which "with the clouds of heaven there came one like a son of man . . . to him was given dominion and glory and kingdom, that all peoples, nations, and languages should serve him." Did Jesus have this celestial being in mind? He never seemed to act domineeringly or to glorify himself. In the book called Enoch, which was considered by many Jews in the time of Jesus to be scripture, the term "the son of man" appears a number of times. This refers to a servant or agent of God in the victorious "Day of the Lord." This may be more what Jesus had in mind when he called himself the Son of man. Did the idea of such service tie in with Jesus' conviction that he would eventually be put to death?

Eighty-one times in the gospel accounts the term "Son of man" seems to be found on the lips of Jesus. On the other hand, a term which the early church came to use extensively in relation to Jesus, "Son of God" is only twice reported to have been used by Jesus—both times in John. Jesus spoke of God not only as *his* father, but *your* father, *our* father. However, he definitely thought of himself as in some way especially close to God. He spoke of himself as "the Son": "No one knows the Father except the Son" (Matt. 11:27). There are several similar references in John.

How did Jesus become the Son of God? is a question that bothered early Christians. Mark hints that Jesus became the Son of God by adoption at the time of his baptism. Hebrew kings in a somewhat similar way were considered sons of God. Matthew and Luke suggest that Jesus was begotten by the Holy Spirit's serving in place of a physical father. John believes that Jesus existed from the beginning of time as God's Son.

However Jesus considered himself, there grew upon him that which is evident in his attitude in connection with his trial and crucifixion: a conviction that he had come into the world to suffer and die for its salvation. The Matthew compiler notes that Jesus came to a full realization of his divine sonship after the Resurrection: "All authority in heaven and on earth has been given to me. Go therefore and make disciples of all nations, baptizing them in the name of the Father, and of the Son and of the Holy Spirit" (28:18-19).

We face other problems in connection with Mark's passion announcements. If Jesus on three occasions told his followers that "the Son of man must suffer many things, and be rejected by the elders and the chief priests and the scribes, and be killed, and after three days rise again," why were the disciples so surprised and stunned at the time of Jesus' arrest and crucifixion? Why did they not expect the Resurrection? Did they think Jesus was using some figure of speech they could not understand? Could Mark, looking back forty years later, have made Jesus' predictions about his death more complete than they were? Mark's information was second hand.

We still have the question, Did God plan Jesus' death? Was it

143

foreordained or predestined from the beginning of time? The Matthew account, compiled for Jewish readers, makes much of parallels between the life of Jesus and the Hebrew scriptures. It expresses a conviction that much which occurred had been predicted. The writer of the letter to the Ephesians wrote of "the plan of the mystery hidden for ages . . . This was according to the eternal purpose which he has realized in Christ Jesus" (3:9 and 11).

Jesus' prayer in the Garden of Gethsemane is often quoted: "Father, if thou art willing, remove this cup from me; nevertheless not my will, but thine, be done" (Lu. 22:42). Was the crucifixion the will of God or was it God's will that Jesus not be a quitter, not run away?

Certainly God gives people a degree of free choice. Otherwise we should be machines, automatons. Did not God do the same with Jesus and his enemies? However, some things are determined before our birth. Few people have changed the intelligence with which they were born. We are not especially successful in changing the color of our skin or eyes, the straightness or kinkiness of our hair. Jesus' death was cruel, involving much physical and mental suffering. Did a loving, kind Heavenly Father plan that? If not, why did he not interfere? Does he prevent other people from suffering unjustly?

For Class Discussion

1. Which term best applies to Jesus: Messiah, suffering servant, Son of man, Son of God? Why? Would John's term Logos or Word be better? When was the term Savior used? What does it mean? What does Lord mean? Why is the use of this term confusing?

2. Why did most Jews reject Jesus' own concept of the Messiah?

3. How important is it to recognize Jesus as the Messiah?

4. If Jesus called himself the Son of God what did he mean by the term? What did he mean by the Son of man?

Supplementary Reading

1. Laymon, Charles M. *The Life and Teachings of Jesus.* New York and Nashville: Abingdon Press, 1955. Chapter 20.

2. Steward, James S. *The Life and Teachings of Jesus Christ.* New York and Nashville: Abingdon Press, 1957. Chapter XVI.

CHAPTER 22

'Let Him Be Crucified"

Read: Matt. 26 and 27; Lu. 22 and 23.

Shortly after Peter and the other disciples recognized that they believed Jesus was the Messiah, the Christ, Jesus "set his face to go to Jerusalem" (Lu. 9:51). In telling about this bold move Mark says, "Jesus was walking ahead of them; and they were amazed, and those who followed were afraid" (10:32). Contrary to the usual Jewish custom Jesus went from Galilee to Samaria. However, according to Luke, "the people would not receive him" (9:53). Evidently Jesus crossed the Jordan and spent some time teaching in Perea. He then visited Jericho on his way to Jerusalem. In Jericho he helped both the poor and the rich: Bartimaeus (Mk. 10:46-52) and Zacchaeus (Lu. 19:1-10).

As they were going toward Jerusalem Jesus tried to explain to his disciples what he expected his fate to be, but they failed to understand him. They did not comprehend what he meant by the Kingdom. They were expecting a political government. They quarreled as to which one of them was the greatest. James and John (or possibly their mother) tried to get Jesus to promise that they would have top positions in the Kingdom. Jesus strove to prepare them for the trials and troubles they would face. He attempted to help them avoid hypocrisy, worry and fear; he warned them that they would be brought "before the synagogues and the rulers and the authorities" (Lu. 12:11).

Jesus refused to be the type of Messiah most people expected. He would have nothing to do with setting up the kind of Kingdom his disciples wanted. Yet he would be a Messiah, the kind of Messiah some people had expected, one of peace, good will, love. The prophet Zechariah had dreamed of such a person, not a military leader riding on a charger. He had once proclaimed:

> Lo, your king comes to you;
>> triumphant and victorious is he,
> humble and riding on an ass (9:9).

Why not be this kind of king! Jesus arranged for some one to provide such a beast of burden. On it he rode into Jerusalem. Crowds were gathering in the city for the greatest of the Jews' five annual feasts, that of Passover. To the disciples this seemed a strange way for Jesus to announce his Messiahship, but, they believed, finally their aims were about to be realized. The enthusiasm of the disciples was contagious. Crowds from Galilee were expectant as they came to the Holy City. They broke into praises as they saw groups around Jesus. As was done with royalty, they put their clothes on the road for him to ride over. They waved branches which they broke from shrubbery along the way.

The Pharisees and priests despised this popularity upon the part of Jesus. Luke reports that the Pharisees demanded "Teacher, rebuke your disciples" (19:39), and a bit further along that "the chief priests and the scribes and the principal men of the people sought to destroy him; but they did not find anything they could do, for the people hung upon his words" (19:47-48). For several days Jesus' teaching in the temple area was interrupted by questions upon the part of the opposition, questions asked to embarrass Jesus, to turn people against him.

His opponents were determined to put Jesus to death. He was becoming too popular. Luke says that "they feared the people" (22:2). Matthew notes that they were determined to kill him before the great feast got under way "lest there be a tumult among the people" (26:5). One of the twelve, Judas Iscariot, aided them in their plans by revealing where Jesus could be found at night apart from the crowds.

How can we explain Judas' action? Luke's statement that "Satan entered into Judas" is scarcely sufficient. Numerous attempts have been made to interpret Judas. Was he a rascal or a blunderer? Was he plotting to save his own life when Jewish leaders attacked Jesus and his disciples? Many scholars today feel that Judas was attempting to aid Jesus, to force him to act as the Messiah was expected to act. Like the other disciples, Judas thought Jesus was the Messiah who was to set up a kingdom which would overthrow Rome. Jesus had begun to assert his Messiahship by his triumphal entry and the overthrowing of the money-changers in the temple. Jesus was popular, but he was not making use of his opportunity to rouse the people to a great active hatred of Rome and to murder the Roman guard. If the priests attempted to arrest Jesus, God would send legions of angels to his rescue, and the crowds would rise up to support him as the new Messiah. May not Judas have felt himself very clever taking the leading part in forcing Jesus to be recognized as the Messiah, the conquering king? May he not have attempted to deceive the priests, appear to be a greedy traitor, by asking them to pay him for his deed?

The great event in the Jewish year was the week-long festival of Unleavened Bread begun by the Passover Feast. This commemorated the escape of the Israelites from Egypt under the leadership of Moses. Although the Passover was a home or family celebration, many Jews visited Jerusalem at this time and celebrated with their friends. Jesus and his disciples made up such a group. The synoptic gospels report that it was at such a Passover feast that Jesus ate his last supper with his closest friends. John reports that this meal took place a day before the Passover celebration, possibly a solemn preparatory banquet such as was celebrated by religious brotherhoods. Jesus' farewell meal seems to be closer to the Essene communion meal than to the Passover. We have some suggestion that Galilean Jews observed the Passover a day earlier than those in Judea. In this case both the synoptics and John could be correct. All accounts agree that the last supper was on Thursday night and that Jesus was crucified on Friday. Most Bible scholars find several arguments to back up John's claim that the Last Supper was eaten the day before Passover.

John does not tell of the originating, in connection with this meal, of what we call the Lord's Supper or Communion, Mass or Eucharist. All the synoptic accounts tell of this, as does Paul (1 Cor. 11:23-26). Jesus recognized that he was about to give his life, which in some way would be a sacrifice for others. Taking the most common elements of the meal, bread and wine, he requested that his disciples, "Do this, as often as you drink it, in remembrance of me" (1 Cor. 11:25). Did Jesus consider this a sacrament to be observed at stated times? Or, did he mean that

147

every time Christians eat or drink they should think of him or the things for which he stood? Of the bread he said, "This is my body;" of the wine, "This is my blood." These terms bother some people. Doubtless in the Aramaic which he was speaking Jesus did not use a verb. He evidently meant that this represents his body and blood given as a sacrifice. Certainly as he sat before his disciples he did not think that they were literally eating his flesh and drinking his blood. Roman Catholics assert that at each observance of the mass a miracle takes place at which the bread or wafer becomes actual flesh of Jesus and the wine his blood, although the "accidents" of appearance, taste and smell do not change. This teaching is called transubstantiation. Some Lutherans believe that a part of bread and wine becomes flesh and blood. This is called consubstantiation. Most Protestants consider that these are symbols, that in taking them people may receive spiritual nourishment or strength.

Luke's account of the last supper differs somewhat from that of Mark and Matthew. In all four gospel records Jesus announced that one of the twelve would betray him. Both Matthew and John report that Jesus said it was Judas. Jesus continued to be kind in his treatment of Judas. In Oriental homes yet today the host often selects a choice morsel of food from the common dish and gives it to the special guest. John reports that Jesus thus honored Judas, possibly hoping to win Judas over to another program. It is quite probable that Judas felt superior to the other disciples, convinced that he was about to bring about what all of them wanted, the establishment of Jesus as Messiah and king. Possibly he felt that Jesus saw through his scheme and was lending himself to his program.

John evidently is correct in saying that Judas then left the group. When Jesus and his disciples had sung a hymn they went east of Jerusalem to an olive grove on the side of the Mount of Olives. Luke says Jesus was accustomed to visit this place. Jesus was very conscious of what in general was about to happen to him. He did not want to die. He could have escaped through the dark over the Mount of Olives and down to the wilderness along the Jordan. As long as he stayed there probably no one would bother him. However, he was determined not to be a quitter. He would take the consequences of his teaching, "not as I will, but as thou wilt." It was while Jesus was thus prayerfully coming to his decision that Judas led a crowd of temple guards and others to the place where Jesus had at times quietly met with his disciples. Jesus did not hold back to grasp one more moment of freedom, but, according to John, stepped forward to meet those who had come to arrest him.

Jesus had warned Peter that he would deny him before morning. Peter had insisted that he would always be loyal to Jesus. He now impetuously rushed to the defense of his master with a sword. Jesus took control by demanding "No more of this!" (Lu. 22:51). "Put your sword back into its place; for all who take the sword will perish by the sword" (Matt. 26:52).

Jesus was immediately taken to the home of Caiaphas who served as high priest from A.D. 18 to 36. His father-in-law, Annas, who had been high priest from A.D. 6 to 15, seems to have had some part in the proceedings, according to John. Jesus did not receive a legal, formal trial that night. It might be considered grand jury proceedings. It was evidently an attempt upon the part of Caiaphas and his associates to decide what charges might be brought against Jesus. This did not prove as easy as had been expected. Witnesses could not be made to agree. "At last two came forward and said, 'This fellow said, "I am able to destroy the temple of God, and to build it in three days." ' " (Matt. 26: 60-61). Jesus confused the situation by keeping silent. Finally the high priest demanded that Jesus testify on oath whether or not he was the Christ or Messiah. Just how Jesus dealt with this question and what references were made to the Son of man are rather uncertain. However, this gave the high priest a chance to raise the charge of blasphemy and dramatize it by tearing his clothing. Mark and Matthew mention another meeting the next morning of the chief priests and elders, the Sanhedrin. Possibly this was to legalize the actions of the night before. Lawyers today note that at several points Jesus' "trial" was still not in accord with legal procedure.

At the time of Jesus' arrest most of the disciples slipped away. However, Peter courageously followed at a distance and even came into the courtyard of the high priest. Here he mingled with some of the high priest's servants around a fire. Then Peter's courage wilted before a maid who accused him of being associated

149

with Jesus. Peter denied this. Later the event was repeated. Peter's speaking caused others to recognize that he was a Galilean, for the Galilean accent differed from that of Judea. In the book of Judges we have the record of a group of Ephraimites being discovered by their speech (12:1-6) ; a Levite in Ephraim was similarly recognized as a foreigner (18:3). Peter was angered and "began to invoke a curse on himself and to swear, 'I do not know this man'" (Matt. 26:74). No sooner had he done this than he realized that he had been disloyal to Jesus. "And he went out and wept bitterly." Peter eventually became the great leader of the church. The church's interests and prejudices are at times reflected in the way the gospel account is recorded. However, it is to its credit that the church reported Peter's denial. All four gospel accounts tell of it.

When the gospel records were being written, the church was eager to have the good will of the Roman government. Therefore the fact that Jesus was condemned and crucified by representatives of Rome is dealt with lightly and the blame is placed largely upon the Jews. This is especially true of Luke, which was written for non-Jewish readers. Pilate's headquarters were in Caesarea along the coast north-west of Jerusalem, but Pilate and many of his soldiers were in Jerusalem at the Passover period to see that peace was maintained. While the charges discussed among members of the Sanhedrin were of a religious nature, these would not bear any weight with Roman officials. Therefore, political charges were made. It was asserted that Jesus had forbidden the paying of taxes to Rome and claimed to be a king. Pilate did not recognize Jesus as guilty of any crime, but the priests would not accept this. They insisted that he was a trouble-maker throughout Palestine. Only Luke tells that when Pilate learned that Jesus was from Galilee he sent him to Herod Antipas, who was in Jerusalem for the Passover. But Herod treated Jesus with contempt and sent him back to Pilate. Luke tells that three times Pilate protested that Jesus was innocent, but he gave in to the demands of the crowd stirred up by the priests. His attempt to transfer the crowd's hatred to another man, called in some manuscripts Jesus Barabbas, failed. When some Jews cried out, "If you release this man, you are not Caesar's friend" (John 19:12), Pilate became frightened. He had been criticized by the Jews before. His record was not too good. Countering the high priest at this point would lead to charges which probably would cost Pilate his position.

Mark, Matthew, and John report that Jesus was the victim of horse-play upon the part of Pilate's soldiers. Luke reports such treatment by Herod's soldiers. Matthew and Luke tell of somewhat similar mistreatment by people associated with the high priest.

Jesus was condemned to be crucified. Such a person was required to carry the crossbeam to which his hands were later nailed. The synoptic gospels report that a man named Simon from Cyrene in north Africa was drafted to carry the cross for Jesus. Mark notes that this man was the father of Alexander and Rufus, evidently well known Christians. There was a large Jewish group at Cyrene. Some people think this man was the "Symeon who was called Niger" (Acts 12:1) who was associated with another man from Cyrene. In this case our Simon of Cyrene was doubtless a Negro.

The gospel accounts vary considerably in details of the crucifixion. Evidently about nine o'clock Friday morning Jesus' hands were nailed to the crossbeam and it was fastened to the upright pole already planted on the execution ground called "the Skull," not far outside the city. Crucifixion was a cruel method of execution usually reserved for slaves and desperate criminals. The naked body was suspended by the hands and partially seated on a nail or peg. The torture often lasted two or three days, sometimes longer. Suffering was increased by swarms of flies and the taunts of those watching. Death would finally come by exhaustion.

The Jews had tried to lessen the cruelty of Roman executions by giving the condemned an opiate to drug them. When this was offered to Jesus he rejected it, probably wishing to keep a clear mind. Of the "seven last words from the cross" Mark and Matthew give but one, a quotation from the 22nd Psalm. Jesus doubtless recognized how appropriate this Psalm was to the experience he was having, and probably quoted several verses from it. It is only Luke who records Jesus' prayer, "Father, forgive them; for they know not what they do," and his kind words to one of the criminals crucified with him, "Today you will be with me in

151

Paradise." As the 22nd Psalm ends in a note of triumph so Jesus realized that God had not forsaken him. Luke reports his last words as "Father, into thy hands I commit my spirit."

What did Jesus' death on the cross mean to mankind? The early church made much of it. It helped men to understand God. In some way it brought an ever growing group of people into accord with God. From this a theological term developed, the at-one-ment or atonement. Theologians have quarrelled among themselves as to just how this atonement functions. A large number of explanations have developed. Physicists disagree as to what light is; most of us have difficulty explaining electricity; but all of us know how to use light and electricity. So, regardless of which technical explanation we accept, we can find ourselves brought into accord, into one-ness, with God, through the death on the cross of him of whom Paul said "God was in Christ reconciling the world to himself" (2 Cor. 5:19). Ours has always been a loving God. Calvary, with its spirit of forgiveness, revealed God to men.

For Class Discussion

1. Why were his opponents so eager to put Jesus to death?
2. How do you interpret Judas?
3. What does the term atonement mean to you?

Assignment

1. An inscription was put over the cross of Jesus. According to Matthew what was its wording? Mark? Luke? John?
2. Summarize what Jesus attempted to teach.

Supplementary Reading

1. Laymon, Charles M. *The Life and Teachings of Jesus.* New York and Nashville: Abingdon Press, 1955. Chapters 22, 23 and 24.
2. Stewart, James S. *The Life and Teachings of Jesus Christ.* New York and Nashville: Abingdon Press, 1957. Chapters XVII, XVIII, and XIX.

CHAPTER 23

'This Jesus God Raised Up"

Read: Matt. 28; Lu. 24; Acts 1

The Christ is still alive! Death could not hold him! Such was the electrifying conviction that reunited the followers of Jesus. They had scattered after the crucifixion. Two of the disciples had mourned, "We had hoped that he was the one to redeem Israel" (Lu. 24:21). Something had changed all this. The details of the four gospel accounts of the Resurrection are confusing, conflicting, but that is unimportant. We do not need them. The proof of the Resurrection is in the transformed disciples. They had become new men. Peter had denied knowing Jesus. Now we find him speaking forth courageously unafraid. Jesus' followers were convinced that they had experiences with Jesus after his crucifixion, that God had thus publicly demonstrated that Jesus was the Son of God. They were aflame with overwhelming confidence.

Some one has portrayed this proof of the Resurrection in the following words:

> I showed my friend the empty tomb so as to prove to him that the Christ had risen from the dead. But he believed not. I revealed to him the broken seal and the napkin folded in a corner. But no faith arose in him. I set before him the written record and many other infallible proofs that my Lord was indeed alive. But still he did not believe. "For," said he to me, "I have looked into your heart and I find it selfish, ambitious, proud. I see that it is hot and resentful, envious and grudging. No, your Christ is dead forever more."
>
> Then there came a day when I yearned over my friend and loved him as my own soul. I forgot my proofs, and remembered only his incomparable need. I gave up my

153

argument, and merely stretched forth my hand with an aching tenderness in its touch. I became so concerned for his plan that somehow my own was forgotten and failed, and I did not even care. I sought out the bruises that life had left upon his soul, and in some strange fashion I became a minister for their healing. And then he believed! "For," said he, "I have seen the living Christ walking in the world. I know that he indeed is risen from the dead and become the first fruits of them that sleep in the charnel house of self. Yes, your Christ is alive forever more."

These first followers of Jesus were all Jews. They were considered a bit odd, almost a synagogue of their own. Doubtless neither Jesus nor these who remained loyal to him ever intended to form a new religion. The effort of Jesus had been to speed up the growth of the Jewish religion, make it more thoughtful, more effective, more active, more all-inclusive. He wanted to make it more ethical, moral, less legalistic, less a matter of ritual. He was concerned with the inner life. As has happened a number of times since, religion had become degenerate. Those who had a vision of greater possibilities, of larger service for their religion, became unpopular. Before long they found themselves pushed outside the group to which they had belonged. The new wine could not be contained in old wineskins.

At first the Jews paid little attention to this new group growing up in their midst. But as it showed vigor and took on strength the Jewish leaders decided it must be destroyed.

The majority of Jews did not recognize Jesus as the Messiah, the Christ. They could have accepted his teachings without ascribing Messiahship to him, but they also rejected his advanced ideas. He had gone too far beyond current Jewish concepts. The better educated Jews recognized that their ideas had evolved during the centuries, but they were quite content with what they had. They wanted to maintain the status quo religiously. They were in no hurry to make further developments.

Why did most Jews reject Jesus? A twentieth century Orthodox Jewish writer, Rabbi Joseph Klausner, has given two primary reasons. He believes that, in the first place, Jesus was too universal, not putting enough emphasis upon his nation or race. In the second place, he says, Jesus put too much emphasis upon the love of God. This would counteract the justice of God. These people seem to have forgotten that one of their own prophets, Micah, had put love and justice together in his famous question: "What does the LORD require of you but to do justice, and to love kindness and to walk humbly with your God?" (Mic. 6:8). Therefore, a new religion was founded.

How do we know that this new religion, Christianity, is better than the great religions already in existence, Judaism, Hinduism, Buddhism? Jesus himself gave a basis by which we may judge, "You will know them by their fruits" (Matt. 7:16). One has but to examine the standard of living, the health, the happiness of the average person of other religions and compare these with the average Christian to make his own conclusions. Other religions were searching for God, for truth. The religion of Jesus is the religion of maturity.

We might well raise another question at this point: What is Christianity? Is it a creed? Is it a way of life? Is it the church? What is it?

The followers of Jesus soon came to recognize themselves as a group of people called apart, a church. How the church got under way, how it came to be named, its persecution and subsequent spread, the leaders it developed, the problems it faced, the solutions it worked out, and its contributions to our own life and thinking constitute the remainder of this book. Our chief source materials are two: The Acts of the Apostles, and the letters of early church leaders. This is exciting history. The world was beginning to turn from paganism to a moral concept of human relations. These writings are essential to the Christian scriptures. The words of Jesus were not sufficient. The cross, the resurrection, and the exaltation of Christ are a part of the Christian message. These had to be proclaimed and interpreted. This is a part of the apostolic witness, necessary to the Christian Bible.

In Luke's account of the early church he shows the same interest he expressed in his first volume. To him Christianity has no limits of race or sex; it is for all people. In his opening verse he points out that in his first book he dealt with all that Jesus began to do and teach "until the day when he was taken up." He implies that he proposes to report what Jesus continued to do through his church.

The first two paragraphs of Luke's second volume are a more detailed repetition of the last paragraph of his first volume. If one were to read only Luke's Gospel account, he would be led to believe that the Ascension took place the same day as the Resurrection, but in the Acts we find another of those frequent forty day periods. During this time Jesus charged his disciples to stay in Jerusalem until they were convinced they had the truth, the Holy Spirit. They were to be sure they knew just what his message was before attempting to give it to others. He did not want them to be blind guides leading the blind, lest both fall into a pit. He wanted them to be well prepared, organized, self-confident.

Luke also says that during these forty days Jesus was telling his disciples about the Kingdom. But in the sixth verse he indicates that the disciples were dull of understanding. They still failed to grasp what Jesus meant by the Kingdom: "Lord, will you at this time restore the kingdom to Israel?" Is this not one of the most pathetic questions in our Bible? They still could not give up the idea of a political kingdom with a physical throne and crown. They still had in mind a picture of Jesus' overcoming the Romans and becoming a royal successor to David, making Israel a more powerful nation than ever before.

The eighth verse gives Jesus' last command to his disciples, the Great Commission. The command to spread the gospel to all mankind is in each of our five records. It is the important thing. The words differ from account to account and the setting differs. The Matthew account puts it in Galilee. In Luke's earlier account, in the generally accepted appendix to Mark, and in John, the commission seems to be given in a room in Jerusalem rather than on the Mount of Olives. Note the concentric circles in the commission as given in Acts. Start right here in town, go to the country-side round about, but do not stop there. Spread the message to the neighbors to the north whom most Jews despised, and then go on to the entire world. Know no limits. The Christian message was not to be confined to the home region. Nor was it something for export only. It must apply equally to all people everywhere. How much did the disciples comprehend by "all the world?"

156

The account in Acts gives the great commission as Jesus' last words to his disciples. A cloud took him out of their sight and they saw him no more, as in the Old Testament a cloud was said to hide God from view. The only apparent direction to get away from the earth is up. Therefore we speak of Jesus as ascending.

In their amazement there came to the disciples the assurance that "Jesus, who was taken up from you into heaven, will come in the same way as you saw him go into heaven." How are these words to be taken? Many early Christians took them literally. They believed that these eleven men would some time soon see Jesus come back and complete his task as the Messiah, drive out the Romans, and set himself up in Jerusalem as king. They had agreed that Jesus was the Christ, the Messiah, but he had not fulfilled what they expected the Messiah to do. Doubtless, they reasoned, he planned to return soon and complete his task.

Many scholars are convinced that Jesus himself did not believe or preach that he would return. However, the early church soon adopted this concept. There is some reference to it, or at least a hint about it, in every New Testament book except Galatians, Ephesians, Philemon and Second and Third John.

As years passed and the men who had been closest to Jesus died, Christians realized they had been wrong. How should the promise that Jesus would return be interpreted? There was the promise of Jesus with which the Matthew account concludes, "I am with you always." The Ascension was not the last time men were convinced that Christ was present. When Paul listed post-Resurrection appearances of Christ he said, "he appeared also unto me" (1 Cor. 15:8). But, despite the conviction of the continuing presence of Christ, the idea of a "return" of Jesus did not completely die out. A new emphasis on this developed in the middle of the nineteenth century. Today there are three schools of thought.

In the Revelation to John there is reference to Satan being bound a thousand years. This has given rise to two of these schools. The premillenarians say the world is getting worse and worse. When it gets so corrupt, so sinful that it can get no worse, Jesus will come to the rescue and bind Satan for a thousand years, a millenium. Such people logically rejoice in indications of evil as these show that Jesus will soon return. The second group are the postmillenarians. They recall the conviction of Jesus that the Kingdom of God would grow like mustard or leaven. They feel that the world is growing better and better. When perfection is reached, the Kingdom will have achieved its fulfillment; after a proving time of a thousand years Jesus will return. This group emphasizes that we are preparing the way for the second coming or advent of Jesus.

A growing third group has no specific name. Its emphasis is spiritual. It draws its support from the picture in the book printed last in our Bibles. In this Jesus is shown standing at the door constantly seeking admission: "Behold, I stand at the door and knock; if any one hears my voice and opens the door, I will come in to him and eat with him, and he with me" (Rev. 3:20). This group emphasizes that the spirit of Christ is always trying to come to men but he will not knock the door down. Individuals must accept Christ; the return is personal as men allow this spirit to enter their lives.

In connection with the return of the disciples from the Mount of Olives to Jerusalem their names are given. Each of the synoptic gospels lists the twelve but their order varies. However, in each list the name of Peter appears first. This suggests that Peter was recognized as the leading disciple.

Another name emphasis appears in the 14th verse. The eleven disciples with the brothers of Jesus, some women, and Mary devoted themselves to prayer. Why does the record report "some women and Mary?" Little had been said about Mary since the birth stories. Here is the beginning of holding Mary in special reverence. She was the nearest they now had to Jesus. To some uncertain degree she represented Jesus.

Others joined the group so that we are told there were 120. Peter assumed leadership and suggested that some one should be elected to replace Judas among the twelve. He felt that the new member should be a man who had associated with the group from the beginning. Twelve was a sacred number. Evidently the twelve disciples were thought of as being symbolically related to the twelve tribes of Israel. There had been a reference in Luke's gospel account (22:30) to the disciples' judging the twelve tribes. When James lost his life a bit later nothing seems to have been done about electing a successor to him. Perhaps the early

Christians felt that James would serve as a judge in the next life but Judas had eliminated himself.

In what way Judas committed suicide is a question to which we have no definite answer. In Acts we read that he fell headlong and burst open in a field which he had bought. In Matt. 27:5 we are told he hanged himself. Acts 1:25 sums up Judas' action by saying that he "turned aside, to go to his own place."

Two men were nominated for the vacant position. One was Joseph Barsabbas who must not be confused with Barabbas whom we have already met or with Joseph Barnabas or Judas Barsabbas whom we meet later. The second nominee was Matthias. It fell to the lot of the latter to join the eleven. Nothing more is heard of either Joseph Barsabbas or Matthias, although several apocryphal writers use the name of Matthias to give authority to their writings.

The newly formed twelve were to be "witnesses to the resurrection." There is reference to "this ministry and apostleship." It was said that Matthias was "enrolled with the eleven apostles." The word apostle had already been used in the synoptic gospels, but disciple was the more common word. It is well to note the difference between the two words. "Disciple" means learner; "apostle" one who is sent forth. These two terms represent the change in emphasis of the work of the twelve.

For Class Discussion

1. What are the important things to recognize about the Resurrection? In 1 Cor. 15:3-8 Paul tells of evidences of the Resurrection but does not mention the open tomb. Why?

2. For what reasons, other than those suggested by Klausner, did most Jews reject Jesus?

3. Why do we say that the Christian religion is better than any other?

4. What other reform groups have been cast out of the mother group?

5. To which theory of the second coming of Jesus would you subscribe?

6. What denominations put special emphasis upon premillenarianism?

Assignment

1. In your own words tell what Jesus' Great Commission was.
2. How would you sum up what became of Judas?
3. Why was Matthias selected? What do we know about him?
4. What is the difference between "disciple" and "apostle"?

Supplementary Reading

1. *The Interpreter's Bible*. New York and Nashville: Abingdon Press. Vol. 9, 1954. Pages 3-35.
2. Phillips, J. B. *New Testament Christianity*. New York: The Macmillan Company, 1956.
3. Weatherhead, Leslie D. *Manner of the Resurrection*. New York and Nashville: Abingdon Press, 1960.

CHAPTER 24

"Speak No Man in This Name"

Read: Acts 2-5.

Seven weeks had passed since the Resurrection. The second greatest Jewish festival, Pentecost, had arrived. Great numbers of Jews abroad were in Jerusalem every Pentecost. Although Passover was considered the greater festival and drew the larger crowds, it was too early in the spring for smooth passage on the Mediterranean. The sea at Pentecost time was ideal. If Jesus insisted that his good news was to be shared with people in the uttermost parts of the world, now was the apostles' chance. They had been together for ten days since their last group experience of the presence of the Christ. They had busied themselves recollecting the teachings of Jesus. They had been much in prayer. Christ's message and their task were becoming organized in their minds. Now they were convinced they had the truth and were ready to share it.

Jesus had promised that his followers would receive the Holy Spirit, the spirit of truth. The early church was sure this had taken place, but evidently it was not sure when. Was it not through the Holy Spirit that they perceived the Resurrection? John suggests that Jesus gave the disciples the Holy Spirit the first time they saw him after the Resurrection: "He breathed on them and said to them, 'Receive the Holy Spirit'" (20:22).

Luke, writing half a century after the event, makes the receiving of this conviction a moving experience. The conclusion that the early Christians received the spirit of truth is not pictured as a calm, quiet growth. This may have been an especially impressive prayer meeting. Luke doubtless had difficulty learning just what took place. He does not say there were wind and fire. He would remember that he had quoted John the Baptist as saying (Lu. 3:16), "He who is mightier than I . . . will baptize you with the

Holy Spirit and with fire." Is this what occurred on this day that is sometimes called the birthday of the church?

What can we say about the speaking in other tongues? Evidently there was much excitement. People were greatly impressed by the message of the apostles. Who were present? They were all Jews or at least people who had accepted the Jewish religion. They could all speak some form of Aramaic. In informal, idiomatic conversation it would be difficult to understand one another. In impressive, somewhat formal, public speaking that might not be so difficult.

Let me give an illustration. I once took some students to a neighboring city to meet and hear the British social worker from the east end of London, Murial Lester. We had an informal chat with her at the supper table. Most of us had considerable difficulty understanding her vocabulary and pronunciation. We then went to the auditorium, which was crowded with expectant enthusiastic people. When Miss Lester stepped forward there was a hush. Some people were sitting on the edge of their chairs. She was gripping her listeners. We were stirred by her ideas and forgot about what seemed "peculiarities" of speech.

May not this have been similar to the experience that first Christian Pentecost day in Jerusalem? Not all early Christians would have agreed, or all today. There are other references in Acts to speaking in tongues (10:46 and 19:6). Stories are told of people today who have found themselves speaking in a language they had never been taught. However, Jesus is never reported to have spoken thus. About thirty years before Acts was written, this speaking had become a problem. The church at Corinth in Greece evidently asked Paul about it. He gives an interesting reply in 1 Cor. 14:13-19, concluding, "I would rather speak five words with my mind, in order to instruct others, than ten thousand words in a tongue."

Not all people were impressed by the apostles. Some accused the apostles of having had too much new wine (of being happily drunk). Peter pointed out that this could not be, as it was but nine o'clock in the morning. They could not have had enough wine by then to be drunk.

Peter went ahead to claim that this was the realization of the Old Testament prophet Joel's belief that God had declared he

162

would pour out his Spirit upon all flesh (Joel 2:28-32). While we agree with Peter that this was what was taking place, we can apply the same quotation to many experiences since the time of Peter. Peter boldly proclaimed that Jesus, who had been put to death by lawless men, had been raised up by God, "having loosed the pangs of death." He is the Messiah, the Christ. He is more than the Messiah expected by the Jewish people. "God has made him . . . Lord." He is our supreme master, the one we are to obey. It is by him we are to be judged. He has poured out the Holy Spirit upon the apostles. Within fifty days of the crucifixion the evidence of the Resurrection given by the apostles convinced thousands. There was no illusion here. The apostles were speaking from definite experience.

Doubtless we have but a resume of Peter's sermon. We wonder how accurate Luke's reports of various sermons were. He learned about them years later second or third hand. Many who heard Peter were impressed and exclaimed, "Brethren, what shall we do?" Peter instructed them to think this thing through, get a new mind about it. Then they themselves should join the Christian group, seek a clean start and symbolize this by baptism. If they did this, they too would receive the spirit of truth, the Holy Spirit. About three thousand accepted this invitation. They became students of the apostles and joined in fellowship with them, eating and praying with them. They "had all things in common; and they sold their possessions and goods and distributed them to all, as any had need." More details about this communal living are given later.

About three o'clock one afternoon Peter and John, still good Jews, went to the temple. We presume that this John was the son of Zebedee and brother of James. However, it is not impossible that it was John Mark. They came through the eastern gate of the temple. It may be that they were spending their nights at Bethany as this is not the approach one would naturally make from the city of Jerusalem.

At the temple gate a beggar called to Peter and John. They had doubtless had such an experience many times, but this beggar had the good fortune of getting their attention. Peter and John had no money to give him. He did not get what he asked for, but got something much more important—self-confidence. With assurance Peter told him that he could walk and helped him to his feet. Probably no one had ever done this before; few people had showed personal interest in the beggar. He was so startled and pleased by this new experience that he actually walked. The "leaping" may be a bit exaggerated. We must remember that the record was written fifty years or more later by a man who got his information second or third hand.

People who had noticed this beggar from time to time were astounded. Peter saw his chance to tell them about Christ. He never let pass an opportunity to witness for his new religious outlook. His address is quite similar to that which he had given on Pentecost. However, he first denies that the healing of the beggar is "by our own power or piety." The healing is because of faith in the name of Jesus. One's name is the symbol of the person himself. Peter's hearers are accused of being responsible for the crucifixion of Jesus. They must rethink the whole situation that "times of refreshing" may come to them. He pointed out that the Jews were fortunate in being the first people to whom God had revealed himself through his servant.

The first reported attack upon the early Christians came not from the Pharisees with whom Jesus had had so much difficulty, but from the Sadducees. Under Roman control the high priest was always a Sadducee. To maintain their positions the priests were eager to keep peace lest the Romans take away some of their power. Luke suggests that Peter and John were arrested because their teaching was contrary to the Sadducees' denial of any resurrection. However, this action tended to advertise the new religious outlook. Consequently the Christian group increased to five thousand. Peter and John were proving to be good witnesses to Christianity.

The next day Peter and John were brought before the Sanhedrin or Council over which the high priest presided. Luke seems to be a bit uncertain about the high priesthood. Caiaphas was the legal high priest, but his father-in-law Annas, a former high priest, still had great power. Even facing the Sanhedrin Peter bore his testimony. He pointed out that the beggar now very evidently was able to walk. This man's healing or saving came through Christ. "There is no other name under heaven given among men by which we must be saved." The English word "saved" and the English word "healed" are the same word in Greek. Peter pointed out that the one whom members of the Sanhedrin had rejected could do more than heal a cripple's feet.

The Sanhedrin were startled by the boldness of Peter and John. Most people cowered before the Council, but here were men of the common people, not trained by rabbis or appointed to positions of importance, who spoke forth courageously. They were not considered "unlearned and ignorant" as the King James version states it, but rather "uneducated, common." They were far from ignorant. They were men inspired by a movement worth dying for. Members of the Sanhedrin recognized Jesus as the source of this inspiration. There was too much evidence that the beggar had actually been helped through Peter and John. They had become heroes in the eyes of the crowds. No punishment could be given, but perhaps a repetition of such an experience could be prevented. Certainly a stop must be put to the statement made from time to time that Jesus, whose death had been caused by the Sanhedrin, had been raised up by God. Therefore, representing the government, the Sanhedrin ordered that Peter and John were never again to speak or teach in the name of Jesus.

Peter and John would not be cowed. They replied, "Whether it is right in the sight of God to listen to you rather than to God, you must judge; for we cannot but speak of what we have seen and heard." We admire the Old Testament story of Daniel's putting his religious convictions ahead of government orders. We shall eventually examine the book printed last in our Bibles. It reflects a time when some Christians allowed themselves to be thrown to the lions or burned as torches for the emperor's garden parties rather than obey orders of the government which they felt contrary to their religion. What had Jesus taught about allegiance to God in contrast to allegiance to government (Matt. 22:21)?

When Peter and John returned to the Christian group a prayer meeting of gratitude was held. Acts 4:31 reports that this was followed by the receiving of the Holy Spirit. This is probably a repetition of the story given in Acts 2:1-4. Luke may have thought that these reports represented two different events.

As in Acts 2 the story of receiving the Holy Spirit is followed by a report of the early Christians' having all things in common, a communal type of living. Could this have been adopted from the Essenes? Many of the group sold their real estate and turned the proceeds over to a common treasury. Although Luke says "as many as were possessors of lands or houses" did this, he indicates that the action was voluntary. A Levite from the island of Cyprus, named Joseph, is the first such volunteer mentioned. Since there were several other Josephs in the early Christian record he was given the nickname "Son of Encouragement" which in the Aramaic language used by his associates is Barnabas. He eventually became one of the leaders of the Christian community, definitely encouraged the new religious outlook.

One of the group, Ananias, wanted praise similar to that given Barnabas. He and his wife agreed to a scheme whereby they expected to get favorable publicity at a low cost. They sold some property and kept back part of the proceeds, claiming that they were giving it all to the apostles. Peter severely reprimanded Ananias for his dishonesty, his trying to deceive not only men but God. This so shocked Ananias that he dropped dead. His body had scarcely been buried when his wife suffered a similar experience. Thus two perfectly good names were spoiled for future use. Would not Jesus have found some kinder way to handle this situation? However, this whole experience increased people's respect for the apostles, especially for Peter. The Christian community grew extensively. In this chapter we find the first use of the word "church" as referring definitely to Christians. The term had been used in the Septuagint Old Testament in reference to Jewish groups. The word means "called out." Some distinction between Christianity (although the word "Christian" had not yet been coined) and Judaism was beginning to be made.

The remainder of the fifth chapter of Acts deals with another story of apostles' being imprisoned and then warned not to preach any more in the name of Jesus. Many Bible students think this is another couplet, retelling the story of Acts 4:1-22. It is an emphasis upon the theme of the entire book of Acts: Nothing can stop the gospel. In this account we are not told how many apostles were imprisoned. By some method which they considered an agency of God, they escaped. The next morning they were again found in the temple teaching their religious convictions. They were taken to the Sanhedrin and reprimanded by the high priest for teaching in the name of Jesus. Once more Peter was the spokesman, insisting, "We must obey God rather than man."

Again he delivered to the Council a short sermon. This sermon is an excellent summary of the conviction of the early Christians, their confession of faith or kerygma.

This caused members of the Council to want to have the apostles executed. However, the apostles found a friend in court. Not all the Sanhedrin were Sadducees. An outstanding Pharisee was one of the members. He was Gamaliel, a teacher in the Jerusalem training school for rabbis. Saul or Paul, whom we shall soon meet, was one of his students. He came eventually to be considered by Jews as one of their seven greatest rabbis and given the title of Rabban. Gamaliel advocated a "wait and see" policy with the apostles. He insisted that the apostles' movement would soon die out unless it had the backing of God. In the latter case "You might even be found opposing God." Luke tells that Gamaliel gave two illustrations of popular rebellions which had failed. One of these under the leadership of Judas of Galilee had taken place A.D. 6-8. He inspired the group which became Zealots. However, the reference to Theudas raises a problem. We have two records of Theudas' leading such a thwarted rebellion, but this took place ten or twelve years after Gamaliel came to the defence of the apostles. It was easy for Luke, writing a half century later, to confuse details of a speech that none of the Christian group had heard.

Gamaliel's advice was taken by the Sanhedrin who, after beating the apostles, again warned them not to preach in the name of Jesus, but released them.

For Class Discussion

1. What groups emphasize speaking in tongues today? What should be our attitude toward them?
2. In Acts 4:19-20 Peter and John defied the government. Under what circumstances should Christians do this?

Assignment

1. What was Paul's attitude toward speaking in tongues?
2. Acts 4:6 refers to Annas and Caiaphas. Identify each.

3. In Acts 4:27 Peter and John refer to Herod and Pilate. Identify each.

4. Identify: Barnabas, Sapphira, Gamaliel.

Supplementary Reading

1. *The Interpreter's Bible*. New York and Nashville: Abingdon Press, Vol. 9, 1954. Pages 36-87.

CHAPTER 25

"Seven Men of Good Report"

Read: Acts 6, 7, and 8

The earliest Christians were quite human. From time to time they quarreled among themselves. Luke gives two instances when the disciples disputed about who of their number was the greatest (9:46 and 22:24). Luke begins his sixth chapter of Acts by saying that among the Christians "the Hellenists murmured against the Hebrews."

Who were the Hellenists? The word is related to the Greek word for Greece "Hellas." Hellenists were Jews who had come under the influence of Greece. Probably most of them had lived outside of Palestine. They had learned the Greek language and adopted certain Greek customs. They were much more liberal than the "Hebrew" Jews who had endeavored to stay clear of all Greek influence. The Hellenists had come to recognize that there were good things in the Greeks and Greek civilization. They did not feel that the Jewish religion and ways of life had reached perfection. They were willing to accept changes, improvements. Therefore they tended to pay more attention to the teaching of the apostles than did the Jews now called Hebrews. The word Hebrew itself suggested the past, older ideas, conservatism. A large part of those impressed by Peter's preaching at the time of Pentecost were Hellenists. Many of these were ready for Christianity. Greek thinking exerted a great influence on the Christian religion. It is sometimes said that Christianity has two parents, Hebrew theology and Greek philosophy.

The Hellenists complained that "their widows were neglected in the daily distribution." The widows of Hellenists were probably lonely women who had lived abroad much of their lives and had returned to Palestine after the death of their husbands. Luke seems to take for granted that his readers will know what is meant by "the daily distribution." At this point Luke is probably using source material that has already explained this term. It evidently is a part of the communal living referred to in 2:44-45 and 4:32-37. The Christian community had taken upon itself the responsibility of seeing that all its members were provided with the necessities of life. Probably food was distributed each day, although the reference here does not preclude the possibility that a cash distribution was made daily.

The twelve apostles did not deny the accusation, but pointed out that it was impossible for them to preach the word of God and serve tables at the same time. They suggested that seven men be selected to handle the commissary. This "pleased the multitude." Each man elected had a Greek name. Evidently the group which had made the criticism was assigned the job of working out a solution. All may have done well the task to which they were appointed. The only two later mentioned, Stephen and Philip, are reported to be preaching. This type of early church activity soon came to be shared in by people other than the twelve. The seven are never in the Bible called deacons, but the Greek verb used here in connection with serving tables is diakoneo. Doubtless this is the origin of the office of deacon, but when we first meet men definitely called deacons their tasks are more than administrative. The appointment of the seven may have marked the beginning of two distinct groups of Christians, the Hellenistic and the Hebrew. The former soon took the gospel to non-Jews and became responsible for the growth of the new religion.

When the early Hebrew leader Moses appointed Joshua as his successor he "laid his hands upon him" to invest him with some of his authority (Num. 27:20 and 23). In a somewhat similar way the apostles laid their hands upon the seven. Such a ceremony was later used with new converts to symbolize their receiving of the Holy Spirit. The seventh verse notes that among those joining the Christian fellowship were a great many priests. We have no further reference to this interesting addition to the Christian community. The Essenes had their own priests. Could these be Essene priests rather than temple priests? The early church and the Essenes had much in common. How much influence did these priests exert upon the development of Christian thought?

Just as we have in America churches composed originally of

people who came from certain foreign nations; so in Jerusalem there were synagogues of Hellenists from various Mediterranean regions. It was in these synagogues that Stephen, one of the seven, gave witness to his Christian convictions. Jesus had done considerable of his early preaching in synagogues. Later Paul made extensive use of similar opportunities. With all three people opposition developed among synagogue members who disapproved of the new doctrines. Arguing could not overcome the logic of Stephen's presentation. As with Jesus, his opponents resorted to lying, producing false witnesses. Luke tells this story twice. He probably combines two sets of source material. In his first notation he says that these men testified that Stephen had spoken blasphemously against Moses and God (6:11). Two verses farther on he reports the witnesses as saying, "This man never ceases to speak words against the holy place and the law."

When Stephen had an opportunity to speak he did not waste time rebutting these false charges. Rather like Peter, he grabbed the chance to give further testimony to his new religious outlook. Like all the sermons given in the first thirteen chapters of Acts, Stephen's address reviews the evolution of religion through the Old Testament and implies that the teachings of Jesus are the next forward step. The traditions and temple are only temporary. Christ superseded these. Some of the details given in this address do not agree with the records of our Bible. This is probably due to the fact that Stephen as a Hellenist read the Septuagint translation of the Hebrew scriptures. Possibly the blame should be put on Luke or the author of his source material who was familiar with the Greek. At times the Septuagint paraphrases the Hebrew instead of literally translating it, or translates a Hebrew text different from the one on which our English versions are based. What we have of this address largely deals with Moses in whom Stephen saw a parallel to Christ. As Moses, rejected by his fellow Israelites as an arbitrator, was chosen by God to be the deliverer, so was Jesus. Their ancestors killed the prophets; in like manner, Stephen points out, his listeners murdered the Righteous One. This is a term Peter had used in referring to Jesus in Acts. 3:14.

The Chinese say that in a debate the man who first runs out of arguments resorts to his fists. Likewise Stephen's persecutors

171

turned to violence and illegally stoned him to death. They did not consult the Roman authorities. His dying sentences resemble those of Jesus. Stephen's last words are: "Lord Jesus receive my spirit; Lord, do not hold this sin against them." So died the first Christian martyr. Our word "martyr," one who gives his life for a cause, comes from the Greek word for witness, one who tells what he has seen.

Luke then reports the story of the other member of the seven about whom we know anything after his selection. Philip resembles the Old Testament prophets, or spokesmen for God, in going about from place to place with his message. He was truly an evangelist, that is one who shares the good news. He seems to be the first person to take seriously Jesus' great commission to be his witness in Samaria (Acts 1:8). This was easier for the broader-minded Hellenist to do than for the more conservative Hebrew with his great disdain for the Samaritans.

In one of the Samaritan cities Philip had such success in "proclaiming Christ" that he attracted crowds and so helped a number of people that they came to consider him a miracle worker. As Moses came into contact with Pharaoh's magicians (Ex. 7:10-13), so Philip found a competitor, a man named Simon. Simon seems to have had messianic ambitions. He had amazed people with magic and had come to be called "that power of God which is called Great." However, when groups were baptized as Christians, Simon joined them. He had been startled by the things Philip did but probably failed to grasp Philip's message.

The apostles, being Hebrew in their outlook, scarcely knew what to make of Philip's success. Therefore, they sent Peter and John to investigate. This committee approved what Philip had been doing. As representative of the church in Jerusalem, Peter and John laid their hands on Philip's converts who thus became convinced that they had the spirit of truth, the Holy Spirit.

Simon believed this was some magic power much greater than any he had possessed. He coveted this ability and offered to buy the secret from Peter and John. This use of money to obtain spiritual ends has come to be called "simony" in remembrance of this Simon. Doubtless Simon wished that he and all concerned could forget about it, for Peter severely reprimanded him. The results were not as drastic as Ananias suffered under Peter's reprimand.

In reply to a statement of Peter which was very close to a curse, Simon begged, "Pray for me to the Lord, that nothing of what you have said may come upon me."

Philip's experience in the region of Samaria influenced Peter and John, for we read that they returned to Jerusalem, "preaching the gospel to many villages of the Samaritans." This signifies a definite forward step, the accepting of non-Jews into Christianity.

Luke gives a second story of Philip's foreign mission enterprise. Philip felt directed by God to go along the road south from Jerusalem toward Egypt. On this road he found an African Negro on his way back to his native Ethiopia south of Egypt. This man, a eunuch, was secretary of the treasury of the queen of Ethiopia. He must have been a convert to Judaism, for he had gone to Jerusalem to worship, and was reading Second Isaiah, doubtless in the Septuagint translation, when Philip found him. The ruling family of Ethiopia claims descent from the Queen of Sheba and the Hebrew King Solomon. Friendly relations between Ethiopia and the Hebrew people existed much earlier than New Testament times. Another Ethiopian eunuch stationed in Jerusalem six hundred years previous had been on friendly terms with both the king and the prophet Jeremiah (Jer. 38:7-8).

When Philip found him the Ethiopian was reading Isa. 53:7-8, the Suffering Servant passage. He confessed that he was confused by what he was reading. Philip used this as a starting point for explaining Christianity. Did he believe that Jesus had become God's Suffering Servant? Philip's description of Christianity as the best religion was convincing. The Ethiopian suggested that he would like to be accepted as a Christian. He asked Philip to initiate him by baptism. Some early Greek copies of Acts report that the Ethiopian proclaimed what was probably the earliest form of the baptismal creed, "I believe that Jesus Christ is the Son of God." No reference is made here to the trinity. Philip then returned to his home in the Roman city of Caesarea on the Palestine coast. We hear nothing more of the Ethiopian. By 341 a Christian church was in existence in Ethiopia. Could these Christians be spiritual descendants of Philip's convert?

Luke was interested in the spread of Christianity toward Europe. Therefore he tells no more about its outreach in other directions. Before the great Christian missionary Paul reached

Rome there was a Christian community there. Probably this had been started by men who had become Christians as a result of Peter's Pentecost sermon and had returned to Rome. Doubtless churches were similarly started all across north Africa. Before long there was a strong church in Alexandria, Egypt. Very early a Christian group was organized in southern India by a man named Thomas. Tradition says that this was one of the twelve apostles.

Assignment

1. What information do we have about Stephen?
2. What was the theme of Stephen's address?
3. Identify: Simon of Samaria; the Ethiopian eunuch.

Supplementary Reading

1. *The Interpreter's Bible*. New York and Nashville: Abingdon Press, Vol. 9, 1954. Pages 87-117.
2. Marcel, Simon. *St. Stephen and the Hellenists*. New York: Longmans, Green & Co., 1958.

CHAPTER 26

"Who Was I to Withstand God?"

Read Acts 9, 10 and 11; Gal. 1

In connection with the stoning of Stephen and the succeeding verses we find three references to Saul. Those who stoned Stephen laid their garments at the feet of Saul who "was consenting" to the death of Stephen. We are then told that Saul took an active part in the persecution of the church. In Acts nine we really meet this man. He is the outstanding character of the remainder of the New Testament. Not only is he the hero of Acts, but much of the rest of the Christian scriptures is composed of letters written by him after he became Christianity's leading exponent.

Let us get acquainted with Saul. He was a Hellenist, a Jew born about the same time as Jesus, and brought up in the city of Tarsus in Cilicia the southern part of what is now Turkey. Saul was proud of his birth-place. He once spoke of it as "no mean city" (Acts 21:39). Tarsus was about ten miles back from the Mediterranean on a river deep enough to allow sea-going vessels to come to the city. The caravan route from the Euphrates River and that from the great city of Antioch north of Palestine joined a few miles east of Tarsus. These routes connected with shipping at Tarsus and also turned north there through the Taurus mountains thirty miles from the city. This route led to the cities in the interior of Turkey. Tarsus was therefore a prominent trade center. It was also a manufacturing center, specializing in Cilician cloth made of the hair of goats which were raised in great numbers in the mountains. This was especially useful for tents, sails and awnings.

Tarsus had one of the three great universities of the Mediterranean world. The philosophical teachings there influenced Saul, although his strict Jewish parents doubtless never allowed him to enroll as a student. The city was chiefly Greek, but Romans,

Jews and other Orientals made it a cosmopolitan center. Asiatic mystery religions had their adherents in Tarsus. They doubtless had some influence on Saul.

Saul's family traced their ancestry to the tribe of Benjamin. They named their son in honor of ancient Benjamin's greatest hero, the first king of Israel. They were strict Pharisees. The son later wrote regarding his own Phariseeism that he was "as to righteousness under the law blameless" (Phil. 3:6). When probably about twenty years old, he became a pupil of Gamaliel in the rabbinical training school in Jerusalem.

For outstanding service to the Roman government an ancestor of Paul had been given the honor of being classed as a Roman citizen. This honor, carrying with it certain privileges, was handed down from father to oldest son. Saul was proud of this distinction. He was fluent in Greek and spoke Aramaic, the language of the Jews. He may have spoken Latin. He could also read the language in which the scriptures of the Jews were written, Hebrew. However, most of the quotations from the Old Testament which he made in his writings are from the Greek Septuagint. Although among Jewish people he was always called Shaul or Saul, he also had a Greek name Paulos or Paul which he used in dealings with non-Jews. It is by Paul that we know him best.

We know nothing about any brothers of Saul. We do know that he had a married sister living in Jerusalem. This sister's son was able to befriend his uncle some years later. Was Paul a married man? Not during the period of his life that we know him. There is some suggestion that he was a widower at that time.

Paul apparently was not in Palestine during Jesus' ministry. He evidently returned after the crucifixion and discovered the growing Christian community. He probably belonged to the Cilician synagogue at which Stephen spoke. It was doubtless beneath the dignity of an aristocratic young rabbi to throw stones, but he took care of the outer garments of the men who participated in the lynching. Saul approved of this killing and took an active part in persecuting Christians. "Entering into house after house, he dragged off men and women and committed them to prison" (Acts 8:3). In his own testimony given later he said, "I persecuted this Way to the death, binding and delivering to prison both men and women" (Acts 22:4).

This persecution scattered the Christians "except the apostles" throughout Palestine and to a considerable distance north of it. The apostles were not yet extensively persecuted, perhaps because they were Hebrews, less heretical from a Jewish viewpoint than the Hellenists. Some Christians had gone north to the ancient Syrian capital, Damascus, Saul learned. He had himself commissioned by the high priest to visit Jewish groups in Damascus and bring back to Jerusalem in bonds any whom he found preaching the Christian doctrine.

Saul was so enthusiastic that on his two hundred mile trip to Damascus he evidently did not take time out for a siesta or noon rest. At least as he neared the city he was traveling during the noon hour (Acts 22:6). He had listened in on Christian meetings, had heard preaching about love and kindness, but doubtless thought such talk not sincere. However it would be impossible for him to forget the impression the death of Stephen made upon him. Could we describe what occurred to Saul on the Damascus road as a sunstroke? We have three reports of this experience in the book of Acts. Paul refers to it four times in his writings. The accounts contain minor contradictions. We cannot determine just what the experience of Paul's associates was. Later he was convinced that he had seen "Jesus our Lord" (1 Cor. 9:1) just as truly as the eleven did at the time of the Ascension. Saul realized that his attitude toward Christianity was wrong. He wanted to do what he could to counteract his error. Sometime in this transforming experience he became convinced that his special task was to take the gospel to the non-Jews, the Gentiles. Whether this came on the Damascus road (26:17), through Ananias (9:15), or later at Jerusalem (22:21) is uncertain. In this experience Saul became, to use his own phrase, "a man in Christ."

Saul was befriended by two Damascus men, Ananias and Judas. This should have wiped away some of the blot cast on these names by Judas Iscariot and the husband of Sapphira. After a period of fasting, and of being ministered to by these men, Saul recovered his sight and was baptized as a Christian.

Just what did Saul do after his conversion? The account given

177

by Luke and accounts given by Paul himself in his letters (Gal. 1:16-21 and 2 Cor. 11:32-33) do not agree. Luke says that immediately Saul started preaching in synagogues in Damascus, that the Jews there plotted to kill him, that he escaped by night and went to Jerusalem. There he was sponsored by Barnabas and presented to the apostles. Paul says that after his Damascus conversion he "went away into Arabia" but does not reveal whether that was near Damascus or as far south as Petra. He then says he returned to Damascus, where he may have done some preaching. Three years later he went to Jerusalem, where he spent a couple of weeks with Peter and James the brother of Jesus, but saw no other apostles. Our tendency is to depend upon Paul's own record rather than that which Luke secured second-hand. Luke says that the Jews in Damascus plotted to kill Saul. Paul himself says that the governor of the Nabatean king, who had leased Damascus from the Roman emperor, guarded the city in order to seize him. Both accounts say that he escaped in a basket over the wall or through a window in the wall.

Luke indicates that the Christians in Jerusalem did not trust Saul when he returned. They evidently thought that his claim to be a Christian was a trap to get evidence against them. However, Barnabas, the man who had sold his field for the benefit of the Christian community, believed Saul, told others his story, and got Saul to preaching among the non-Christian Hellenists. These people were about to treat him as they had treated Stephen. Therefore the Christians took him to Caesarea, the Roman city along the Palestinian coast. From there he went to his home town of Tarsus in Cilicia. In Galatians Paul says that he went into the regions of Syria and Cilicia, that he was still not personally known to the churches in Judea. Did he exclude the city of Jerusalem from his reference to Judea? Luke indicates that with Saul no longer either the instigator of persecution or the chief object of the persecution, the Christian community throughout Palestine had a period of peace and growth.

Before continuing with the story of Saul, Luke relates a series of events in which the apostle Peter was the chief character. In his travels Peter found a Christian group at Lydda west of Jerusalem. Today the Israel air-field is at Lydda; also the east-west and north-south rail lines cross there. Here Peter had an experience

178

somewhat similar to that which he had had in the temple grounds; he gave a bed-ridden man such confidence through Christ that he got out of bed. This led others to Christianity in Lydda and the coastal plain (in Hebrew the word is Sharon).

While Peter was at Lydda he received word from Joppa the coastal town just to the west, that a leading Christian woman there had just died. The major city of Israel today, Tel Aviv, developed early in the twentieth century as a northern suburb of Joppa. It is now much larger than the ancient town and largely surrounds it. Peter was invited to Joppa, whether to conduct a funeral or with the hope that he might revive the beloved Tabitha (or Dorcas) is uncertain. Peter's reputation as a miracle-worker was enhanced by his reviving the woman who was considered dead. There Simon Peter found another Simon, a tanner, with whom he stayed for some time.

Many intelligent Romans and Greeks were dissatisfied with their religion. These religions were polytheistic. Their gods were pictured as quarrelsome and immoral. Individuals here and there felt there must be but one supreme power and that that power must be highly ethical. Judaism taught these two things and therefore made an appeal to some non-Jews. However, the Jews felt that they were a superior group, God's pets. They also required circumcision of all male members. Non-Jews felt this was an unnecessary mutilation of the body. As a result Gentiles who became interested in the Jewish religion fell into two groups. One known as converts swallowed their pride and became Jews. The other supported synagogues by their attendance and financial contributions. However, they would not accept the elements of Judaism which they felt were undesirable—these people were called Godfearers.

In the tenth chapter of Acts we meet one of these latter men, Cornelius, an officer in the Roman army. He was stationed in the Roman capital of Judea, Caesarea, a port and garrison city built thirty miles north of Joppa by Herod the Great. Caesarea was the home of Philip the evangelist. Cornelius had heard of the Christian religion. Word came to him that the outstanding Christian, Peter, was at Joppa. He at once sent three of his men to Joppa to invite Peter to visit Caesarea and explain Christianity to him.

179

While these men were on their way to Joppa Peter went up on to the roof of the house of Simon the tanner to pray. He was hungry, but something else was greatly bothering him: Should non-Jews be accepted into Christianity without their first becoming Jews? Philip's activity had Peter concerned. He had brought Samaritans and the Ethiopian eunuch into the Christian fold. The latter was already interested in the Hebrew scriptures. The Samaritans had much in common with the Jewish religion. They worshiped Yahweh and accepted the Torah. But where should this stop? Should converts be received from beyond the fringe groups? What did Jesus mean when he instructed the apostles to take the good news to all the world? Could Gentiles really be classed as unclean? One dreams about the things that are prominent in his mind. Here Peter's hunger and his problem about non-Jews were combined in a dream or vision. He saw a sheet or sail let down before him. In it were animals and other life which Jews classed as unclean, flesh which must not be eaten. Peter heard a voice which he considered divine telling him to kill and eat. He insisted that he had never been unorthodox at this point. Twice more he heard the same command.

As Peter tried to interpret this experience he was called downstairs to meet the men whom Cornelius had sent. The next day he went to Caesarea with them. When he met Cornelius he indicated how he had interpreted his vision: "God has shown me that I should not call any man common or unclean." This was a crucial point in Christianity. In Peter's acceptance of Cornelius the new religion burst the bonds of Judaism. Peter adopted something of the attitude of the Hellenists, but he was soon to learn that many of the Hebrew Christians strongly disapproved of his action. Peter did not compromise. To Cornelius he stated that God shows no partiality, that Jesus is Lord of all; "every one who believes in him receives forgiveness of sins through his name."

Doubtless there were many questions and answers which Luke does not record. Other Jewish Christians were with Peter. They were amazed that the spirit of truth, the Holy Spirit, was received by Cornelius and his associates. This was recognized even before the converts were baptized. Apparently other Christians then helped Peter baptize his new friends.

180

Word of this accepting of uncircumcised Gentiles into Christianity soon reached the church at Jerusalem. When Peter returned he was criticized. It is interesting that the immediate criticism was social rather than religious. Luke had already recorded two instances when Jesus was accused of the same fault: "This man receives sinners and eats with them" (Lu. 15:2 and 19:7). However, when Peter had recounted his experience, exclaiming, "Who was I that I could withstand God?" the Jerusalem Christians "glorified God." This approval may have been half-hearted, temporary. Why did Luke bother to give the details of Peter's conversion of Cornelius a second time? It is well to remember that Luke was writing for the early church. This new experience of early Christianity could not be stressed too much.

Luke follows this report with another example of the expansion of Christianity beyond the confines of Judaism. After Stephen was stoned to death some Jewish Christians fled along the Mediterranean coast north of Palestine. They did not hide their new religion but shared it with others. At first they preached only to Jews. But at Antioch of Syria in the coastal region, some 300 miles north of Jerusalem, the good news was also given to Greeks by some of the Christian Hellenists. Exceeded in size only by Alexandria and Rome, Antioch had a famous library, theatre, amphitheatre, stadium, and baths. Its main street had a regular series of street lamps. Statues lined five miles of streets. Some streets had been paved with white marble as a gift from Herod the Great. Antioch had been the capital of the former Seleucid empire.

"Here a great number that believed turned to the Lord." Quite a few Jews lived in Antioch. They had taken part in a local quarrel in A.D. 39. As a result their synagogue had been burned. They were out of favor with the authorities. This probably explains why they could not successfully oppose the growth of Christianity in Antioch. As with Philip in Samaria the Jerusalem church felt it should investigate. Evidently Barnabas had risen to a position where he was well respected by the apostles. The church appointed him to investigate the situation at Antioch.

Barnabas apparently approved the work of the Antioch church which now included Greeks. He probably felt that the church in such an important city should have skilled leadership. It needed a leader who understood both Jewish and Greek outlooks. Therefore he went on to Tarsus, another 100 miles, where he found Saul whom he brought back to Antioch. For a year the two men served as joint pastors of the church. What had Saul been doing since he was spirited out of Jerusalem? Neither he nor Luke answers this question. Doubtless he was busy preaching in this region and perhaps to a considerable distance beyond. He developed his theology. When he came to Antioch, and a year later became a missionary for the Antioch church, he had already been matured by experience.

Although in this survey we have used the word "Christian" a number of times, this was to some extent an anachronism. It was after the church had been established at Antioch that the word was coined. Christians were called those of the Way (shortened from "the Way of the Lord" adopted from Isaiah 40:3), disciples, or the church. Among themselves the most general term was brothers. The term occurs 51 times in Acts. The word Christian was probably not used much during the first fifty years of the church as it appears only three times in the Bible, here, in Acts 26:28 and 1 Pet. 4:16. Evidently the Greek word for Messiah or anointed one, Christos, was accepted by this time. The word "Christian" meant a partisan of Christ, as "Herodian" meant a partisan of Herod. The Hebrew idea of the Messiah would mean nothing to Greeks. They could not understand why one with oil on his head should be especially honored. The term Christian may have originally been a term of derision, something like the word "greaser." On the other hand, it is possibly related to the common Greek name, Chrestus, meaning "good."

The concluding paragraph of the eleventh chapter indicates that the Antioch church had grown into a sense of responsibility. It sent relief to the Jerusalem church. Non-Biblical history records a famine in Judea at this time. The Jerusalem Christians, with their communal living and expectation of an early return of the Messiah, may have used up their capital. Probably many of them had lost their positions as employees of non-Christian Jews. They were in need. The Antioch church came to their rescue. Paul and Barnabas acted as its agents in taking relief to the mother church.

182

Assignment

1. What occurred to Saul on his way to and in Damascus?
2. What were Gentiles who became Jews called? Gentiles who accepted much of the Jewish teaching but did not become Jews?
3. What two elements of Judaism appealed to intelligent Gentiles? What two elements did they dislike?
4. What specific criticism did Jerusalem Christians make of Peter after his conversion of Cornelius?
5. How did Peter interpret the vision he had at Joppa?
6. Acts 11:22 refers to Barnabas. What two items have we had about him earlier in Acts?

Supplementary Reading

1. *The Interpreter's Bible.* New York and Nashville: Abingdon Press, Vol. 9, 1954. Pages 117-154.
2. Davies, A. Powell. *The First Christian.* New York: Farrar, Straus and Cudahy, 1957.

CHAPTER 27

'We Turn to the Gentiles'

Read Acts 12, 13 and 14.

The growth of Christianity brought strong opposition from the Jews. To get their good will, the new king, Herod Agrippa I, had one of the apostles, James, killed "with the sword," probably beheaded. It is possible that his brother John was executed at the same time. Luke makes no report as to what eventually became of any of the other apostles.

We have not met this Herod before. He was the grandson of Herod the Great. His father was executed by Herod the Great, so was never a ruler. Agrippa was sent to Rome where he was a schoolmate and friend of the boy who was to become the emperor Caligula. In A.D. 37 Caligula made him "king" over the territory which had been ruled by his uncle Philip. He was also given a section further to the north. Two years later, when his uncle Herod Antipas was exiled, Agrippa was given his territory as well. In A. D. 41 Rome withdrew its governor and put Agrippa over all the territory that had been ruled by his grandfather. Three years later he died at the age of 53.

After the execution of James, Agrippa's next move to please the Jews was to imprison Peter. As a result of prayer Peter escaped from prison at night. He went to the home of John Mark's mother, where a group of Christians were assembled praying for him. Tradition says that this was where the Last Supper was celebrated by Jesus and his disciples. It was at least one headquarters of the Jerusalem church. When the maid came to the door in answer to Peter's knock she recognized his voice but was so excited that she ran back to tell the others, without unfastening the door. The group did not believe her. They thought it must be Peter's guardian or accompanying angel. When Peter finally got in he told his story and asked that James, the brother of

Jesus, and other Christians be notified of his escape. Peter then "went to another place," into temporary hiding. Doubtless the other apostles soon disappeared from the territory controlled by Herod Agrippa.

James, the brother of Jesus, had become the head of the Jerusalem church. Luke never bothers to explain who this James was. We get our information from Paul. During the life of Jesus, James and his other brothers failed to appreciate him, opposed him. Paul says that after the resurrection Jesus made a special appearance to James (1 Cor. 15:7). He and the other brothers of Jesus were among those meeting in the upper room previous to Pentecost. He was a strict Hebrew, probably a Pharisee. He did not have the vision of the Hellenists. His blood-relationship to Jesus caused him to be highly respected by the Christian community at Jerusalem.

As if he believed that vengeance is characteristic of God, Luke tells of the inglorious death of Herod Agrippa. This occurred at Caesarea after a group who had been trying to curry his favor had shouted that he was a god. Agrippa did not rebuke them. The Jewish Roman historian Josephus gives a vivid account of this event. The symptoms of the cause of Agrippa's death which he describes suggest strangulated hernia. A number of things in Acts are reported by Josephus. A few Bible authorities feel that Luke read Josephus before writing Acts. If this is true Acts was written later than is generally believed. Upon the death of Agrippa Roman procurators were again appointed for Judea.

Luke now returns to his hero Saul. The church at Antioch, to which Barnabas and Saul had been ministering, took seriously Jesus' last command to preach the gospel to the ends of the earth. If they were to be true followers of Jesus they must take responsibility in sharing the story of Jesus beyond their own community. They became convinced that this would be no easy task, that it demanded the best ability to be found among the Christians at Antioch. Therefore they decided to send out Barnabas and Saul as their representatives. Having dedicated itself to a foreign mission program, the Antioch church held a committal service and sent off its missionaries.

Conditions around the Mediterranean invited such an enterprise. Saul expressed this realization a bit later by stating: "When

185

the time had fully come, God sent forth his son" (Gal. 4:4). Roman peace had done away with closed national frontiers and pirates. Roman engineers had constructed great roads across the empire. Rome had given the Mediterranean world a common language. Missionaries could travel from one end of the empire to another. Wherever they went they found people speaking Greek. Poverty, taxation, overpopulation were causing men to seek for a better way of life. Morally, civilization was at its lowest. People had become disgusted with the religions of Greece and Rome. They were searching for an improved life. Even the Jews were dissatisfied and, more than ever before, were hoping for the coming of the Messiah.

Sailing from Seleucia, the seaport sixteen miles west of Antioch, Barnabas and Saul disembarked at the eastern end of the island of Cyprus about a hundred miles south-west. They took John Mark, Barnabas' nephew (or possibly cousin) with them as an assistant. No information is given as to his duties. Barnabas had originally come from Cyprus; he would be at home there. A few natives of Cyprus had already become Christians. It was some of these who had first preached Christianity to Greeks at Antioch (Acts 11:20). We are told that Barnabas and Paul preached in the synagogues. When they reached the Roman capital at the far end of the island the Roman proconsul interviewed them and "believed." Like Peter in Samaria, Barnabas and Saul had trouble with a Jewish magician and "false prophet." Like Peter, Saul severely reprimanded him, calling him a son of the devil, enemy of all righteousness. It is interesting to note that this magician was sometimes known as Bar-Jesus or son of Jesus. Jesus was a fairly common name. This same paragraph contains another interesting name notation. Luke refers to Saul, "who" he says, "is also called Paul." This is the last time in our Bible that he is called Saul, other than in reports of his conversion experience. The name he used in dealing with Gentiles now becomes his regularly recognized name.

From Cyprus the missionary party sailed north-west to the southern edge of what is now Turkey. They landed at Perga eight miles up the river from the coast. There Mark left Paul and Barnabas and returned to Jerusalem. Why? Numerous answers have been suggested. The other members of the group went across the mountains into the interior of Turkey where they organized churches. In a letter Paul wrote to these Galatian churches he says that he first came to them because he had been ill (4:13). He may have developed fever in the swampy Perga district and gone into the mountains for his health. It is possible that under these conditions the young man Mark thought it best to go home rather than make a strenuous mountain journey which meant a climb of 4000 feet. He may have felt that his mother needed him. He could have opposed the work with Gentiles. It is also possible that he was jealous of Paul who was taking the leadership over Mark's uncle Barnabas. Could it be that Mark did not want to get too far away from a young woman in Jerusalem?

Although Paul had doubtless done extensive preaching in the region of Tarsus, the first preaching in Turkey we find him and Barnabas doing was in Antioch of Pisidia. This was one of sixteen Antiochs built about 300 B.C. by the general of Alexander who founded the Seleucid empire. It is quite possible that Paul's success with the Roman procurator of Cyprus caused him to attempt to win members of the Roman colony in Antioch. The Seleucid kings had planted groups of Jews here and in other cities of this section. Although Paul had already considered himself an apostle to the Gentiles, he was always concerned about the Jews' accepting the next step in religious development. He spoke of the gospel as being "to the Jew first and also to the Greek" (Rom. 1:16). Accordingly, on their first Sabbath in Antioch Paul and Barnabas went to the synagogue and accepted an invitation to speak.

Only Paul's address is given. It has much in common with those of Peter and Stephen. With its numerous Biblical quotations it held the attention of an audience of Jews and Jewish sympathizers. Paul traces the history of the Hebrew people but jumps from David to "great David's greater son," Jesus. He gave expression to the basic Christian convictions. Jesus is the Messiah expected by the prophets. The people of Jerusalem did not recognize him and put him to death. God did not allow him to see corruption but raised him from the dead. There are witnesses to this in Palestine. Those who put their faith in him find a freedom not found under Mosaic law. How much more Paul said and how accurate Luke's resume is we do not know. We

187

should expect Paul to include himself among the witnesses to the risen Lord, for he was strongly convinced that Christ had appeared to him on the Damascus road.

Paul gave special recognition to the God-fearers in his audience. After the service they and some of the Jews urged Paul and Barnabas to continue the next Sabbath. Doubtless these Christian missionaries had many conversations during the week. The next Sabbath a great crowd came to hear them. Some of the Jewish leaders were jealous of the popularity of these strangers. They contradicted them and attempted to make fun of them. Paul and Barnabas pointed out that they had given their own group the first opportunity to hear of Christ. They had fulfilled their obligation, but since they had been rejected "we turn to the Gentiles." This became the pattern Paul followed as he visited other cities. It is in connection with this experience that Luke uses the term "Paul and Barnabas" rather than "Barnabas and Paul." Paul has come into his own.

Evidently the missionary team was able to organize a church in Antioch among the God-fearers. Probably some Gentiles who had become Jews and possibly some regular Jews joined these. They found joy in their new religion. Luke is convinced that God's plan of Christianity's going beyond Judaism is definitely being fulfilled here. Here Paul and Barnabas became primarily preachers of the gospel to Gentiles. Despite an active persecution stirred up against them, they were happy about their success. As they left Antioch they were convinced that the expansion of Christianity was the will of God. Did they have in mind Jesus' instruction to his disciples which Luke records twice in his gospel account (9:5 and 10:11): "Wherever they do not receive you, when you leave that town shake off the dust from your feet as a testimony against them."

Paul and Barnabas went approximately a hundred miles southeast to Iconium, a Galatian city. Here their experience was quite similar to that at Antioch. Probably a larger percentage of Jews was included among the converts to Christianity. The Jewish opposition enlisted some Gentiles in molesting the visitors. They went so far as to throw stones at them. Note that in the fourth verse Luke calls Paul and Barnabas apostles. This is the first time they were given this title.

188

The apostles went about twenty miles south to Lystra. There Paul healed a cripple in much the same manner as Peter and John had done at the temple in Jerusalem (Acts 3:1-10). The natives of Lystra became excited and proclaimed in their local language that the gods had visited them. They already had at least two traditions about deity visiting their community. They thought that Barnabas was the leading Greek god Zeus, corresponding to the Latin god Jupiter. Barnabas was probably the larger, older man. His leadership was still acknowledged. Paul was considered to be the Greek Hermes or the Latin Mercury, the messenger god. This was because Paul was the chief speaker.

Paul and Barnabas were embarrassed. The priest of the local temple to Zeus lost no time in producing oxen to sacrifice to the visitors where the cripple had been healed. To stop this the apostles tore their garments as a dramatic demonstration that they thought such action blasphemy. They vehemently insisted that they were men just as human as those about them. Again, like Peter, they grabbed the opportunity to bear witness to their understanding of God. Theirs was not just one of the gods, but the "living God who made the heaven and the earth." The very short address given here differs from any we have had previously in Acts. The audience had no Jewish background. Arguments from the Bible would carry no weight. God has been lenient, in the past but he has never left himself without a witness. Paul implied that now they must rethink their religion, become responsible people. Probably before Paul had a chance to tell of Christ as God's great witness, Jews from Antioch and Iconium caught up with the missionaries and interrupted their preaching.

The people of Lystra felt "let down" when they learned of their mistake. Therefore it was easy for the Jews to poison their minds against the apostles to the degree that they stoned Paul, leaving him for dead. Other Christians appeared and Paul was revived. Undaunted, he stayed in the city until the next day when he and Barnabas went on to Derbe, probably twenty-five miles south-east. Here they met with success; no opposition is recorded.

From Derbe they courageously retraced their steps, again visiting Lystra—where they evidently had some success—Iconium, and Antioch. Probably they attempted no public speaking but spent time with the Christian groups they had founded. These doubtless needed to be "strengthened." They would have many questions about the new religion. They would need to be warned to expect opposition. Paul and Barnabas could speak from experience. Luke says that they appointed elders in these new churches. The churches were doubtless patterned largely upon the Jewish synagogues. The synagogues had elders or rulers who directed the activities of the organizations. However, in his letter written to these churches a little later Paul makes no reference to elders. It may be that they did not yet have any official position but were rather the fathers or older respected men of the group.

After some preaching in Perga, Paul and Barnabas went to the chief port of the region and sailed to Antioch of Syria, their starting point. Here they made their report emphasizing their success among the Gentiles.

For Class Discussion

What kind of people should the church send into foreign service today?

Assignment

1. What did we have in the second chapter of this survey about the John referred to in Acts 12:12?
2. What experience did Paul and Barnabas have at Antioch of Pisidia?
3. Make a map indicating the travels of Paul, Barnabas, and Mark discussed in this chapter.

Supplementary Reading

1. *The Interpreter's Bible.* New York and Nashville: Abingdon Press, Vol. 9, 1954. Pages 154-194.
2. Perowe, Stewart. *The Later Herods.* New York and Nashville: Abingdon Press, 1959.
3. Wright, G. E., and Filson, Floyd V. *The Westminster Historical Atlas to the Bible.* Philadelphia: The Westminster Press, Rev. 1956. Pages 95-96.

CHAPTER 28

"Come Over to Macedonia"

Read Acts 15 and 16; Gal. 2

The welcome Paul and Barnabas were given at Antioch of Syria had its dark side. They had scarcely told the good news of the acceptance of Christianity by numerous Gentiles when a number of Hebrew Christians arrived from Jerusalem. This group taught: "Unless you are circumcised according to the custom of Moses, you cannot be saved." Circumcision was the symbol of becoming a Jew. Paul and Barnabas had paid no attention to this. Neither had Peter with Cornelius and his household. Now the first foreign missionaries were told that most of their converts were not saved, had no part in Christianity. There was danger that the church would split in two at this point. Paul was a good Jew and did not want to see a complete break between Hellenistic and Hebrew Christians. It was decided to go to Jerusalem and try to work out an understanding with the mother church.

On the way to Jerusalem Paul and Barnabas met a number of Christian groups in Phoenicia and Samaria. Probably there were churches in the Phoenician port cities of Tyre and Sidon; Luke later reports groups there, but does not tell when they were founded. In Samaria church groups had grown up as a result of Philip's preaching. These people would rejoice that many who did not have limited Jewish outlooks had become a part of the Christian fellowship.

In Jerusalem the party from Antioch were met by Christian Pharisees who maintained much of the rigidness they had had before their conversion to Christianity. Again they insisted upon circumcision. Luke reports that Peter retold his experience with the Gentile, Cornelius. He pointed out that God had given him and his associates the Holy Spirit: "He made no distinction between us and them . . . therefore why do you make trial of God?

. . . We believe that we shall be saved through the grace of the Lord Jesus, just as they will." Barnabas and Paul told what "God had done through them among the Gentiles." James, the brother of Jesus, was presiding at the conference. Despite his Hebrew outlook, he was won over by the report of these experiences. He declared, "My judgment is that we should not trouble those of the Gentiles who turn to God."

Probably the question of requiring Gentile converts to be circumcised was not the only one raised at the Jerusalem conference. Whether or not Christians should be required to follow the Jewish dietary rules must have been discussed. Was the rule against eating pork and other "unclean" flesh dropped? The question of whether Jewish Christians might eat with Gentiles, Christian or otherwise, may also have come up. Possibly this was not solved. Accepting Gentiles without requiring circumcision did not necessarily include eating with them. This limitation of the Pharisees may have continued with the Hebrew Christians. It seemed necessary for the more conservative Christians to save face. Consequently four rules were set up for "the Gentiles who turn to God." They were asked "to abstain from the pollutions of idols and from unchastity and from what is strangled and from blood."

This recommendation of James was adopted and published in a letter to be taken to the churches. Two local men were appointed to return to Antioch with Paul and Barnabas. One was Judas called Barsabbas, probably a Hebrew and possibly a brother of one of the men nominated as a successor to Judas Iscariot. The other was Silas, a Hellenist with whom we shall get acquainted later. The letter contains the four requirements. The rule "to abstain from the pollutions of idols" is clarified to read, "abstain from what has been sacrificed to idols." Many Gentiles worshiped idols. As with the Jews, only the best animals were sacrificed. A small part of the meat was burned. The remainder was eaten. Not only was it grade "A" prime meat, but many people felt that the meat had taken on some special value; that eating it would transfer some virtue from the god to the person. Christians must not in this way reverence idols.

The letter says that Gentile Christians are to abstain "from blood and from what is strangled." These two points are the same. Some early New Testament manuscripts omit the reference to what is strangled in both statements. Jewish people were very strict about blood. They did not understand what life is. They knew that a person or animal losing blood also loses life. Life belonged to God and blood was life, so must be poured out to God as sacrifice. All animals must be killed in such a way that the blood was well drained off.

Unchastity is the fourth item from which Christians must refrain. We take it for granted that no Christian would be unchaste. However, it has been said that chastity is the only completely new virtue that Christianity brought into the world. This may not be a fair statement in light of the Jewish moral code, but it enables us to see why this point was emphasized.

In his speech James quoted Amos to indicate that it had been expected that Gentiles would seek the Lord. He quoted from the Greek Septuagint which uses the term "Gentiles" in place of the term "Edom" found in our Hebrew Bible. James concluded his talk by pointing out that in every large Gentile city there was a group of Jews, suggesting that some of these would become Christians and their scruples should be respected.

If it were not for Paul's letter to the Galatian churches we should accept Luke's report of the Jerusalem conference and its sequel without question. But Bible students are perplexed as to how to reconcile Paul's report in the second chapter of Galatians. Paul tells of his conversion and his visit to Jerusalem. He then says that fourteen years later he went again to Jerusalem. This seems to be the next time he went there. However, in the last paragraph of the eleventh chapter of Acts Luke tells that Paul and Barnabas took financial help to Jerusalem from the church at Syrian Antioch. Various solutions for this problem have been suggested. Apparently the most satisfactory is this: We have already noted indications that Luke had several different sets of materials, scraps of writings, from which he compiled his history of the early church. Probably in one he found a report of Paul and Barnabas' taking aid to the Jerusalem church; in another he found a report of the Jerusalem conference. It is quite possible that both reports refer to one trip these men made to Jerusalem, rather than to two separate trips as Luke believed.

If Paul in Gal. 2 is referring to the Jerusalem conference of

Acts 15 several other problems arise, but it is unnecessary for us to examine these details. Paul wrote in an argumentative mood. The group whom Luke calls "some believers who belonged to the party of the Pharisees" (15:5) Paul calls "false brethren secretly brought in, who slipped in to spy out our freedom . . . that they might bring us into bondage" (Gal. 2:5). Paul reports that his mission to the uncircumcised Gentiles won the blessing of these at the Jerusalem conference. He says that he and Barnabas were asked to remember the poor. Could that refer to his bringing aid to Jerusalem at that time? However, Paul is silent about the four requirements made of "the Gentiles who turn to God."

Luke tends to play down dissension in the church. He reports that when Paul and Barnabas and those sent from Jerusalem with the letter arrived at Antioch there was rejoicing. In time the visitors were "sent off in peace." Paul indicates that matters did not go so smoothly. Peter also went from Jerusalem to Antioch and joined in the mixed fellowship, eating with Gentile as well as Jewish Christians as he had done with Cornelius. Then there came a group of the conservative Hebrew Jewish Christians from Jerusalem ("from James"). They had been defeated on the question of requiring circumcision, but they were not willing to compromise on the question of eating with uncircumcised Christians. They would accept them into Christianity as second class citizens. They were so insistent that Peter and even Barnabas were temporarily won over. Paul, with a much wider experience of associating with Gentiles reprimanded Peter. He recorded "I opposed him to his face." It is interesting that although writing in Greek Paul slips back to the Aramaic word for rock, Cephas, rather than use the Greek Peter.

Paul not only disagreed with Peter but had a dissension with his fellow missionary, Barnabas. Paul's growing popularity and his attitude about eating with Gentiles were doubtless a part of it. However, it was brought to a head when plans were being made for a second missionary journey. Barnabas wanted to take his relative Mark with them. Paul evidently thought Mark unreliable. Therefore it was agreed that Barnabas would take Mark and go to the island of Cyprus, the original home of Barnabas. Paul would take Silas and go north and west by land. We hear nothing more about Barnabas in Acts. Paul no longer needed his guidance

194

and evidently did not hold a deep grudge against him. He makes a few unenthusiastic references to Barnabas in his letters. Mark seems to have lived down whatever criticism of him Paul had. In two of Paul's letters, written several years later from prison in Rome, he mentions that Mark is visiting him at the time.

Paul and Silas visited churches in Syria and Cilicia. Possibly these had been started by other missionaries from the church at Antioch. We have been told nothing of the founding of these churches, except that in Gal. 1:21 Paul reports that after his conversion and trip to Jerusalem he "went into the regions of Syria and Cilicia." He now visited the scene of his early Christian activity, probably including his home community, Tarsus. Paul and Silas then reached Derbe, the eastern extreme of Paul's first missionary journey. At Lystra Paul was encouraged by finding a young man whom he had brought into Christianity on his first visit. This definitely compensated for his being stoned there. This young man, Timothy, had a Jewish mother who had also become a Christian, and a Greek father. Timothy accepted Paul's invitation to join his mission party. Paul had had enough trouble about the matter of circumcision. He had won and could afford to be lenient. He was not trying to persuade Jews to break with their traditions. Since Timothy was half Jewish Paul circumcised him. This was in accord with a statement Paul made in a later letter: "To the Jews I became as a Jew, in order to win Jews" (1 Cor. 9:20). Doubtless he wanted to cooperate with the request of James that he try not to offend Jewish Christians.

Luke does not give details of Paul's visit to the churches. He says only that Paul reported on the decisions of the Jerusalem conference. As a result of his visit the churches were strengthened. Paul and his party went on westward through Turkey but with little success, although within a generation this region had numerous Christian groups. He probably met with strong Jewish opposition which he interpreted as being the work of the Holy Spirit. He considered going into the region along the south shore of the Black Sea. However, he felt directed to pass by this region and go on to the port of Troas. This was a city founded by the successors of Alexander the Great near the ruins of ancient Troy, famous for the war fought over the beautiful Helen.

At Troas Paul found himself facing Europe. Probably he had

been eager to take the Christian message to Europe. It is quite possible that he dreamed of the opportunity of preaching in the capital of the Roman empire. Probably for him "all roads lead to Rome." Certainly Europe was in Paul's mind. From the statement in the next paragraph that "we made a direct voyage" it would seem that Luke had joined Paul at Troas. This is the first of what are called "we-passages" in Acts reporting times when Luke seems to have been traveling with Paul. Luke probably urged the extension of the mission enterprise. It is possible, but quite unlikely, that Luke was not with the missionary party, that he used a diary of Paul or some one else who accompanied Paul and at certain points forgot to change "we" to "they." As Peter at Joppa had had a vision relative to the matters that were on his mind, so Paul had a vision in which he saw a man of Macedonia —northern Greece—inviting him to come over "and help us."

Thus Paul and Christianity went to Europe. Probably Hellenists converted at Pentecost had established churches in Europe, but Paul's visit is the first Christian enterprise there about which we know. The party, now composed of four missionaries, sailed from Troas past the island of Samothrace to the port of Neapolis. From there they went into the interior to the city of Philippi, probably Luke's home. Philippi had been named in honor of the father of Alexander the Great, Philip of Macedon. It had later become a Roman colony with numerous retired Roman soldiers. Its people proudly called it "Little Rome."

The Jewish community at Philippi was probably not large enough to have a synagogue. A small Jewish group, possibly only women, had a meeting place along the riverside where they gathered each Sabbath. Paul and his friends went there the first Sabbath they were in Philippi. As rabbis they were asked to speak. This brought about the first Christian conversion in Europe of which we have record. A well-to-do business woman, probably a convert to Judaism, but possibly one of the God-fearers, became convinced of the truth the missionaries were telling. She and her household were baptized. She had come from Thyatira in Lydia, a part of what is now western Turkey. Luke calls her Lydia, but this may have been a nickname because of her home community. Some years later Paul wrote a very friendly letter or two to the Christians in Philippi. In this correspondence he does not mention the name Lydia but speaks of two women, Euodia and Syntyche who "have labored side by side with me in the gospel." Possibly one of these was Lydia. She is spoken of by Luke as a seller of either the very expensive purple dye or cloth so dyed. At one time only royalty could afford such cloth; thus our expression, "to the purple born." The city from which she came was famous for weavers and dyers of wool and linen. She may have been an agent of one of the guilds of weavers. The four missionaries accepted Lydia's invitation to make her home their headquarters.

Paul and his associates had suffered from the Jews. Now they were beaten up as Jews "advocating customs which it is not lawful for us as Romans to accept or practice." The accusation was doubtless superficial. The real criticism was that the Christian group had interfered with the unethical financial gains of some Philippians. A girl who was a soothsayer, possibly a ventriloquist, was making money for her owners. She started following Paul and his friends about, embarrassing them by yelling about them. Paul was annoyed and finally turned to the girl and in some way changed her entire program. Luke suggests that he drove an evil spirit out of the girl, much as he had reported that Jesus had cured people of evil spirits (Lu. 7:21 and 8:2). When her owners saw that they could not make financial gain as they had done before they stirred up an anti-semitic attack. They dragged Paul and Silas to the magistrates with the accusation that "These . . . Jews . . . are disturbing our city." Without an opportunity to make a defense, the preachers of the Christian gospel were beaten and turned over to the jailer. He was warned not to let them escape. As a precaution he put them into the inner dungeon and fastened their feet in stocks.

Despite their mistreatment, Paul and Silas witnessed to their fellow prisoners by prayer and song. When an earthquake suggested the possibility of escape the men did not try to get away. The jailer feared that his prize prisoners had escaped. In order to avoid the suffering and fate which Peter's jailers at Jerusalem had experienced (Acts 12:19) he was about to commit suicide. Paul stopped this. The jailer was so startled by the entire action of these men that he envied something in their makeup. These dignified, cultured, well educated rabbis were not discouraged by the rats and fleas of their imprisonment. Yet the Roman officer was about to take his own life! How did they get that way? What was their secret? What could he do to have what they had? Paul answered at once: "Believe in the Lord Jesus, and you will be saved." This did not mean, Sign your name to a creed about Jesus and you will get to heaven. The jailer was not asking anything about heaven. What Paul was telling him was, Follow the teachings of Jesus and you will have the healthy outlook we have.

The jailer accepted Paul's invitation. Even before he was baptized he put his new religion into practice—he washed the wounds that had been inflicted upon Paul and Silas. After his baptism he took them to his own apartment and provided a meal. Two questions might be raised about this prison baptism of the jailer "and all his family." Would this quickly arranged midnight baptism in a jail suggest that immersion was the form used? Does "all his family" suggest infant baptism?

The next morning Paul and Silas insisted upon pointing out to the magistrates that as Roman citizens they had been illegally treated. They probably showed their citizenship certificates. This brought an apology from the frightened officers. Paul and his companion did not rush away. They took their time to visit Lydia and "the brethren." This possibly refers to Luke and Timothy, but it is more probable that other converts had been made. Eventually the church here became one of the most loyal of all those Paul organized. Paul and Silas then moved on along the paved military highway to Thessalonica to plant seeds of Christianity in a great commercial city. Some months later Paul wrote a letter to friends he made in Thessalonica. In it he recalls that "we had already suffered and been shamefully treated at Philippi" before going to Thessalonica (1 Thess. 2:2).

Assignment

1. What was the purpose of the Jerusalem conference?
2. What four requirements did the Jerusalem conference make of "Gentiles who turn to God?"
3. What was the Macedonian vision?
4. What other visions have we previously had in Acts?

5. What did Paul and Silas mean by the answer they gave the Philippian jailer? (In other words, What is the meaning of "believe" and "saved?")

6. What seems to be the home of (a) Timothy, (b) Luke?

Supplementary Reading

1. *The Interpreter's Bible.* New York and Nashville: Abingdon Press, Vol. 9, 1954. Pages 195-225.

CHAPTER 29

"To the Church of Thessalonians"

Read Acts 17:1—18:22; 1 Thessalonians

Paul and Silas had been imprisoned at Philippi as Jews, but at Thessalonica it was the Jewish community that made trouble for them. This port city had attracted a large number of Jews. Generally known as Salonika, the city today is the second largest in Greece. Among its modernistic buildings are structures which were standing in the time of Paul. Salonika played an important role in the first and second World Wars.

For three Sabbaths Paul preached in the synagogue proclaiming Jesus as the Christ. It is said that he "argued with them from the scriptures" evidently pointing out that Jesus is the culmination of the evolution of Hebrew religion. Some Jews were won, but most of Paul's converts were Greeks, people who were dissatisfied with their own religion and did not find the Jewish religion completely to their liking. Luke points out that some leading women were among the converts. Generally a woman took the religion of her husband, regardless of what that was. Christianity was causing people to break with precedent. Luke does not tell much about Paul's experience in Thessalonica. However, Paul a little later wrote two letters to the Thessalonican Christians. In these we get a more complete picture. After he was no longer accepted in the synagogue he evidently continued his propagandizing for his religious convictions. His appeal was chiefly to those who did not know God. His message was to turn "to God from idols, to serve a living and true God, and to wait for his Son from Heaven, whom he raised from the dead" (1 Thess. 1:9-10).

A group of jealous Jews stirred up a mob and attacked the house of Paul's host, Jason. When they could not find Paul they dragged Jason and his friends before the city authorities. They accused them of harboring trouble-makers who were guilty of treason, putting Jesus before Caesar as king. Of course Paul had not called Jesus king, but Messiah or Christ. This word would be unknown to the government authorities. Evidently Jews interpreted it to them as king. Paul and his associates may have considered as a compliment the strong accusation: "These men who have turned the world upside down have come here also."

When Jason and his friends were required to put up bond that there would be no more trouble with the Christians, Paul, Silas, and Timothy went forty-five miles south-west to Beroea (sometimes called Berea). Again the missionaries spoke in the local synagogue. Luke pays the Jews of Beroea a high compliment, saying that they "were more noble than those in Thessalonica, for they received the word with all eagerness, examining the scriptures daily to see if these things were so." These were more free from prejudice, willing to investigate for themselves. Paul made converts at Beroea, apparently mostly Greeks. We hear nothing more about the church there, except that when Paul made his last journey to Jerusalem taking an offering from the western churches "Sopater of Beroea" was one of those who accompanied him (Acts 20:4). When Jews from Thessalonica arrived at Beroea to make trouble for Paul, his Christian friends took him by sea out of Macedonia to Athens. Silas and Timothy remained awhile.

Athens was a cultural and artistic center. Along with Tarsus and Alexandria it had one of the three great universities of the Mediterranean world. Politically and commercially it was of no importance. Athenian society was based upon slavery, giving its citizens time for art, poetry, philosophy and general speculation. As usual Paul gave his first attention to his fellow Jews. He also talked "in the market place every day with those who chanced to be there." This attracted the attention of some philosophers who invited Paul to Mars Hill or the Areopagus where a council met from time to time to discuss social and philosophical questions.

Paul's Athens address is much different from any others we have recorded. His audience was not familiar with the Hebrew scriptures. Therefore there would be no value arguing from them. It is also much different from the address he gave at Lystra. Paul had been observant as he came into Athens. Among the many temples and statues or idols he found an altar with the inscription, "to an unknown god." Paul probably was not the first preacher who had used this altar as the starting point for his address, but it gave him a point of contact with his listeners. Paul began by complimenting the men of Athens for being very religious—not "too superstitious" as the King James committee translated the Greek. Paul then proceeded to proclaim a monotheism, a god in whom "we live and move and have our being." Showing his familiarity with Greek culture, he quoted from a Greek poet, Aratus, who two hundred years before had written, "For we are indeed his offspring." If this is true, Paul argued, then we should have a much greater concept of God than was represented in the Athenian statues. The God who made the world does not live in the shrines or temples of Athens. Paul's disapproval of statues was expressed in a letter he later wrote: "Claiming to be wise, they became fools, and exchanged the truth about God for images" (Rom. 1:22-23).

Paul's statement that "in him we live and move and have our being" had a note of familiarity to his audience, for a Greek poet had said about the same thing. This concept is in accord with Jesus' statement to the Samaritan woman at Jacob's well, "God is spirit" (John 4:24). We too are spirits. We *have* bodies. We might well ask, Does God have a body? While many think of God as not having a body, might we not say that the universe is God's body? As we are in every part of our bodies, so God is in every part of the universe. Our bodies are composed of atoms. A large part of every atom is empty space. Physicists report that the empty space in an atom is in about the same proportion as the empty space in the universe.

Paul again appealed to certain philosophers by speaking of the unity of human nature, that basically all men are alike. While the Revised Standard Version quotes Paul as saying "he made from one every nation of men" many early New Testament texts say "of one blood." Paul's recognition of the essential oneness of men has been collaborated by recent scientific discoveries that from the standpoint of blood and intelligence there are no significant racial differences.

Up to this point and even when he called upon men to rethink their religion Paul probably met with general approval from his philosophical listeners. But his reference to Jesus as the judge of mankind whom God had raised from the dead was in general unacceptable. Some mocked him. Others were courteous enough to say that they would hear him again. However, one member of the council of the Areopagus "joined him and believed." He and others may not have continued in their new convictions long. We have no New Testament reference to a church at Athens. Paul later refers to a Corinthian family as "the first converts in Achaia" (1 Cor. 16:15). Athens was the first place Paul had visited in Achaia.

Still traveling alone, Paul went south to the great commercial center of Corinth, the largest and wealthiest city of Greece. It was located near where the Corinthian canal is now. By use of the canal, ships going from eastern to western Greece are able to save two hundred miles. The Roman emperor Nero attempted to cut such a canal in A.D. 66-67, but sharp enough instruments were not available. A road had been made over which small ships were dragged on rollers. Larger ships were unloaded and the cargo taken over the isthmus and loaded onto other ships. The east and west ports made Corinth a sailor's town with its temples and temple prostitutes. An ancient writer reports that one temple had a thousand prostitutes connected with it. With its suburbs Corinth had a population of 600,000.

Paul thus proposed to take Christianity to a very difficult city. Shortly after reaching Corinth he got acquainted with a Jewish couple, Aquila and Priscilla. They were among those who in A.D. 49 were ordered out of Rome. A Roman writer of this time reports that the Jews had been expelled because of a disturbance instigated by a man named Chrestos. Could this mean the preaching of Christianity in Rome? Aquila and his wife were very friendly with Paul and continued so for a number of years, helping him in his Christian preaching. Paul does not list them as his first converts at Corinth. May it be that they had become Christians before leaving Rome? Like Paul, they were tentmakers by profession. Paul stayed with them and worked at their common trade.

It is quite possible that Paul planned no campaign here but simply expected to do what preaching he could in the synagogue on the Sabbath until he got word that it was safe to return to

Macedonia. However, as elsewhere, Luke gives the feeling that God took the initiative. Paul stayed at Corinth eighteen months. He established a vigorous church which he visited on at least two later occasions and to which he wrote at least four letters.

In time Silas and Timothy arrived from Macedonia. They probably reported that it was not yet safe for Paul to return to that section. They also gave an encouraging account of the church at Thessalonica, and possibly those at Philippi and Beroea. Perhaps this report stirred up Paul to more vigorous preaching, with the result that he soon was not welcome in the synagogue.

Paul did not go far from the synagogue. He began giving addresses and answering questions in a house next door. Although his letters to the Corinthian church indicate that most of his converts were non-Jews, Paul won over the ruler of the synagogue, Crispus. A little later the Jews turned against their new synagogue ruler and "beat him up." His name was Sosthenes. He may have been considered too friendly to Paul. Possibly he became a Christian; a man by that name was associated with Paul in writing a letter to the Corinthian church (1 Cor. 1:1). Was he the same man?

Paul became convinced that God was with him in his mission to Corinth despite his being dragged before the tribunal and charged with being a law-breaker. The proconsul, Gallio, would not listen to the charges, saying "I refuse to be a judge of these things."

Before returning to Antioch of Syria Paul wrote two letters to the church at Thessalonica. These are the beginning of Christian literature, the first Christian documents to survive. We are fortunately able to date these letters. About the beginning of the twentieth century an inscription was found which indicates that Gallio became proconsul in A.D. 51. Paul wrote his letters about a year earlier—A.D. 50.

Before examining Paul's letters it might be well to note a statement in the last paragraph of the last book of our Bible to be written. In speaking of the writings of Paul the author says, "There are some things in them hard to understand, which the ignorant and unstable twist to their own destruction, as they do the other scriptures" (2 Pet. 3:16). Regardless of how much we admire Paul we shall at times have to agree with the author of 2 Peter.

Paul was much concerned about his first European churches. He knew they would have plenty of trouble. It would seem that when he left Beroea he sent Timothy back to Thessalonica to investigate and be of any assistance he could. He had now come to Paul at Corinth with an encouraging report which Paul acknowledges in his letter. It is quite possible that Silas was sent to Philippi and that Paul wrote a similar letter to the church there after Silas reported at Corinth. If so, such a letter has been lost. Could it have been a copy of his letter to the Thessalonians?

Paul congratulates the Thessalonians for their faithfulness to Christianity, saying that they have become an example to other Christian groups not only in Macedonia but also in Achaia. Paul includes Silas (or Silvanus, of which Silas is an abbreviation) and Timothy as authors of the message, using the term "we" more often than in any other of his letters.

Paul points out that he is indebted to no one at Thessalonica, that he did nothing to please men but to please God. He notes that he and his associates earned their own living there "that we might not burden any of you." In a letter written some years later to the church at Philippi he acknowledges that the Philippians helped him while he was in Thessalonica "once and again" (4:16). He notes that their becoming Christians had caused the Thessalonians to suffer as had Christians in Palestine. He had warned them to expect this and is very happy that they have withstood temptation to deny their new religion.

Most of Paul's converts at Thessalonica had had little if any relation with Judaism and its moral standards. Paul reiterates what he had taught them when he was with the Thessalonians, that they must abstain from all immorality, and honor marriage. They must avoid being meddlers and respect manual labor.

Paul had emphasized his expectation of a return of Christ. Timothy evidently had brought word that the Thessalonians were disturbed because some of their number had died before the Lord had returned. Would these miss the glory to be experienced when Christ comes back? Upon the second coming, Paul writes, "the dead in Christ will rise first; then we who are alive." Both groups shall always be with the Lord. The coming back of the Lord is referred to several times in this letter. He will return when least expected "like a thief in the night." Therefore it behooves all to keep busy, live moral lives, and have constant fellowship with God.

As far as we know Paul had had little or no previous experience in writing to his churches. Word evidently soon reached him that his letter had not been entirely satisfactory. He realized that it did not please the Jewish element in the church. His teaching about the second coming had been misunderstood. Idlers and busybodies were still making trouble for the church. Paul felt called upon to write a second letter to his friends at Thessalonica.

His first chapter is again of congratulation and commendation. In the second chapter he gets down at once to the purpose of his letter: "Now concerning the coming of our Lord Jesus Christ." A report had got circulated, Paul and his associates did not know just how, that the day of the Lord had already come. Paul then makes a statement which seems to contradict the teaching of his first letter which suggested that Christ might come at any moment. In his second letter he says that Christ will not come until after the rebellion has taken place and the man of lawlessness has been revealed as he explained to them when he was in Thessalonica. We do not have the advantage of knowing what Paul taught about this when he was preaching in Thessalonica. Its interpretation varies greatly. The rebellion is a falling away from the faith within the church. Was the man of lawlessness a Roman emperor or a Jewish leader who would strenuously oppose Christianity? Old Testament Jews had expected some one to attack God and his people before what they called the day of the Lord. "Taking his seat in the temple of God, proclaiming himself to be God" (2:24) suggests a repetition of something that had occurred on two previous occasions: one of the causes of the Maccabean Rebellion in 168 B.C. had been the erection of a Greek altar in the temple area at Jerusalem; in A.D. 39 or 40 the Roman emperor had tried to have his statue set up in the temple as an object of worship. Whatever Paul had in mind as the man of lawlessness, he was an anti-Christ, a term not used by Paul but employed by the later New Testament writer of 1 and 2 John.

Paul condemns those who "did not believe the truth" and thanks God for those saved through "belief in the truth." He expresses confidence that the Thessalonian Christians will "do the things which we command." The command is that the Christian group have nothing to do with idle, shiftless members. Evidently Paul found some such among those who formed the church when he first preached in Thessalonica. Probably his emphasis upon the return of Jesus gave an added excuse for being idle. If Jesus was to return soon, why spend time working; why not rather meditate upon Christ? Paul, always on the job, endeavoring to make every minute count, refuses to tolerate any laziness. "If any man will not work, let him not eat" (3:10). Calling oneself a Christian gives him no excuse for depending upon others for support. Did Paul want these excluded from the common meal, the Lord's Supper?

For Class Discussion

1. Does the accusation against Paul and his associates at Thessalonica describe Christianity today? Is the world upside down, needing to be put right side up?

2. Why are some churches and church school classes called Berea, but seldom by the name of any other group mentioned in this chapter?

3. Who in early American history used Paul's command, "If any one will not work, let him not eat?" How did the situation that caused this differ from that at Antioch?

Assignment

1. In what way were Paul and his associates at Thessalonica charged with treason?

2. What did Luke commend about the Beroeans?

3. In his Athens address what did Paul say about (a) God, (b) people?

4. Why did Paul write 2 Thessalonians?

Supplementary Reading

1. *The Interpreter's Bible*. New York and Nashville: Abingdon Press, Vol. 9, 1954. Pages 225-247. Vol. 11, 1955. Pages 245-339.

2. Barnett, Albert E. *The New Testament—Its Making and Meaning.* New York and Nashville: Abingdon Press, 1946. Chapters II and III.

3. Goodspeed, Edgar J. *An Introduction to the New Testament* Chicago: University of Chicago Press, 1951. Chapters I and II.

4. McCasland, S. Vernon. *The Religion of the Bible.* New York: Thomas Y. Crowell Co., 1960. Chapter 28.

CHAPTER 30

'Paul an Apostle . . . Through Jesus Christ"

Read Paul's letter to the Galatians.

Taking Priscilla and Aquila with him Paul sailed directly east from the port of Corinth to Ephesus. After speaking in the synagogue there Paul left his companions at Ephesus and went on by ship to Caesarea. Before going to his headquarters at Antioch he visited the church at either Caesarea or Jerusalem—Luke is vague as to which.

Luke never records anything about Paul's letter writing. It would seem that at Antioch Paul heard bad news. Despite the agreement at the Jerusalem conference some of the Hebrew Christians had gone among Paul's Galatian churches and preached that it was essential that one must be circumcised, become a Jew, a "descendant of Abraham," before he could be considered a Christian. They claimed that Paul was not an authority, had not been appointed as one of the twelve apostles. Paul was obliged to spend some time in Antioch before going to the Galatian region to straighten out this matter. Therefore he wrote a letter in hot haste in which he vigorously defended his stand. Not all scholars give this as the setting for Paul's letter to the Galatians. Some think that it was written under similar conditions after Paul's return from his first missionary journey. Other dates and places have been suggested.

This is Paul's first really great letter, a vehement charter of religious freedom, a declaration of independence. He strikes out from the shoulder in his first sentence: "Paul an apostle—not from men nor through men, but through Jesus Christ and God the Father." An apostle is one who is sent. No man had commissioned him. He had his commission from the highest possible source. He is astonished that his converts are becoming turncoats, taking up with a pseudo gospel. His is the gospel of Christ. One who teaches contrary to it is accursed.

To support his contention that his apostleship is from God, Paul reminds his readers of his own conversion experience from orthodox Judaism when Christ appeared to him. He tells of his visits to Jerusalem. In connection with the first visit he cleverly refers to James the brother of Jesus as an apostle—he was not one of the twelve, but people would hardly dare say he was not an apostle. Paul points out that in connection with the Jerusalem conference the pillars of the church "saw that I had been entrusted with the gospel to the uncircumcised . . . and . . . gave to me and Barnabas the right hand of fellowship, that we should go to the Gentiles" (2:7-9). He emphasizes that he made this trip to Jerusalem "by revelation," not called by the church authorities there. Paul has nothing to do with any "apostolic succession," any feeling that the original twelve or the family of Jesus had automatic special power. He notes that Titus, an uncircumcised Greek, was with him and was accepted by the Jerusalem Christians without being circumcised.

To point out that Christianity is a new religion, Paul tells of his experience at Antioch after the Jerusalem conference. Like Paul, Peter associated freely with Gentile Christians. But when some of the Hebrew Christians arrived from Jerusalem Peter slipped back into his earlier habit of refusing to eat with the uncircumcised. This custom had developed among Jews probably to keep their group from being absorbed by the Gentiles. To the orthodox Jew meals were a religious observance, preceded by ritualistic washing, started with a blessing, and accompanied by discussion about God and his Torah. Only "clean" food which had had a tenth of it offered to God might be eaten. To eat with people who did not observe these rules was considered denying God. In telling of Jesus' criticism of some of these regulations Mark adds an editorial explanation, "Thus he declared all food clean" (7:9). We cannot imagine Paul refusing to eat with Titus or his many Gentile converts, but Peter had had a much more limited experience and could be swayed by fellow Hebrew Christians. Paul tells of his reprimanding Peter and then states his own Christian conviction: "a man is not justified by works of the law but through faith in Jesus Christ," that is, observing regulations does not make a man righteous.

Paul proceeds to ask the Galatians if it is by the law that they became Christians, received the spirit of truth. The Judaizers insisted upon following all the detailed regulations attributed to Moses. Many of these were physical, including circumcision. Paul asks, "Having begun with the Spirit, are you now ending with the flesh?" (3:3) Abraham did not observe the laws of Moses—he lived long before Moses. Abraham was a man of faith and righteousness. Therefore obeying the Hebrew laws does not make a man a descendant of Abraham. Men of faith are the real spiritual sons of Abraham. No one who for his salvation depends upon observing the laws of the Torah will be saved, for no one is able to observe every regulation.

Law is not bad, but the good can be the enemy of the best. Law has its place. It is like the custodian who takes a boy from his home to the teachers. When he has been delivered to the teachers the boy has no more need for the custodian. The law brought us along the way to Christ, but now that we have Christ we no longer need these detailed regulations. Through faith in Christ we have become the spiritual offspring of Abraham, regardless of race, status or sex. Circumcision with that which it symbolizes is no longer necessary. These who seek salvation by observing the law are slaves. Now we are released from slavery, recognized by God not as slaves, but as his children. When people had come far enough along in their spiritual evolution that they could understand the will of God, Christ was sent that we might have the gospel of freedom.

Paul points out to his non-Jewish readers that they have been rescued from a religion that bound them by regulations about the observance of numerous special days and rituals. He begs them not to slide back into a similar bondage. In an allegory of Abraham's two sons, Ishmael and Isaac, Paul points out that those who refuse the new covenant of faith can no longer claim to be Abraham's children. They lose their heritage.

The gospel of Christ is unlimited. Christ set us free. Do not revert to slavery. If you require circumcision then you must require all the detailed regulations of the law. Snobbishness and divisiveness are contrary to the spirit of Christ. Neither Jewish Christians who have been circumcised nor Gentile Christians who have not should feel superior to each other. Paul expresses confidence that his readers will understand and accept his teachings. He then throws in an important warning that there is danger in freedom, that freedom from the old law implies self-control. Christians must never forget to love their neighbors as they love themselves. Those whose concern is with the physical are in danger of "the works of the flesh." Without God's spiritual help these are what man will produce. Paul makes a list of these and then warns "that those who do such things shall not inherit the kingdom of God" (5:21). On the other hand those who have the Holy Spirit have qualities which Paul calls the fruit of the Spirit; "against such there is no law." These spiritual matters are what are really important.

Kindness, helping the other person, is essential to Christianity. Paul may have the Thessalonian idlers in mind when he insists that "Each man will have to bear his own load" (6:5), not expect others to do his work for him. On the other hand help should be given those who need it: "Bear one another's burdens, and so fulfill the law of Christ" (6:2). Men get from life what they put into it. Those who emphasize physical things will find their satisfaction soon destroyed, while "he who sows to the Spirit will from the Spirit reap eternal life" (6:8).

Paul concludes his letter by summing up his conviction about circumcision: it is completely unimportant; those who insist upon it break the law at many points and are simply seeking self-satisfaction in being dictatorial. The important thing is to become a new man, a man of faith activated by love.

For Class Discussion

1. What groups today refuse to eat with other people? To what extent do their reasons correspond to those of orthodox Jews of Paul's day?

2. Do any Christian groups today over-emphasize legalism, form or ritual?

3. In Marcion's edition of Christian writings he puts Galatians at the beginning of Paul's letters. Why?

Assignment

1. How did Paul's report of the Jerusalem conference in Galatians differ from that of Acts 15:22-35?
2. What does Paul say about Abraham?
3. To what did Paul compare the Hebrew law?
4. What does Paul consider the (a) works of the flesh, (b) fruit of the spirit?

Supplementary Reading

1. *The Interpreter's Bible.* New York and Nashville: Abingdon Press, Vol. 10, 1953. Pages 427-593.
2. McCasland, S. Vernon. *The Religion of the Bible.* New York: Thomas Y. Crowell Co., 1960. Chapter 29.

CHAPTER 31

"I Belong to Paul"

Read Acts 18:23-20:1; 1 Corinthians

After spending some time in Antioch Paul visited the Galatian churches on the way to Ephesus. This great port on the western coast of Asia Minor was the fourth largest city in the Roman empire. The harbor was beginning to silt in in Paul's day. Later it became completely filled and the city was abandoned. In Ephesus Paul learned that another preacher had been there before him. This was a Jew named Apollos who had been born in Alexandria, Egypt. He was an eloquent orator who had a limited knowledge of Christianity. He seems to have been better acquainted with John the Baptist. When he spoke in the synagogues at Ephesus, Aquila and Priscilla took him aside and endeavored to bring him up to date in his Christianity. He had later gone on to Corinth with the blessing of the Ephesian Christians. When Paul reached Ephesus he asked the followers of Apollos if they had received the Holy Spirit. They answered, "No, we have never even heard that there is a Holy Spirit." After further explaining, Paul gave these people Christian baptism and they became convinced that they had the Spirit of Truth.

His years of experience seem to have given Paul smoother strategy. He was able to make addresses in the Ephesian synagogue for three months before he was stopped. He then rented a lecture room in the hall of Tyrannus where he spoke daily for two years. Some early copies of Acts report that Paul had the use of his lecture room from eleven in the morning until four in the afternoon. Possibly another teacher used the same room during the earlier hours and still another in the evenings.

Along with his success as a preacher Paul gained a reputation as a miracle worker. A group of Jewish brothers tried to imitate Paul with interesting unpleasant results. Some people who practiced magic were so impressed by Paul that they burned their extremely expensive books and gave up their deceptive practices.

Paul's ministry was not confined to the territory around Ephesus. As a port opposite Corinth, Ephesus had numerous visitors from the Greek city. Two different groups from the church at Corinth visited Paul to discuss problems with him. One group was "Chloe's people" (1 Cor. 1:11), probably servants or slaves of a Christian woman of Corinth. They reported on the quarrels in the Corinthian church. The other group contained at least three men, Stephanas, Fortunatus and Achaicus (1 Cor. 16:17). The first of these was the man whose household "were the first converts in Achaia"; Paul looked upon him as one of the best leaders of the Corinthian church. These men brought with them a letter from the Corinthian Christians asking advice on a number of problems.

Paul had already written a letter to the church at Corinth (1 Cor. 5:9). Therefore what we call First Corinthians was not Paul's first letter to the Corinthians. In referring to this letter Paul goes on to remind his readers that he has instructed them not to associate with immoral men. Do we have this first letter? It is quite possible that we have a part of it. In the Revised Standard Version New Testament 2 Cor. 6:14 to 7:1 is separated from its context by extra spaces. This section does not fit well into the matters discussed in the sixth and seventh chapters. It begins, "Do not be mismated with unbelievers." This could well be a part of Paul's first letter to the Corinthians.

In a long and varied letter Paul shows his skill as a patient teacher. The problems with which Paul deals in this letter give us a picture of the first century churches. With no precedent, no traditions, there were many difficulties to be worked out. The first problem with which Paul dealt in this letter was that of divisions or sects within the Corinthian church. Paul had founded the church and some of its members were intensely loyal to him. However, the visit of the flamboyant orator, Apollos, with his limited understanding of Christianity, had developed an Apollos "fan club." Possibly Peter had also visited Corinth, or perhaps there were other visitors from Palestine. Some people felt that Peter, as the leading member of the original twelve disciples, should have their supreme loyalty. Thus the church was dividing into at least three quarreling cliques. Paul was much disturbed by this. None of these people wanted personal followers. "I decided to know nothing among you except Jesus Christ and him crucified" (2:2). The Corinthians must grow from childish loyalties to become mature spiritual men. "I planted, Apollos watered, but God gave the growth" (3:6). All are servants of God. "We are fellow workmen for God" (3:9). Paul, Apollos, Peter must be forgotten. Complete loyalty must be given to Christ and God.

As in Thessalonica so in Corinth some new Christians who did not have the moral emphasis of the Jewish religion were falling short at certain ethical points. This is not surprising when we know their environment. There was a man living with his stepmother. There were those who were boastful. Others were adulterers and homosexuals. Others were drunkards. As Paul has written before, so he insists again that these things must not be tolerated. Bringing lawsuits against one another in heathen courts is not Christian. Because an act is legal does not make it right or helpful. Our bodies belong to God. They must be properly taken care of and never misused. They are temples of the Holy Spirit.

These were probably not the problems about which the Corinthian church had asked Paul's advice. His discussion of them did not make the Corinthians happy. In the seventh chapter Paul turns to the matters about which the Corinthians wrote him. The licentiousness among the Gentile Christians was doubtless another source of division in the church. To avoid immorality it is well for Christians to be married. Husbands and wives should respect one another. Paul still feels that he is living near the end of the age, that the Lord will return soon. It is his personal conviction that the unmarried might well remain that way. Thus they could give their time and energy to "the affairs of the Lord." However, marriage is no sin, and some people would be better married.

Then there was the question about food offered to idols. This was a problem of Christian freedom. We might expect Paul to quote the ruling of the Jerusalem conference and drop the matter. But Paul refuses to depend upon law, either the Torah or rulings of the church. Rather he appeals to intelligence and love. Evidently some of the Corinthian Christians were arguing that "all of us possess knowledge," that idols are of no value and therefore there was no harm in eating meat that had been offered to them. Paul agrees that in general this is true, but points out the importance of love, of protecting the weak brother, the former idol worshiper. To such a person eating meat offered to an idol would be reverting to his heathen practice. If eating at the home of an unbeliever, do not ask about the meat. If some one brags that the meat has been offered as a sacrifice, then do not eat it, for the sake of the conscience of the other man. "If food is a cause of my brother's falling, I will never eat meat, lest I cause my brother to fall" (8:13).

Paul next turns to a discussion of Christian worship. Evidently some questions had been raised in the letter he received. He commends the Corinthians for following his teachings, but in the same breath tackles one of the problems rising out of his teaching of Christian freedom. If Christians are not under laws, is it not all right for women to take part in worship services with their heads uncovered? Paul had to deal with a local situation. In Corinth the badge or sign of its many prostitutes was to go about bare-headed. Normally there should be no rule requiring a Christian woman to cover her head. However, the reputation of Christians must be protected. Therefore it was only proper that in Corinth Christian women should not be seen outside their homes with their heads uncovered. It might be thought that they were a group of prostitutes. Is Paul completely in accord with his teaching to the Galatians, that in Christ there is no distinction between male and female (3:28)?

The Lord's Supper at Corinth had degenerated into something other than a loving commemoration of the death of Jesus. It was a full meal. The Jerusalem practice of having meals in common was to some extent being followed. Possibly this had been introduced by the Peter clique. But the meal was disorderly. Some rushed to eat ahead of others. Individuals even became drunk. Wealthy members humiliated the poor. Paul proceeds to repeat what he has once told them of the simplicity of the supper originated by Jesus "on the night when he was betrayed." This is the first written account of the Lord's Supper we have and is today the most used of all the records.

217

Another cause of dissension in the Corinthian church was the fact that individuals varied in their abilities. Paul points out that all these abilities—he lists nine—are given through the Holy Spirit. For a person to have one of these gifts does not make him superior over a person who has some other ability. Our physical bodies must have different parts and organs if they are to function. So must the church, the body of Christ. In place of dissension, Paul emphasizes the essential of Christian life—love. In this 13th chapter Paul gives his most beautiful poetic expression. Far more important than any talents or gifts are faith, hope and love; "but the greatest of these is love." Through love all friction, dissension, cliques can be done away. "Love is patient and kind. . . . Love does not insist on its own way . . . endures all things."

"Speaking in tongues" was being practiced by some members of the Corinthian group. This may have been a carry-over from emotional expressions of heathen religion, or it may have been introduced by visitors from Jerusalem as an imitation of the Pentecost experience. Paul felt that there was far less value in this than in prophesying, that is preaching or explaining Christianity. His summary should have been conclusive: "In church I would rather speak five words with my mind, in order to instruct others, than ten thousand words in a tongue" (14:19).

Services of worship must be orderly, "for God is not a God of confusion but of peace" (14:33). What does Paul mean when he says that "women should keep silence in the churches" (14:34)? In 11:5 Paul takes for granted that women pray and prophesy or preach in church services. His statement in the 14th chapter that "If there is anything they desire to know, let them ask their husbands at home" may suggest that Paul is forbidding gossip and chatter in church.

Evidently some Corinthian Christians challenged the idea of human resurrection, perhaps of a future life. Paul argues that that would make liars of him and others who had been preaching about Christ's resurrection. He feels that without such a belief men would not live moral lives. After insisting upon a resurrection Paul points out that the seed itself which is planted does not come up again. So a human body will not be restored like it was buried: "It is sown a physical body, it is raised a spiritual body" (15:44). He expects the return of Christ soon—before all his readers have died: "We shall not all sleep" (14:51). When Christ returns, those still living will be changed "in the twinkling of an eye" to join those who will be raised imperishable. Therefore people should be active in the work of the Lord, knowing that such work will receive its award.

Paul concludes his letter by giving directions for collecting an offering for the Christians in Judea, and promises to visit the Corinthians soon. Paul indicates his friendliness for Apollos, who evidently has returned to Ephesus. Paul says he has urged him to visit Corinth again and is assured he will eventually do so. Paul sends greetings from the Corinthian friends, Aquila and Priscilla, who are with him in Ephesus, and then once more insists "Let all that you do be done in love" (16:14).

Paul's letter did not have the effect he had hoped. The factions were to some extent brought together, but against Paul. Despite various commendations, he had "stepped on the toes" of the divergent groups. Moreover some Jewish Christians had arrived with glowing letters of commendation. We do not know from where they came, but they claimed to have far more authority than Paul. Like those who had gone to Galatia they insisted that Paul was not a real apostle. They caused the Corinthians to believe that "His letters are weighty and strong, but his bodily presence is weak, and his speech of no account" (2 Cor. 10:10).

Paul evidently made a hurried visit to Corinth that Luke does not include in his account. This was not a pleasant experience. After his return to Ephesus he wrote a "stern letter." Apparently the last four chapters of our 2 Corinthians constitute a part of this "stern letter" meant to "kill or cure." In it he lashes out against the visitors who claim that Paul is not an apostle and who lord it over Paul's converts. Paul asks sarcastically, "Did I commit a sin . . . because I preached God's gospel without cost to you" (11:7). He points out how much more he suffered for the gospel's sake than did these "superfine" or superlative apostles. He may be unskilled in speaking but not in knowledge, he insists. He did not allow the Corinthians to support him financially while he was with them lest he be suspected of self-interest. His opponents have even used this as an argument that Paul is not a true apostle.

Paul warns the Corinthians that he will soon visit them for a third time. Titus is sent to Corinth with the letter. Paul plans to complete his mission in Ephesus. He will then go to Corinth, hoping to meet Titus on the way.

Luke reports that before Paul left Ephesus his success there got him into trouble. Great crowds came from long distances to Ephesus to worship at a famous shrine of the goddess Artemis. It had become one of the seven wonders of the world. Many bought silver miniatures of the shrine to take home and use as worship centers. Demetrius, a leader among the silversmiths, realized that, to the extent that Paul's religion increased, his business would decrease. He incited a frenzied mob to attack Paul. Fortunately Paul was protected by friends while the town clerk calmed down the crowd. He insisted that the Roman courts would hear any charges the group wanted to bring against Paul and his associates in a legal manner.

As Paul hurried north to meet Titus he began to regret that he had written his "stern letter." Titus was not at Troas. Although he was urged to stay, Paul hurried on to Macedonia. There they met, and Titus broke the good news that Paul's "stern letter" had been successful. The troublemakers had been punished and most of the Corinthian Christians were ready to welcome Paul. This brought peace to Paul, who took time out to work with the churches in Macedonia before going on to Corinth. He was quite concerned about an offering the churches of Greece were raising to send to Judea. He remained in Macedonia to supervise the collection of this offering there and to give the Corinthian church time to complete its gift. Paul wanted to avoid becoming involved again in financial questions with the Corinthians. Meanwhile he wrote the Corinthians a thankful letter. This is most of the first nine chapters of our 2 Corinthians. In it he relates how painful the controversy had been to him and how relieved he now is that it is finally a matter of the past. He expresses his appreciation to God for working through him and renews his appeal for mutual love and understanding. In one paragraph Paul reiterates the great themes of all his letters: "God was in Christ reconciling the world to himself" (5:19), and "If any one is in Christ, he is a new creation" (5:17).

Shortly after sending this fourth letter Paul reached Corinth. Luke says that Paul spent three months in Greece, but gives no details. Luke's primary purpose was to relate how the gospel spread and new churches were founded. He was not concerned with the problems of the early church and how they were worked out.

For Class Discussion

1. What problems in the Corinthian church are found in churches today?
2. Why do some Christian groups today insist that women must keep their heads covered in church buildings? Why do some forbid women to preach in their churches?

Assignment

1. Make in your own words a summary of 1 Cor. 13.
2. Make a chart showing what we seem to have of each of Paul's four letters to the Corinthians.
3. In what connections have we had earlier reference to (a) speaking in tongues, (b) meat offered to idols?

Supplementary Reading

1. *The Interpreter's Bible.* New York and Nashville: Abingdon Press, Vol. 9, 1954. Pages 247-264; Vol. 10, 1953, Pages 1-425.
2. Barnett, Albert E. *The New Testament, Its Making and Meaning.* New York and Nashville: Abingdon Press, 1946, Chapter I.
3. Goodspeed, Edgar J. *An Introduction to the New Testament.* Chicago: University of Chicago Press, 1937, Chapters IV and V.
4. McCasland, S. Vernon. *The Religion of the Bible.* New York: Thomas Y. Crowell Co., 1960. Chapter 30.

CHAPTER 32

'To All God's Beloved in Rome"

Read Acts 20:1-6; Romans

While making his third visit to Corinth or just after that, while he was visiting churches in Macedonia, Paul wrote his longest letter. This letter was addressed to "all God's beloved in Rome," headquarters of the empire that ruled the Mediterranean world. It is the weightiest, most carefully worked out of all Paul's letters. It was not hurriedly got together to meet some problem or problems that had just come up. Paul had never been in Rome. He had not founded the church there. The Roman church was doubtless founded by Jews or God-fearers who had been converted to Christianity at the time of the first Pentecost after the resurrection. However, it soon became chiefly a Gentile church. Paul, therefore, as the apostle to the Gentiles, felt a degree of responsibility for this church in the heart of the Roman world. His letter might well be called "the gospel according to Paul."

From Paul's experience he knew the kind of problems that arise in churches. Perhaps he could prevent these from rising or "nip them in the bud" for the Roman church. He would deal with such problems in advance and give an organized outline of his own concept of Christianity. His letter was also to prepare the way for his visiting Rome, perhaps secure an invitation from the Christians there. He tells his readers that "without ceasing I mention you always in my prayers." For a long time he has been wanting to visit Rome and be of some help there, "that we may be mutually encouraged by each other's faith" (1:12). He has often intended to visit Rome "but thus far have been prevented." Throughout the letter Paul is kind and uncritical. Near the end he explains that his work has been that of founding churches. Therefore, despite his wish to visit Rome, his real task has kept him from doing so. He feels that his work in the eastern part of the empire has been completed. He wants to open up missionary activity in Spain, but on the way to Spain he will visit Rome.

Paul reports that he cannot go to Rome immediately, for first he must take the offering from the churches of Macedonia and Achaia to the saints (Paul's favorite word for Christians) in Jerusalem. For more than a year Paul had been supervising the collecting of this offering. One might ask why Paul did not send a bank draft—such facilities were available in his day. At many points Paul was a good psychologist. The offering he was taking to Jerusalem was to do much more than alleviate the economic distress of members of the mother church. It was to bridge over the gulf between the conservative Jewish Christian group in Palestine and the more liberal Gentile churches in Greece. In 1 Corinthians (16:1) he said that he had directed the Galatian churches to send a similar offering. Paul could point out that some of the drachmas he had with him had been given by a man in Corinth who had for a period of time done without one meal a day in order that the Jerusalem Christians might have money with which to buy food; other drachmas were from a woman in Thessalonica who had taken in washings to earn money to add to this offering. Thus the members of the earliest church would be more friendly to these new and strange Christian groups. To bind the groups together even more, some men from Greece and Galatia went to Jerusalem with Paul.

Paul's letter to the Romans is very general. Its teachings could apply to any Christian group. He does not deal with special Roman problems, has no local color. Only in the first and 15th chapters is Rome mentioned. Since some of the earliest copies of this letter do not have any reference to Rome, it is suggested that Paul wrote his letter as a summing up of his Christian convictions, and had copies sent to several churches. Paul sensed a turning point in his ministry. To go to Jerusalem was dangerous. Possibly he would never be allowed to visit Rome or come back to any of his churches. Some of the earliest copies did not have the 15th and 16th chapters.

This leads to a problem that has bothered all students of the New Testament. The problem is the 16th chapter of Romans. This chapter appears to be a letter of commendation upon the part of Paul for Phoebe, a deaconess of the church at Cenchreae, the eastern port of Corinth. Evidently Phoebe was about to visit a city in which there lived a number of Christian friends of Paul. Therefore he sent with her (or possibly ahead of her) a letter of introduction. Paul sends greetings to twenty-six people whom he names, two others whom he mentions specifically, and certain groups. He knows in whose homes different church groups meet. Would Paul know this many individuals in Rome? Among those to whom Paul sends greetings are three of his kinsmen, two of whom had been his fellow prisoners—Luke does not tell of Paul's having any prison experience before this, other than a few hours in Philippi; evidently Paul's treatment had unpleasant details omitted by Luke. Paul sends greetings to a woman who has treated him like a son and to Priscilla and Aquila whom we last noted were in Ephesus. All this seems to fit Ephesus much better than Rome. Rom. 16:17-20 is a paragraph of warning about "those who create dissensions and difficulties." This does not fit the atmosphere of the first fifteen chapters.

Most scholars are convinced that this 16th chapter is a separate note written by Paul from Corinth to the church at Ephesus which he has very recently left; a note to introduce Phoebe to Christian friends there. Some, however, do believe that this 16th chapter was written to the Roman Christians. They ask why Paul would have told the Ephesians that Priscilla and Aquila had risked their necks for his life, or that Andronicus and Junias are men of note among the apostles. Others suggest that this chapter is but the ending of a longer letter to the Ephesians; that the main part of the letter has been lost. Another suggestion is that copies of Paul's general letter we call Romans were sent to various churches and that this 16th chapter was added to the copy sent to Ephesus.

Paul's theme is sin and salvation—particularly Christ's part in salvation. He believed that the gospel is "the power of God for salvation." His theme is summed up in 1:17: "He who through faith is righteous shall live." To Paul faith meant dependence upon God: thinking through the will of God, doing his will, and having spiritual fellowship in union with him. Sin is falling short, failing to hit the mark.

Punishment comes upon all ungodliness and wickedness. Greeks claiming to be wise have foolishly turned to the worship of man-made images. Many have become homosexuals, and commit numerous other sins. "Though they know God's decree that those who do such things deserve to die, they not only do them but approve those who practice them" (1:32). God shows no partiality. Jews too are unrighteous. Having the law does not save the Jews unless they very carefully obey the law. Jews have no right to pass judgment upon Gentiles. "All men, both Jews and Greeks, are under the power of sin" (3:9). All men are slaves of impure impulses. The function of the law is to give knowledge of sin.

Righteousness, escape from sin and punishment, is revealed through Christ. Observing rules and forms does not bring an understanding of the character and righteousness of God. We must recognize our own shortcomings and through Jesus Christ find the qualities of God. In 3:24-25 Paul uses a number of words that are difficult to understand—justified, grace, redemption, expiation. In somewhat legal terminology Paul says that God gives us who have faith in Jesus much more than we deserve. We are all sinners, but in some way he helps us overcome the consequence of our sin. Faith does not destroy the law but is much greater than the law. Abraham was our great forefather. The important thing about him was his faith, not his observance of rules or ritual, such as circumcision. He is the spiritual father of both Jews and Gentiles. Therefore we too must live by faith. If Judaizers show up with their claim that Christians must first become sons of Abraham, that is Jews, Paul has already answered them.

Through Jesus and his death man has been made at peace with God. Reconciliation has taken place. This is a cause of rejoicing. Although it is not definitely expressed in the Old Testament, Jewish leaders had developed the idea that men sinned because Adam sinned. With this in mind Paul points out that salvation and God's grace have come through one man, Christ Jesus. Through him we can be made righteous, have a new life. As death no longer has dominion over Christ, so when we become fully Christian sin will have no dominion over us. The reward for enslaving ourselves to God is eternal life. Paul realizes that he himself has not yet attained sinlessness. "I do not do what I want, but I do the very thing I hate" (7:15). Sin seems to Paul to be a personality dwelling in his flesh. "I of myself serve the law of God with my mind, but with my flesh I serve the law of sin" (7:25). However, Christ lived in a body and overcame sin. Therefore we live in the hope that the Holy Spirit will enable us to do the same. "In everything God works for good with those who love him" (8:28). "If God is for us, who is against us?" (8:31). Absolutely nothing can separate us from the love of God.

Paul next takes up a problem which must have greatly bothered him and many of the Gentile Christians: Why have most of the Jewish people rejected Jesus? They are his kinsmen and certainly should have the benefits that Christ brought to mankind. Their desertion of Jesus does not mean that God's purpose has failed. There is no automatic value in being a physical descendant of Abraham. Many people of Israel have been more concerned with law than with faith. Their zeal for God is not enlightened. God's demands upon Jew and Greek are alike. Faith comes only from understanding and accepting the Christian message. It must be taken to both groups. Paul tells his Gentile readers that they must appreciate that the Christian message came through the Jews and that they should be grateful to the Jewish religion. They should be glad that Christianity has not been confined to the Jews. It is his conviction that the Jews will return to the gospel which originated among them, so that eventually "all Israel will be saved" (11:26).

Paul's final contribution is his ideal of Christian behavior, how a Christian should conduct himself in the world, in relation to government, and as a church. Next to the Sermon on the Mount this is the best summary the Bible gives of how a Christian should live. It is all summed up in the word *love*: "Love does no wrong to a neighbor; therefore love is the fulfilling of the law" (13:10).

Christians must give their whole selves to God. Whatever ability one has is not to be boasted about but dedicated to the service of God. Try to excel others in kindness. Tribulation and persecution may come, but be patient and help those who persecute you. As far as possible live peaceably with all. "If your enemy is hungry, feed him; if he is thirsty give him to drink" (12:20). "Overcome evil with good" (12:21). Cooperate with government. Pay your taxes "for the authorities are ministers of God" (13:6). As did Jesus, Paul says that the commandments concerning relations with others can be summed up in the requirement, "Love your neighbor as yourself" (13:9).

This love for all means that there is room for a variety of outlooks in the church. "Then let us no more pass judgment on one another, but rather decide never to put a stumbling-block or hindrance in the way of a brother" (14:13). "Nothing is unclean in itself; but it is unclean for any one who thinks it unclean" (14:14). However, love may cause us to refrain from things we feel are right in order that we may not injure some one who has a different concept. Evidently there had been some problem about food; probably meat offered to idols, or possibly food which Jewish Christians still considered unclean. "The kingdom of God does not mean food and drink but righteousness and peace and joy in the Holy Spirit" (14:17). "We who are strong ought to bear with the failings of the weak, and not to please ourselves" (15:1). "Christ did not please himself" (15:3).

After this one possible reprimand Paul closes his letter by saying "I myself am satisfied about you, my brethren, that you yourselves are full of goodness, filled with all knowledge, and able to instruct one another" (15:14). He then explains that because of the necessity of taking the offerings of the Greek churches to Jerusalem he is not able to visit Rome immediately, but "I know that when I come to you I shall come in the fullness of the blessing of Christ" (15:29).

For Class Discussion

1. Does it really matter what one believes?
2. Why did not more Jews follow Jesus? What are the Jewish attitudes toward Jesus today?
3. What is the duty of the Christian today toward (a) the government, (b) his employer, (c) those with whom he works, (d) people of other races, (e) those who do not agree with him?

Assignment

1. What is the problem of Rom. 16?
2. In Romans what does Paul say about (a) Abraham, (b) Adam?

3. How does Paul deal with the fact that most Jews rejected Jesus?

4. Why is the King James translation of Rom. 1:13 likely to be misunderstood by present day readers?

Supplementary Reading

1. *The Interpreter's Bible.* New York and Nashville: Abingdon Press, Vol. 9, 1954. Pages 353-668.

2. Barnett, Albert E. *The New Testament: Its Making and Meaning.* New York and Nashville: Abingdon Press, 1946. Chapter IV.

3. Barrett, C. K. *The Epistle to the Romans.* New York: Harper & Brothers, 1957.

4. Goodspeed, Edgar J. *An Introduction to the New Testament.* Chicago: University of Chicago Press, 1937. Chapter VI.

CHAPTER 33

'Ready to Die at Jerusalem"

Read Acts 20:3—26:32

Was it murder or robbery that was plotted against Paul by some Jews at the port of Corinth? As Paul was about to sail from Cencreae he learned of the plot and went instead by Macedonia. Were Jews trying to get rid of a heretic, or was the offering Paul was taking to Jerusalem the temptation? Representatives of Macedonia, Asia and Galatia were with Paul. These went on to Troas. After a visit in Philippi Paul continued to Troas, evidently accompanied by Luke, as the account in Acts says that "we" came.

A week was spent in Troas. On Sunday the group of people there interested in Christianity gathered in a third-story room for a common meal, fellowship and instruction. Was it by this time the habit of Christians to meet each Sunday, later called the "Lord's Day?" Paul preached until midnight. The meeting was disturbed when a young man named Eutychus, having gone to sleep, fell out of the window. Paul said he was not dead and evidently took care of him. The meeting then continued until daylight. Paul took a ship that did not stop at Ephesus as he was eager to get to Jerusalem for Pentecost. Could it be that Paul had too many enemies in Ephesus, that it was not safe for him to stay there? However, at the port of Miletus he had an opportunity to meet with some of the men of the Ephesian church.

Evidently the plot of the Jews against Paul had made him pessimistic as to the outcome of his visit to Jerusalem. He tells the Ephesians they "will see my face no more." He warns them that they will be attacked by outsiders and have internal strife. They must be patient with one another and help the weak. He quotes a statement of Jesus found nowhere else in the Bible, "It is more blessed to give than to receive." Thus Paul bid farewell to what soon was one of the most important churches of the first century. Ephesus became the center of Christianity and remained so until that honor was taken over by Rome.

Paul and his party sailed to Tyre in Phoenicia where they found an active Christian group about which we had not heard before. The Christians insisted that Paul should not go to Jerusalem, but he would not be stopped. In his report Luke emphasized parallels between Paul and Jesus. In Lu. 9:51 he had said that Jesus "set his face to go to Jerusalem." At Caesarea, the Roman port nearest Jerusalem, the group stayed at the home of Philip, one of the seven "deacons," and his four unmarried daughters. Here Paul received a similar warning. The prophet Agabus, whom we had met in Acts 11:28, dramatically told Paul not to go to Jerusalem, saying that he would be bound by the Jews and delivered to the Gentiles. Actually the Jews attempted to lynch him and he was rescued by Gentile officers. Paul insisted that he was "ready not only to be imprisoned but even to die at Jerusalem for the name of the Lord Jesus." Evidently Luke had joined in the attempt to keep Paul from Jerusalem, for he reports "we ceased and said, 'The will of the Lord be done'."

Since Paul insisted upon going to Jerusalem, the Christians there tried to make the best of the situation. He and his party went to visit James, brother of Jesus and head of the mother church. Apparently none of the original twelve was in Jerusalem at the time. James and his associates rejoiced in Paul's accounts of Christian growth in Turkey and Greece, especially among Gentiles. However, they told Paul that ugly rumors were afloat among the Jews. It was claimed that he had been instructing Jews abroad to quit circumcision and other Jewish traditions. Paul's circumcising Timothy to prevent this kind of report (16:3) had not impressed his opponents.

James suggested that possibly Paul's personal loyalty to Judaism might be publicized by his taking part, along with four other men, in purifying ceremonies. Paul would pay the expense. Luke, as a Gentile, seems not quite to understand what vow these men had taken and what was to be done about it. James pointed out that the church had already decided that Gentile Christians were not required to observe Jewish ceremonies, and gave again the decision of the Jerusalem conference.

In conforming to this plan Paul went to the temple. Here Jews from Asia, doubtless ones who had made trouble for Paul in Ephesus, stirred up a mob who were determined to lynch Paul. However, word of this got to the Roman guard stationed in the Tower of Antonia built by Herod the Great at the north-west corner of the temple grounds. Soldiers immediately broke up the mob and rescued Paul, taking him to the Tower for protective custody.

Luke, who seems to have remained close to Paul for the next four years, gives considerable detail of Paul's experiences. He tells nothing more about the churches. It would almost appear that the Christian group at Jerusalem deserted him. Luke draws an extensive parallel between the treatment of Jesus and that of Paul. He makes no criticism of the Roman officials, placing the blame for Paul's troubles on the Jews. We may recall that Luke was writing chiefly for Gentile readers. He seems to have been eager to commend Christianity to the Roman authorities of the time when he did his writing.

As Paul was being taken to the Tower, apparently chained to a soldier on each side, he spoke to the officer, who was surprised that he used Greek. The officer thought he had found an Egyptian Jewish revolutionary leader. Josephus tells that this Egyptian led thirty thousand (not a mere four thousand as Luke reports) to the Mount of Olives. Most of these followers were killed or captured but the leader disappeared. Paul said he was from Tarsus in Turkey and asked permission to address the crowd. We wonder that the mob could become quiet enough to hear Paul. In an address in Aramaic (which Luke, for his Gentile readers, calls Hebrew) Paul pointed out that he was a strict Jew trained as a rabbi by Gamaliel. He emphasized that he had persecuted people of "the Way" to death until his conversion on the Damascus road. In telling of his conversion he noted the part played by "Ananias, a devout man according to the law, well spoken of by all the Jews who lived there." He also mentioned that later, while praying in the temple, he had been commissioned by God to go to the Gentiles. Despite this attempt to prove himself a law-abiding Jew the mob shouted "Away with such a fellow from the earth!"

Paul was taken into the barracks by the Roman officer "to be examined by scourging." Paul asked, "Is it lawful for you to scourge a man who is a Roman citizen, and uncondemned?" This brought fear upon the Roman officer who had great respect for Roman citizenship. In fact he had paid good money to some high official to get such a recognition for himself. Paul was able to say that he had inherited his honor, that he came from a family respected by the Roman government.

To find out what the trouble was all about, the officer (tribune) the next morning ordered priests to present their charges. When Paul spoke up, the high priest ordered him struck on the mouth. Paul retorted "God shall strike you, you white-washed wall," a term meaning artificial, a false front. When he was told that this was the high priest, he apologized.

Paul realized that some of his accusers were Pharisees, but most of the priests were Sadducees. He got them to quarreling among themselves by suggesting that they were finding fault with him for believing in the resurrection of the dead. Because of the dissension among his accusers Paul was returned to the barracks by the officer. Paul became convinced that God was with him and that he would have a chance to bear witness to his religion in Rome.

A group of Jews made a vow that they would neither eat nor drink until they had killed Paul. Their scheme was to make an attempt to have Paul brought before the council, and murder him on the way. Paul's sister's son learned of the plot and notified his uncle who had him tell the tribune. By nine o'clock that night the tribune had Paul on the way to Caesarea under the protection of 470 soldiers. Josephus reports that the Jewish population was on the verge of revolt. The representatives of Rome were taking no chances. Since Paul was a Roman citizen any trial held would need to be conducted by a Roman court. Therefore he was sent to the Roman capital of Judea where the procurator or governor, Felix, would hear the case. Luke gives the gist of a Latin letter the tribune sent to Felix in which he pictured himself as a protector of Paul, a Roman citizen who was attacked as guilty of some unimportant infraction of Jewish law.

Felix was a brother of a favorite of the Roman emperor Claudius. This brother secured the appointment of Felix as

232

procurator of Judea in A.D. 52. The province was badly disturbed when Felix took over. He maintained a form of peace by cruel repression. His third wife was a daughter of King Herod Agrippa I, whom he had persuaded to desert her husband and to defy Jewish law further by marrying him, a non-Jew. While Paul was being held at Caesarea a conflict arose between Jews and Syrians in the city. This was finally referred to Rome for decision. About this time Felix was recalled and tried for official misconduct. Through the influence of his brother he was acquitted, but he was not given back his position.

After a few days the high priest, some associates, and a Roman lawyer went to Caesarea to bring accusation against Paul. They accused him of being an agitator. As the priests had accused Jesus of advocating anti-Roman actions when bringing him before a Roman procurator, so now Paul was similarly accused in order to turn the procurator against him. Paul denied being an insurrectionist but quickly admitted that he was a member of "the Way." He pointed out that some Jews from Asia attacked him but they had not come to Caesarea to press their accusations. Felix knew something about Christianity. He recognized where the trouble lay and announced that he would wait until the tribune came from Jerusalem before he would make his decision.

Felix ordered that Paul be kept in custody but be well treated, given some liberty. A bit later Felix and his Jewish wife had an interview with Paul. They were impressed by Paul, with the result that Felix had several conversations with him. He greedily hoped that Paul would pay him a bribe for his release. As a consequence, when Felix was recalled to Rome two years later he left Paul in custody in Caesarea. He should have released him, but this might have incited the Jews to send to Rome stronger accusations against Felix. Therefore when the new procurator, Festus, came Paul was still in prison.

Festus, a man of ability and rather good character, found the situation left by Felix in Judea almost impossible. He did not remain long as procurator. He had scarcely arrived at Caesarea when he made a visit to Jerusalem, hoping to get the favor of the Jewish leaders. They took advantage of this and urged that Paul be brought to Jerusalem for trial. They again hoped for a chance to kill him on the way. Festus insisted that trials were held in Caesarea, but invited the Jewish leaders to come there and make their charges. When they did this Festus decided to ingratiate himself with the Jews and suggested to Paul that it might be well to transfer the trial to Jerusalem. Paul realized that a fair trial was almost impossible there. It perhaps would not be much better at Caesarea. Paul therefore made use of his right as a Roman citizen and announced, "I appeal to Caesar."

Herod Agrippa II was the son of Herod Agrippa I, who had put James the disciple to death. He did not inherit his father's kingdom but in A.D. 53 was given territory east of the Sea of Galilee. This included a little more than that which had been governed by his great-uncle Philip. As a senior ruler for Rome he, accompanied by his sister, came to Caesarea to welcome Festus. The latter told Agrippa about Paul. Agrippa expressed an interest in Paul; so an interview was arranged.

A group of prominent local men attended this interview, as did Agrippa's sister. Festus explained that he still did not know what charges to report to the emperor when Paul was sent to Rome. Paul's address is quite similar to that made on the steps of the Tower of Antonia in Jerusalem. It could be appreciated by Agrippa, who was classed as a Jew but not a very devout one. Much of Paul's address could not be understood by Festus, who interrupted by proclaiming, "Paul, you are mad; your great learning is turning you mad." Paul turned to Agrippa for confirmation that what he said was true, that his actions had not been hidden. Agrippa evidently resented being appealed to against Festus. Sarcastically he told Paul, "In a short time you think to make me a Christian." The Moffatt translation reads, "It won't be long before you believe you have made a Christian of me." The Goodspeed translation reads "You are in a hurry to persuade me and make a Christian of me." The King James translators missed the point when they had Agrippa saying, "Almost thou persuadest me to be a Christian." Agrippa and Festus agreed that Paul had done nothing to deserve even imprisonment. Agrippa went so far as to tell Festus "This man could have been set free if he had not appealed to Caesar."

Assignment

1. What had we previously had about Agabus?
2. What two charges did Jews from Asia make against Paul at the temple?
3. How does Paul's story of his conversion in Acts 22 differ from that in Acts 9? How does the account in Acts 26 differ from the other two?

Supplementary Reading

1. *The Interpreter's Bible.* New York and Nashville: Abingdon Press, Vol. 9, 1954. Pages 265-331.

CHAPTER 34

"What Has Happened Has Served to Advance the Gospel"

Read: Acts 27-28; Philippians

Did Luke remain with Paul during his Caesarean imprisonment? It appears so. Perhaps during this time he collected much of the material he included in his gospel account and the early part of Acts. When Paul and other prisoners were taken to Rome we find "we" being used again. Another friend, Aristarchus of Thessalonica who had come from Greece with Paul, was also along. In a gripping description of the voyage Luke pictures the dominant personality of Paul who, although a prisoner, exerted an influence in every crisis. The centurion in charge of the prisoners allowed Paul to visit the Christian group at Sidon on the coast of Phoenicia. This is the only reference we have to a church there.

Sailing north of the island of Cyprus the ship put in at a port in what now is the south-west corner of Turkey. There the prisoners were transfered to a vessel going from Alexandria, Egypt, to Italy.

This ship had great difficulty making progress westward, so swung to the south and along the southern coast of the island of Crete. Since it was too late in the fall for safe traveling in the Mediterranean Sea, Paul suggested that the winter be spent in the harbor town of Fair Havens, or in a nearby city. However, the centurion, the captain of the ship, and the ship's owner decided to attempt to reach Phoenix near the western end of the island. Soon a tempestuous northeastern wind drove them south to the tiny island of Cauda. In the protection of this island the sailors took what precautions they could to strengthen the ship and make it less subject to the strong winds. The next day they threw overboard the ship's cargo and spare equipment. Because neither sun nor stars could be seen they soon lost their bearing. Luke's account of the storm is one of the most vivid in literature. When Paul tried to persuade the crew to winter at Fair Havens he had predicted loss of life if they did not do so. He now was more optimistic, saying that no lives would be lost, that God promised him he would reach Rome.

For two weeks the ship drifted westward, coming to the island of Malta south of Sicily. Malta will be remembered as being under constant bombardment during much of World War II in an attempt upon the part of Germany and Italy to take it from the British to use as a stepping-stone to north Africa. As they neared the island the sailors tried to abandon ship in the life-boat. Paul notified the soldiers of the plan. The latter cut adrift the little boat and thus forced the sailors to remain with the ship. Paul seemed to take charge. He ordered the passengers to eat. Everything possible was then thrown overboard in order to run the ship closer to the shore. Fearing that the prisoners might escape, the soldiers planned to kill them, but the centurion's respect for Paul prevented this. By swimming and floating on material from the ship all got to land.

The natives of Malta kindly received the shipwrecked people, building a fire to enable them to get warm and dry. Paul busied himself gathering sticks for the fire. Wakened by the heat, a small European snake "fastened on his hand." The natives thought that Paul was a criminal who was being punished by their god of justice and vengeance. However, when Paul shook the snake into the fire without its doing any harm, they decided he was a god, much as people of Lystra had thought that Paul and Barnabas were gods. Luke reports that the governor of the island entertained "us" for three days. How many are included in "us" we do not know. Paul was able to heal the father of the governor. Many others of the island were cured. How much credit for this belongs to Paul and how much to Dr. Luke is not reported. The natives gave them gifts and furnished food for the remainder of the journey.

After three months the party left on another Alexandrian ship which had wintered at the port of the island. After stops in Syracuse, the capital of Sicily, and Rhegium, in the "toe" of Italy, the ship went to the Bay of Naples, the regular port of arrival for grain ships supplying Rome. Luke reports that a Christian group entertained the party for seven days. Probably the centurion had all his prisoners and soldiers stay there for a week to get their "land legs," get rested for the 150 miles tramp along the paved highway to Rome. It is possible that only Paul and his close friends and some guards stayed for the week.

About forty miles south of the capital Paul and his friends were met by a group of Christians who had walked that distance to meet him. Ten miles farther on they were met by a similar group. When they reached Rome Paul was allowed to rent living quarters. Here he stayed with a Roman guard—probably chained to his wrist.

In this great world capital with its more than a million people Paul would not be able to go to the synagogue as he had elsewhere. Therefore he invited the Jewish leaders to visit him. Paul pointed out that he had done nothing against the Jewish religion. He had no criticism to make of his nation, but, because of his understanding of the messianic hope, he had been turned over to the Romans. The Roman authorities "wished to set me at liberty," but to avoid further trouble with his Jewish accusers he had appealed to Caesar. Paul's Jewish listeners reported that they had heard no accusations against him. However, they would like to learn about his sect and religious ideas, as what they had heard about the group was not good.

These people later returned to Paul for an entire day's explanation of his teaching. Again he pointed out from the Hebrew scriptures the evolution of religion leading to Jesus. As usual, some saw value in his logic while to many it was heresy. Luke, of course, wrote his record a number of years after the events and depended to a large extent upon his memory and understanding of what would logically take place. By the time he reached Rome Paul had developed rather good strategy with the Jews. In his letter to the Romans he had gone into detail to express his hope that Israel would return to the gospel. It is not likely that at this time he would tell his Jewish listeners that they were dull, deaf and blind. Matthew had quoted the famous statement from the sixth chapter of Isaiah attacking people for their slowness in accepting his message. Matthew used it in connection with a discussion of parables. Mark and Luke hinted at the same quotation in this connection. John used a part of it in his lament over the failure of many Jews to accept Jesus despite his miracles. It is natural that Luke should use it in closing his account of the growth of the church. He thus attempted to explain to the Gentile readers why so many Jews had not accepted the gospel. The quotation fit Luke's purpose much better than it fit Paul's. Once more Paul turned to the Gentiles.

Luke concludes his account by saying that under Roman guard Paul kept open house in the capital for two years, preaching and teaching about Christ and the Kingdom openly and unhindered. Thus he ends his book with a note of triumph.

But, what next? What became of Paul? Why did not Luke tell more? There is an ancient tradition that Paul was released, made his visit to Spain, but was again arrested and brought to Rome where he was executed. Clement of Rome, writing about A.D. 95, said that when Paul "reached the limits of the West he gave his testimony before the rulers, and thus passed from the world and was taken into the Holy Place." "The limits of the West" is generally considered to be Spain, although Clement was writing to churches in the East where it is possible that Rome was considered the limits of the West.

On the other hand, if Paul had been declared not guilty of any charges brought against him, it seems that Luke would have said so as it would have been a climaxing victory for his hero. It would also have been a compliment to the Roman government. Luke was eager to build good will between Christianity and Rome. Certainly all religious charges against Paul were dropped. The charge that Paul was "a pestilent fellow, an agitator among all the Jews throughout the world" (24-5), may have been pressed, with the result that he was found guilty and executed.

It has been suggested that the ending of Luke's letter has been lost or that he died before finishing it. However, the last sentence seems to be an artistic ending. If some later editor added it to give the writing a proper ending, we still wonder why he did not tell what finally became of Paul. Luke evidently intended to trace Christianity from its birth in Jerusalem to the capital of the Roman empire; when he accomplished that he quit. It is possible that he planned a third volume telling the next stage in the growth of the church. If so he never wrote the book, for we have no reference to such in any Christian writing. It could also be argued that to tell of Rome's executing Paul would have been contrary to his effort to build good will between Rome and the church. People knew of Paul's death anyway, so why bring up this unpleasant fact! We do not know what the end is.

But we do know something of Paul's activity during his two years in Rome. His preaching and teaching won support for Christianity. He also returned to his writing. Apparently his first letter was to his earliest European church, Philippi. He probably wrote to the Philippians at the same time he wrote to the Thessalonians about A.D. 50. He may have written at other times but we have none of these letters. What in our Bibles is called, "The Letter of Paul to the Philippians," was written from prison. Most scholars are convinced that this was his Roman imprisonment. It has been suggested that it was written from Caesarea, or during an imprisonment in Ephesus—Ephesus was much nearer Philippi than Rome or Corinth was. We also know that Paul sent Timothy from Ephesus to Philippi; in Philippians Paul says he hopes to send Timothy there. However, there is far more evidence to suggest that the letter was written from Rome.

The Philippian church had learned of Paul's plight and had sent Epaphroditus to be of whatever assistance to him he could and to take him a financial gift. This was greatly appreciated by Paul. He would need money for food, rent and perhaps legal council. In expressing his thanks for this aid, Paul reminds the Philippians that they had given him financial support before, while he was at Thessalonica and while he was at Corinth (4:15-16). It is quite probable that when Paul left Caesarea for Rome, Palestinian Christians sent a messenger to churches in Turkey and Greece to tell about it. Because of Paul's shipwreck Epaphroditus arrived in Rome ahead of him. It may be he who organized the groups who walked long miles south of Rome to welcome the Apostle. Perhaps he had taken the lead in arranging for living accommodations in Rome. When Paul got to Rome he apparently found Epaphroditus on hand to act as secretary and perhaps as cook.

Paul was always courteous and grateful. We should expect him to send a note as quickly as possible to Philippi expressing his gratitude. We have such a letter, but at its face value it does not seem to have been written until Paul had been in Rome for quite a while. In the first chapter he points out that "what has happened to me has really served to advance the gospel, so that it has become known throughout the whole praetorian guard." Many have been made confident of their religion and are proclaiming the word without fear. Paul could scarcely say this until he had been at Rome several months, perhaps a year or more. In the second chapter he reports that Epaphroditus has been ill, "near to death." Epaphroditus has discovered that the Philippians had heard of his illness and is much distressed by this. Considerable time would have been involved in the illness of Epaphroditus, his recovery, word to Philippi eight hundred miles away, and messages back again. Paul ends this section with "Finally, my brethren, rejoice in the Lord" (3:1).

But it is not "Finally." That statement is just half way through the book. In the third chapter Paul gives a severe warning about Judaizers who have evidently come to Philippi. It is only in the fourth chapter that Paul gets around to expressing thanks for the assistance the Philippians have sent him.

It has already been noted that both 2 Corinthians and Romans appear to be composite writings. This would seem to be true also of Philippians. We can reconstruct the situation much as follows: When Paul reached Rome he found Epaphroditus there with not only personal and financial help but also with bad news—the Judaizers had not given up; they had come to Philippi insisting that Paul is not to be followed and demanding that Gentiles must become Jews before being recognized as Christians. Epaphroditus also reported that two women among the early converts to Christianity at Philippi were quarreling. It would seem that Paul at once dictated a letter to the Philippians dealing harshly with the Judaizers and entreating the two women, whom he highly compliments, "to agree in the Lord." He then expresses his great gratitude for the aid the Philippians have given him. He notes that they have done this before, saying that, good as the financial help is, the realization that they believe in him, are spiritually supporting him, is even better.

Then a year or so later, when Paul has realized that his imprisonment had given him a chance to preach the gospel without interference from either Jew or Gentile, that he has won soldiers and others who would have paid no attention to him under normal conditions, he wrote another letter to the Philippians. With doubtless an ending which has been lost, this second letter is the first two chapters and the first verse of the third chapter of "The Letter of Paul to the Philippians." During this time Epaphroditus had become ill and had been nursed back to a degree of health but could no longer be of much assistance to Paul. Paul decided to send him back to Philippi but felt it essential to explain this to the Philippian Christians as well as allay their fears and worries about Paul's imprisonment. Appreciation and optimism dominate both letters.

There is a bit of further support to this belief that we have here two short letters of Paul. About fifty years after Paul wrote to the Philippians, a Christian leader, Polycarp, also wrote to the Philippian Christians. In his letter he refers to Paul who "wrote letters to you," which they still had and could profitably use. If some other letter of Paul to the Philippians were in existence it would have been included in the collected writings of Paul, for it would have been at least as important as the 16th chapter of Romans. It would appear that the plural term here refers to the two parts of our present "letter."

In his writing to the Philippians Paul does not argue, does not try to justify or explain his beliefs. Neither does he moralize. Despite the fact that he is in immediate prospect of death he is content and happy. The word "joy," or its equivalents, appears more often than in all his other writings combined. He has learned the secret of contentment. For him "to live is Christ, and to die is gain" (1:21). To depart and be with Christ is far better.

Paul feels a very close bond with his readers. As they have suffered for their religion, so has he. He often uses the term "us" to include readers and writer. He knows the faults of the Philippians and loves them despite their faults. He is eager to have them, like him, "press on toward the goal for the prize of the upward call of God in Christ Jesus" (3:14).

In his eagerness to unite the Christians at Philippi to one mind and one love, Paul pays perhaps his highest compliment to his master in what is called the Hymn to Christ (2:6-11). This is one of the best known poems in the New Testament. Many scholars believe that it was originally composed by some one else since its vocabulary and emphasis differ from that generally found in Paul's writings.

Assignment

1. Outline the experience Paul had during his first visit to Philippi.
2. What did Paul want the Philippians to think about?
3. Make a map showing Paul's three missionary journeys and his trip to Rome.
4. List ten cities visited by Paul and note his experience in each.

Supplementary Reading

1. *The Interpreter's Bible.* New York and Nashville: Abingdon Press, Vol. 9, 1954. Pages 331-352; Vol. 11, 1955, Pages 1-129.
2. Beare, F. W. *A Commentary on the Epistle to the Philippians.* New York: Harper & Brothers, 1959.
3. Goodspeed, Edgar J. *An Introduction to the New Testament.* Chicago: University of Chicago Press, 1937. Chapter VII.
4. Simcox, Carroll E. *They Met at Philippi.* New York: Oxford Press, 1958.
5. Titus, Eric Lane. *Essentials of New Testament Study.* New York: The Ronald Press Co., 1958. Pages 137-138.

CHAPTER 35

'A Prisoner for Christ Jesus"

Read: Colossians and Philemon.

Colossians and Philemon are prison letters of Paul very closely linked together. The great majority of scholars believe they were written from Rome, although there are those who suggest Ephesus or Caesarea. One item that raises a question is Paul's statement in Philippians and Philemon that he hopes after his release from prison to visit Macedonia and Asia Minor. What has become of his plan to visit Spain? Could it be that Paul's years of imprisonment have aged him, reduced his pioneering zest, and increased his desire to revisit old friends?

Colossae, Laodicea and Hierapolis were three small cities in the province of Asia about a hundred miles directly east of Ephesus. They were famous for beautiful wool of a dark purple color. Christian churches had been established there, possibly by Paul. Since Paul says "we have heard of your faith" (1:4) and refers to Christians "who have not seen my face" (2.1), some people feel that Paul never visited these towns. They believe the churches there were the result of his activity in Ephesus. In Acts 19:10 we learn that because of his Ephesian preaching "all the residents of Asia heard the word of the Lord, both Jews and Greeks." The leader of the church, possibly its founder, at Colossae was Epaphras. He must not be confused with Epaphroditus of Philippi. In writing to the Colossian church Paul calls Epaphras a beloved fellow servant, a faithful minister of Christ (1:7). "I bear him witness that he has worked hard for you and for those in Laodicea and in Hierapolis" (4:13).

Epaphras made a long journey to visit Paul and discuss with him a problem which had arisen in the Colossian church. Epaphras remained with him while Paul sent a letter to the Colossians by another helper, Tychicus. Tychicus was one of those who had gone to Jerusalem with Paul to take an offering at the end of his third missionary journey.

The problem presented by Epaphras was a heresy relative to aeons or "elemental spirits," a hierarchy of angelic beings. The idea of angels had been largely absorbed from the Persian religion, Zoroastrianism, while the Jews were in Babylonian captivity about 550 B.C. The Jews around Colossae were mostly a group who had remained in Mesopotamia several hundred years and had finally migrated to the province of Asia. They had brought with them further Zoroastrian ideas about angels or non-human beings. They had mixed up some of these concepts with some Greek philosophical ideas and heathen practices of non-Greek natives in Asia.

We do not know whether followers of this mixture of concepts were members of the church at Colossae or were trying to absorb Christ into their religion and thus make a place for him, but an inferior place.

Members of the group called their ideas a philosophy but Paul considered them an "empty deceit." The chief idea was that there are angelic beings or "elemental spirits" of varying ranks called thrones, dominions, principalities and authorities (1:16). Some believed that the heavenly bodies are the bodies of these "elemental spirits." These were to be worshipped by fasts and feasts, vigils and various ceremonies. Circumcision seems to have been included. Certain things were taboo, must not be touched, handled, or tasted. Only by such worship of the "elemental spirits" and by various acts of magic might people come to God. By climbing such a spiritual ladder one might reach communion with God.

We find many people today who want more and more mystery and magic in their religion. That was true of people of Colossae. The complex mixture of philosophy, astrology and magic appealed to many as superior to the simple teachings of Christianity. This was but one of several "Gnostic" schools that sprung up in early Christianity. Phases of Gnosticism were found outside Christianity as well as in. Gnostics felt that they had knowledge revealed to them by God and that they therefore were superior to people who did not have this revelation. We are familiar with the negative term, agnostic, a person who claims that certain things are not known, cannot be known. The Gnostic was the opposite of this, a know-it-all.

Paul recognizes that these concepts were out of accord with the teachings of Jesus. In his reply he shows a much more advanced and philosophical concept of Christ than we have found thus far. The idea he expresses here is further developed in the Letter to the Hebrews and the writings of John. Paul describes the place of Christ in Christian experience.

Paul puts Christ above all the "elemental spirits" by paying him the highest compliments he can. As Egyptians and Greeks had called kings the living images of certain gods, so Paul says "He is the image of the invisible God" (1:15). As some Jews thought of individuals having a spiritual existence before conception, so Paul calls Christ "the first-born of all creation." He is also the head of the new creation, the church, and "in him all the fulness of God was pleased to dwell" (1:19). No other intermediaries between God and man are necessary. His death on the cross brought man into atonement with God. In contrast to the mysteries taught at Colossae there is one great mystery in Christianity—how Christ can be in us, how the same spirit which was in the man Jesus can also be in us.

As physical circumcision is unnecessary so also are "questions of food and drink or with regard to a festival or a new moon or a sabbath" (2:16). "Let no one disqualify you, insisting on self-abasement and the worship of angels" (2:18), thinking that he knows more than you do. Instead of observing taboos "seek the things that are above." One must put away "anger, wrath, malice, slander and foul talk" (3:8). "Do not lie to one another" (3:9). If one is Christian he must recognize that all men are one; there can be no race distinction. With him "there cannot be Greek and Jew, circumcised and uncircumcised, barbarian, Scythian, slave, free man" (3:11). The distinction taught by Gnostic groups cannot exist in Christianity. We must teach "every man all wisdom" (1:28). We must have "love which binds everything together in perfect harmony" (3:14). "Do everything in the name of the Lord Jesus, giving thanks to God the Father through him" (3:17), not through the "elemental spirits." "Continue steadfastly in prayer . . . Conduct yourself wisely . . . Let your speech always be gracious" (4:2-6)

Paul concludes his letter by sending greetings from men who are in Rome with him. Three of them are Jewish Christians: Aristarchus, Mark, and Jesus who is called Justus. Three are Gentile Christians: Epaphras, Luke and Demas. He then instructs that when the Colossians have read this letter they are to have the Laodiceans read it too, in return for which they are to read the letter from Laodicea.

Do we have this Laodicean letter? Many scholars think it is lost, as is doubtless true of many other letters Paul wrote. However, there is strong weight to the idea that the "Letter to Philemon" is the letter referred to in Colossians. It would seem that Onesimus, a slave of Philemon, ran away from home. Paul had converted Philemon to Christianity. It would appear that Onesimus went as far as he could and finally found himself lost in the great city of Rome. He would be extremely lonely. In time he heard of Paul and knew he would be friendly. He became a helper of Paul's, possibly took the place held by Epaphroditus. Eventually he became a Christian. When Paul learned who he was the question rose, Was it right to keep another man's property? It was finally agreed that Onesimus should return to Philemon. When Tychicus took Paul's letter to Colossae, Onesimus went along taking with him Paul's letter to his master.

This raises some questions. In Colossians Paul refers to Onesimus as "one of yourselves" (4:9). That would look as if Colossae was the home of Philemon and Onesimus. However, we must remember that Colossae and Laodicea were but eleven miles apart, the Christian groups were small and would know each other well. The message for the Colossians is also for the Laodiceans. Paul wrote that Epaphras had "worked hard for you and for those in Laodicea and in Hierapolis" (4:13). The Christians in the three cities were to a large degree one group. It is quite possible that Philemon and Onesimus lived in Laodicea rather than in Colossae.

Despite the fact that he was a Christian, it was probable that Philemon would treat a runaway slave harshly. Paul did not want that to occur. Therefore he took numerous precautions to prevent it. Paul's first precaution was to address his letter not only to Philemon but also to "Apphia our sister and Archippus our fellow soldier, and the church in your house." Apphia may have been the wife of Philemon. Archippus could have been their son, but was more likely the leader of the church to which Philemon belonged. (The suggestion has been made that Archippus was the slave owner in whose house a group of Colossians met, and that Philemon lived in the larger city of Laodicea, but was overseer of churches in Laodicea, Colossae and Hierapolis; that the letter was really sent to Archippus in care of Philemon.) Since two other people and an entire church group were included among those to whom Paul wrote, the owner of Onesimus could hardly keep Paul's request secret. But to play safe Paul secured other witnesses by telling the Christians at Colossae not only to see and read the letter, but also to "say to Archippus, 'See that you fulfill the ministry which you have received in the Lord'" (4:17). This probably meant that Archippus was to see that Paul's request was carried out.

Paul pays compliments to the recipient of the letter and then suggests that he would be doing right to command him, "but for love's sake I prefer to appeal to you" (8). Before he is through, Paul's tone sounds like that of a command: "Yes, brother, I want some benefit from you in the Lord . . . Confident of your obedience, I write to you, knowing that you will do even more than I say" (20-21). His attention is called to the fact that he owes Paul "even your own self." Paul closes with the friendly threat that he hopes to visit him.

The request or demand was that Onesimus be received "no longer as a slave but more than a slave, as a beloved brother" (16). Paul explains that in his imprisonment he has come to love Onesimus as his own son. The name Onesimus means "useful." Paul points out that the young man may have become useless to his owner but very useful to Paul. He would like to keep Onesimus with him but feels he should not do so without the consent of his owner. It looks as if Paul fervently hopes that Onesimus will be forgiven and sent back to Paul.

Was Paul's letter successful? We have no definite proof but much to indicate that it was. If his owner had refused to treat Onesimus kindly he would scarcely have allowed the letter to get into circulation. However, we have much more to suggest the success of this letter. Fifty years after Paul wrote this note Ignatius, the bishop of Antioch of Syria, while on his way to Rome, was visited by a delegation from the church at Ephesus headed by its bishop, Onesimus. A bit later Ignatius wrote a letter to the Ephesian church speaking of Bishop Onesimus as "a man of inexpressible love." He goes on to say that he would like one of the Ephesian men to stay with him as a helper. This entire request is worded in terms similar to those used by Paul to Philemon. He seems to keep reminding the bishop that he is in a situation to do for Ignatius what Philemon had done for Paul. There is much to indicate that Philemon's slave has become Bishop Onesimus. Probably he had been returned to Paul, had become one of Paul's right-hand men when still quite young, had been recognized by the church for his ability and his association with Paul, and eventually had been made bishop of the important Ephesian church.

Paul must have written many personal letters, but this is the only one we have. Why was it saved and the others not? This letter was also addressed to a church group. It had had its influence on church history by the time the letters of Paul were collected and published. There is much to indicate that this collecting was done at Ephesus while Onesimus was bishop. Probably Bishop Onesimus instigated this collecting. If so, he could hardly have done otherwise than include the Philemon letter.

This brings us to the problem of "The Letter of Paul to the Ephesians." On its face it appears to have been written by Paul at the same time he wrote Colossians and Philemon. It would seem to have been delivered by Tychicus on his trip to Asia Minor. The majority of New Testament scholars think otherwise. The earliest copies of the New Testament do not have any reference to the Ephesians in the text of the letter as one may note by reading the Revised Standard Version. Titles to books of the Bible were given long after the books were written. Some of the earliest Bible scholars entitled this book "To the Laodiceans."

Although Paul is referred to as the author in 1:1 and 3:1 and by implication a couple of other places, this seems to be done as a loving compliment to Paul. Whoever the author was, he greatly admired Paul. He thoroughly understood Paul's later thinking, but applied it to a still later situation, a situation in which the conflict between Jews and Christians was a thing of the past. The term Gentile no longer meant a non-Jew, but a non-Christian. The book contains no allusions to local situations. Its style is much different from that of Paul; it has long, involved sentences such as Paul carefully avoided. Its vocabulary is different; it has 82 words not used by Paul; it gives different meanings to a number of Paul's terms. At points it contradicts statements made by Paul.

The writer was probably with Paul during his last years at Rome. It has been suggested that after Luke's "The Acts of the Apostles" was published people came to a new realization of how extremely important to the church Paul was. Acts never refers to Paul's writing, but some one knew he had written letters and set about collecting those he could find. Acts tells of Paul's visiting Galatia, Thessalonica, Philippi, and Corinth—all of them more than once. It was natural to expect that Paul had written to these churches, but who would know about Colossians and the letter to Philemon? Since the collection seems to have been made in the Ephesian community it is quite possible that Bishop Onesimus, knowing about Colossians and Philemon, and of Paul's concern for Rome, made this collection. Such a collection to be copied and sent to numerous Christian centers should have an introduction helping its readers to see how much the teaching of Paul applied to them and their problems at that time. Could Ephesians be such an introduction compiled by Bishop Onesimus? However, there is a Semitic flavor to the letter that suggests that its author was a Jew. Although there are numerous indications that this letter is a later application of Paul's ideas, it must not be forgotten that tradition attributed it to Paul.

The author was a man of great ability and originality. In his essay, seemingly written for general use, he begins the development of a philosophy of religion. He makes a systematic organization of Paul's brilliant but scattered contributions. He presents an answer to the Gnostic teachings that continued to bother the church. Although he gathers together ideas from probably all of Paul's known writings, he naturally makes the most use of Paul's letter to the Colossians. Paul's last letter not only expressed the highest development of his Christian thinking but dealt most with the problem still prominent thirty years later. In this great admiration for Paul the author uses phrases which Paul would never have used. He calls Paul a "holy apostle." He brags about Paul's "insight into the mystery of Christ" (3:4). Paul's idea of the coming of Christ in glory to execute judgement is never mentioned. However, much of Paul's theology is commended to a later generation who "have heard of" Paul (3:2).

The author, in a devotional, prayerful mood, expresses his concern for the church, which is the symbol of Christian unity. He calls the church the body of Christ. Christ is its head, directing its growing up. The author also uses the analogy of the church as Christ's bride. The church and Christ are made one in marriage. Before the coming of Christ only the Jews knew about God. The evil powers of the world brought about disunity among men. Through Christ this disunity has been healed and now all people may know God. To tell this to the world is the task of the church.

The second half of the book gives instructions for implementing the ideas established in the first half. There must be unity within the church. This can be brought about only by love. Christians must never revert to the immoral practices of paganism. The author lists those practices that must be avoided. Family relationships must be pure, considerate: "Husbands, love your wives, as Christ loved the church and gave himself up for her" (5:25). "Finally . . . stand against the wiles of the devil" (6:10-11).

For Class Discussion

1. Why did Paul not attack the institution of human slavery?
2. Could Christianity have developed without Jesus?
3. How can the church be "the body of Christ?"

Assignment

List ten writings we feel sure are Paul's and tell the purpose of each.

Supplementary Reading

1. *The Interpreter's Bible.* New York and Nashville: Abingdon Press, Vol. 10, 1953. Pages 597-749; Vol. 11, 1955, Pages 133-241; 555-573.

2. Goodspeed, Edgar J. *An Introduction to the New Testament.* Chicago: University of Chicago Press, 1937. Chapters VIII, IX, and XIV.

3. Knox, John. *Philemon Among the Letters of Paul.* New York and Nashville: Abingdon Press, Rev. 1959.

4. Moule, C. F. D. *The Epistles of Paul to the Colossians and to Philemon.* Cambridge: University Press, 1957.

CHAPTER 36

"What Must Soon Take Place"

Read: The Revelation to John

Being a Christian was unpopular, dangerous. In Palestine there was persecution from the Jews. As churches were formed elsewhere Jewish persecution spread, but eventually died out. In the summer of A.D. 64 the emperor Nero burned Rome. The reaction to this was so violent that he looked about for some group on which to put the blame. The Christians became his victims. As a consequence many were cruelly treated and quite a number put to death. Nero committed suicide at the age of thirty, but in Greece and the Roman province of Asia the story grew that Nero would soon return to avenge his enemies.

After Nero's death persecution of Christians diminished until the time of the emperor Domitian who came to the throne in A.D. 81. Domitian was often referred to as Nero. His trouble with the Christians centered about the issue of emperor worship. After the death of one of the first Roman emperors people began to speak of him as a god. The Romans and Greeks had many gods in their religions. To add another to the group was not unusual. Soon some sought to win the favor of the emperor by calling him a god while he was still alive. In time politicians saw here an opportunity to center both political loyalty and religious enthusiasm upon the emperor. Eventually every one was required to make public acknowledgment of the emperor as a god. Toward the latter part of his reign Domitian became quite strict in enforcing this. His representatives in the province of Asia determined to carry out his demand completely.

To most Romans this seemed quite simple. Altars to the emperor were erected throughout the empire. Each adult was ordered to put a pinch of incense on the fire on the altar, declare "Caesar is a god," and bow before his image. He was then given a certificate showing his loyalty. In business dealings he could be required to display this, much as one may be asked today to show his license to drive an automobile. However, Jews were exempted. Rome recognized that they had been a nation of their own with their particular religion which insisted that there is but one god. Rome professed to honor the religions and customs of the small nations she had incorporated into the empire. But Christianity had no claim to be a national religion. At first it was considered a branch of Judaism. As the Jews came to be a very small percentage of the church, Christians were no longer given Jewish exemption. Yet no true Christian was willing to acknowledge the emperor as a god.

Christians began to be persecuted for their religion. Some lost their lives. However, many decided they would rather be live heathen than dead Christians. There was danger of Christianity's disappearing. The church could not compromise and continue to be the church.

Some Christian leaders realized that Christians and their Jewish predecessors had had periods of severe persecution before, but had survived. They had escaped from Egyptian bondage. Many small nations had been destroyed by the Assyrians and Babylonians but numerous Jews had returned from Babylonian captivity. The Syrians had attempted to destroy the Jewish religion but had been defeated by the Maccabean Rebellion. God may have sent persecution as punishment and training. At least God would not allow his followers to be completely wiped out. As Isaiah had declared eight hundred years before, there would be a remnant of the faithful left. Roman persecution would not last long. God would take care of that. How to convince the Christian people of this, especially in Asia, was the problem faced by church leaders.

Any preaching or writing which openly encouraged people to refuse to recognize the emperor as a god would quickly be stopped by Roman authorities. Yet the demand, "No Compromise," must be made. It was a Jewish Christian leader of the Ephesian community who worked out a solution. His name was John. The John whose writing we are about to examine called himself a prophet. He had suffered for his Christian convictions, apparently had been imprisoned on the penal island of Patmos. There, he says, he had a series of visions. He was convinced that God through Jesus Christ was giving him a message to the Christian people of the province of Asia.

John wrote his message as an apocalypse. This was a code developed by the Jews several hundred years before. When trouble, persecution, developed, such messages of encouragement, tracts for hard times, were written. They were to assure their readers that God reigns and will be victorious. We have some knowledge of a hundred of these apocalypses. They were so common that they could not seem strange to their early readers. An apocalypse was a writing composed to make an impression, convey a message to a group of people who understood the various figurative expressions. Quite often they were reports of complex visions of things to come. Matter-of-fact government officials could find nothing in such writings to use as a basis for charges against those who wrote or read these apocalypses. They would consider such writings as childish prattle.

Much of our modern painting and sculpture seeks to give an impression, not to duplicate reality. Our oratorios, separated from their music, seem repetitious, almost foolish. The music provides the atmosphere, the feeling; and it helps get across the message. One of our great oratorios, *The Messiah*, carries on the theme of the Revelation to John: "The kingdom of the world has become the kingdom of our Lord and of his Christ, and he shall reign forever and ever" (11:15).

Back in 168 B.C. the Syrians had desecrated the Jerusalem temple in their attempt to force the Jews to adopt the Greek religion. This resulted in the Maccabean Rebellion. Many Jews and many Syrians lost their lives in bloody battles but the struggle reached a standstill. Then some one wrote the apocalypse of Daniel. In it the readers were assured that if the Jews were faithful to God the Syrians would be defeated. Encouraged by this promise, the Jews drove back the Syrians and rededicated their temple in 165 B.C. This writing had been so successful that the Jewish people included it in their canon of sacred scriptures. Thus it was a part of the scriptures used by the Christians in the time of Domitian. The Christians of Asia were familiar with the apocalypse of Daniel. Why not write a modern

255

apocalypse dealing with the situation of A.D. 95? As Daniel had succeeded so should this new apocalypse.

Other elements influenced John's apocalypse. One of these was the collection of Paul's letters to seven church groups, introduced by a general letter, Ephesians. This had become popular among the churches. Why not begin the new apocalypse in the same way? Therefore, after a general introduction, the second and third chapters of John's book are composed of . letters to the angels or messengers (probably pastors) of seven churches in the province of Asia.

Christians there were not only familiar with the Hebrew scriptures. They were also familiar with Greek dramas with their choruses and varied music and sound effects. If similar elements were incorporated in the new apocalypse it would bear an added note of familiarity, would seem something more than Jewish. The result of these various factors was the apocalypse we call the Revelation to John. "Apocalypse" means something discovered or revealed, uncovered, or unveiled. Note that there is no *s* on the word Revelation.

Although most of its readers were not Jewish, the apocalypse uses more of the Old Testament than Matthew does. One scholar finds Old Testament references in 278 of the 404 verses in the book. However, in the entire apocalypse there is not a direct quotation from the Old Testament. The writer considers himself a prophet to whom God speaks directly, not through former writers.

The purpose of this new book was not glibly to assert that everything will be all right. Rather it was to make Christians willing to die, be martyrs, for their religion. It promised great reward for those who thus gave their lives. It threatened severe eternal punishment for those who deserted Christianity by acknowledging the emperor as a god. It also vividly and repeatedly proclaimed in apocalyptic terms that God was about to overcome the forces of evil, that the persecutors themselves would soon be punished, that the church was about to be victorious in its struggle with the empire. This all "must soon take place" (1:1); "the time is near" (1:3 and 22:10). This book is to be read aloud in the churches of Asia immediately. It deals with the urgent problem of John's day. It has no specific message for the twentieth century, save that it emphasizes general truths that apply to all time. The book met with a considerable degree of success. Other apocalypses were written in the same general period. Two of these became popular in the church, the Apocalypse to Peter, and the Shepherd of Hermas. Some churches included all three in their collection of sacred Christian writings. When a list of writings to be the Christian scripture, the New Testament, was considered, some wanted to keep these apocalypses. Others felt that they had served their purpose and were no longer needed. It might be said that the inclusion of the John apocalypse in our Bible was a compromise. However, some churches continued for many years to oppose the use of this book.

The oriental respect for the number seven, considered the number of perfection, appears time and again in John's apocalypse. There are seven beatitudes, and references to seven spirits, seven horns, seven eyes, seven stars. There are letters to seven churches. The main part of the book contains seven series of seven visions with various interludes.

In his general letter in the first chapter, John points out that God is everything: the Alpha and the Omega, the first and last letters of the Greek alphabet. God is eternal, is, was, and will be. He is the *Almighty*, something even the emperor never claimed to be. Much the same claim is made for the Christ through whom the message from God is being given.

As Luke did not confine his messages to Theophilus, or Paul his wisdom to the church at Rome, so John expected people other than those belonging to seven distinct churches in Asia to read and profit from his writing. As with many New Testament writers, he sought to give a personal feeling to his message. Therefore to each of seven churches he addressed a note commending or criticizing it for particular attitudes. However, the message to each is to "be faithful unto death, and I will give you the crown of life" (2:10). To those who willingly become martyrs for Christianity it is promised that they will not be hurt by a second death; they will be kept safe from the trials coming to the world; they will have a blessed and glorious immortality; and will reign with Christ on his throne.

The main part of John's apocalypse consists of a series of visions. These are worded in terms familiar to those who knew their Old

Testament well. They can be organized into three awe-inspiring acts, each of which promises a new world in which the rule of Satan and his agents is destroyed and God rules supreme. Each of these acts is a vigorous assurance that the cruel rule of the Roman emperor is about finished, a new age is about to begin.

The first act, chapters four through eleven, may be called the Roll of Destiny. It opens with a vision of God on his heavenly throne much as is pictured in Isaiah's worship experience in the sixth chapter of his book. As in it, creatures with six wings are proclaiming "Holy, holy, holy is the Lord God Almighty". Seated around the throne are twenty-four elders representing the old and new Israels. Reminiscent of Ezekiel, God has in his hand a scroll written on both sides. It is sealed with seven seals which no one seems worthy to open, until there comes a Lamb which has been killed but is living again. This is Jesus, "the Lamb of God, who takes away the sin of the world" (John 1:29). By his death he was believed to have released God's plan for mankind.

As the first four seals are broken, "the four horsemen of the Apocalypse" appear: invasion, war, famine, and death. Upon the opening of the fifth seal those who have given their lives for the Christian religion are assured that it will be only "a little longer", after a few more have suffered, before they will be released. Upon the opening of the sixth seal "the kings of the earth and the great men and the generals and the rich and the strong" and others earnestly seek to hide from "the wrath of the Lamb" This is followed by an interlude in which "a great multitude which no man can number" proclaim, "Salvation belongs to our God who sits upon the throne, and to the Lamb" (7:10). When the seventh seal is opened, seven angels blow trumpets and new disasters occur: hail and fire, mountains falling into the sea, stars falling from heaven. But when the seventh angel blows his trumpet, loud voices are heard saying, "The kingdom of the world has become the kingdom of our Lord and of his Christ, and he shall reign for ever and ever" (11:15). Again God is called almighty and eternal.

Despite this, some people might not be convinced that the Satanic control of Rome is about to be destroyed and God will take over as eternally supreme. Therefore John presents a second act, the Dragon War (12:1-19:10).

258

"Now war arose in heaven, Michael and his angels fighting against the dragon" who had opposed the Christ. As a result the dragon, or Satan, is cast down to earth, but "his time is short". Out of the sea rises a beast. Beasts represent governments in apocalypses. This one is the Roman empire. To it the dragon or Satan "gave his power and his throne and great authority". Instead of being divine, the emperors are Satanic. (Paul would not have agreed with this.) The beast utters blasphemies against God and makes war on the saints (Christians).

A second beast, religious government, forces men to worship the first beast, causing "those who will not worship the image of the beast to be slain". No one is allowed to buy or sell without the stamp or mark certifying that he has acknowledged the emperor as a god. He must have "the name of the beast or the number of its name" (13:17). John cannot safely give the "name of the beast", but those who know the Hebrew alphabet will have little trouble knowing to whom he refers. "Let him who has understanding reckon the number of the beast . . . its number is six hundred and sixty-six" (13:18). Neither the Hebrews nor the Greeks used numerals. In each case the first letter of the alphabet was considered one, the second two, and on through the alphabet. Greeks were known to speak of Jesus as 888. In the Greek spelling, Jesous, J has a value of 10, E of 8, S of 200, O of 70, U of 400, and again S of 200. Since the emperor Domitian was thought of as the returned Nero the total value of the letters in "Caesar Nero" could be considered his number. To do this in Greek might be too obvious. Therefore John changes the Greek over into Hebrew or Aramaic letters. The total value of these letters spelling "Caesar Nero" is 666. For those who understood Jewish apocalyptical writings 666 had an additional meaning. Seven symbolized completion or perfection. Six represented the inability to reach this, or doom. Three sixes represented evil raised to the nth power.

John reports hearing singing by the martyrs "who follow the lamb wherever he goes" even to death. They do not have the mark of the emperor but of God and the Lamb. He hears an angel proclaiming that "the hour of his judgement has come", while another cries, "Fallen, fallen is Babylon the great, she who made all nations drink the wine of her impure passion" (14:8). The Babylon of Mesopotamia had disappeared as a city. Of course here

Babylon means Rome. Another angel warns that "If any one worships the beast and its image, and receives a mark . . . he shall drink the wine of God's wrath . . . and he shall be tormented with fire and brimstone" (14:9-10).

Another vision shows angels pouring out bowls of God's wrath, plagues, upon the earth. These include ulcers, turning the sea and rivers into blood, scorching heat, darkness, kings of the east assembled to fight the empire, and finally the destruction of "Babylon." John then describes the fall of Rome, pictured as a harlot seated on a scarlet beast. She is drunk with the blood of the martyrs. She is the goddess Roma, considered the mistress of the emperor gods. Although they have other symbolism, "the seven heads are seven hills on which the woman is seated" (17:9). No one can picture a woman sitting on seven hills at once. Rome was built on seven hills. John is treading on dangerous ground here. It is even reported that he was told "The woman that you saw is the great city which has dominion over the kings of the earth" (17:18). This sentence is so dangerous that we wonder if it may have been inserted later. Christians are warned to leave Rome to avoid the calamities about to be experienced there: pestilence, mourning, famine, and fire. As the city burns, kings, merchants, and seamen who have prospered because of Rome throw dust on their heads and mourn, "Alas, alas for the great city." John then hears songs of rejoicing by the martyrs and expressions of happiness from the elders and the beasts around God's throne. These represent Christians and nations from the four corners of the earth, probably the little nations which have been destroyed by Rome. They sing, "Hallelujah! For the Lord our God the Almighty reigns" (19:6).

Possibly his readers still need encouragement. Therefore John presents a third act, the New Jerusalem (19:11—22:5).

In this act the armies of heaven on white horses follow the Word of God, Christ, King of kings and Lord of lords. The beast (the Roman empire) and the false prophet (Antichrist or priesthood of the Roman religions) are "thrown alive into the lake of fire that burns with brimstone" (19:20). John then sees an angel bind the devil or Satan and throw him into a pit. This is sealed over so that Satan will deceive the nations no more for a thousand years.

For this thousand years John sees Christ reigning, along with the martyrs "who had not worshiped the beast or its image and had not received its mark" (20:4). After this Satan is released and attempts to conquer the earth with his army. He is "thrown into the lake of fire and brimstone where the beast and the false prophet were, and they will be tormented day and night for ever and ever" (20:10). John then sees the judgement before a "great white throne." All are judged "by what they had done." Next he beholds "a new heaven and a new earth." The holy city, new Jerusalem comes down out of heaven. "Behold, the dwelling of God is with men" (21:3). The evils of this present existence are no more, "for the former things have passed away." He hears God saying "Behold, I make all things new." John closes his message of encouragement by describing this new world as a magnificent city. This had been the dream and ambition of Jews for several hundred years. The early Christians were city or town dwellers. The park-like city described by John would appeal to them. Who would want to worship the emperor and be deprived of this great prize?

Several of the earlier apocalypses bore as authors the names of people who had lived long before. To carry out the pretense that these ancient men had written the books, instructions were given to seal them until near the time dealt with in the books. However, John has no such pretense. He warns, "Do not seal up the words of the prophecy of this book, for the time is near" (22:10). He insists that no one must weaken the message. Anyone who alters the promise of reward to the martyrs, or punishment for those who worship the emperor, will be severely dealt with (22:18-19). In conclusion John reiterates his promise that God's conquest is to come very soon.

To what extent did John prove correct? In A.D. 96 Domitian was murdered. His successor released many Christians who had been imprisoned. Insistence upon emperor worship was diminished. However, the new emperor ruled but two years. His successor again demanded emperor worship. The Roman government was little changed. But the church was not destroyed. It found new courage. Persecution broke out again but the church survived. Soon Christianity became a recognized religion in the Roman empire. About two hundred years after the writing of

John's apocalypse the emperor became a Christian in name and much of Rome followed him. Many see in this a greater victory for Christianity than John ever dreamed would occur. The cataclysm expected by John and other apocalyptists did not take place, but the gradual growth of the Kingdom of God dreamed of by Jesus is evident.

Was the church right in putting the Revelation to John into the Christian scripture? There was much disagreement at this point. Without it we should miss certain very important verses. One of these is 3:20; "Behold, I stand at the door and knock; if any one hears my voice and opens the door, I will come in to him and eat with him, and he with me." Another is 21:5, "Behold, I make all things new." Doubtless we still need the assurance that is the theme of this book, that good is stronger than evil, that God will overcome Satan, that one with God is a majority, that in the end all evil will be destroyed, and that the unseen world is very near.

For Class Discussion

1. Were those who decided upon the canon of Christian scriptures right in including the Revelation to John?
2. How is the Millennium idea misused today?
3. What values can be found in the Millennium concept?
4. Is our civilization inevitably improving?

Supplementary Reading

1. Goodspeed, Edgar J. *An Introduction to the New Testament.* Chicago: University of Chicago Press, 1937. Chapter XV.
2. Martin, Hugh. *The Seven Letters.* Philadelphia: The Westminster Press, 1958.
3. Laymon, Charles M. *The Book of Revelation.* New York and Nashville: Abingdon Press, 1960.
4. Parsons, Ernest W. *The Religion of the New Testament.* New York: Harper & Brothers, 1939. Chapter VII.
5. Rowley, H. H. *The Relevance of Apocalyptic.* New York: Harper & Brothers, 1946.
6. Sloan, W. W. *A Survey of the Old Testament.* New York and Nashville: Abingdon Press, 1957. Chapter 39.

CHAPTER 37

"He Continues a Priest Forever"

Read the Letter to the Hebrews

A growing respect for Jesus caused various Christian leaders to set about interpreting him, developing a Christology. A philosophy of the Christian religion was coming into existence. We noted this in the "Letter to the Ephesians." It was also mentioned in our discussion of the "Gospel according to John." We find a distinct development in this field in the "Letter to the Hebrews."

Who the author of this "word of exhortation" (13:22) was, to whom it was sent, and when it was written are all questions which the book itself does not answer. There is no universal agreement today regarding the answer. The King James translators entitled the writing "The Epistle of Paul to the Hebrews." Scholars are agreed today that Paul did not write it. Origen, a little after A.D. 200, said that God alone knows who wrote the letter. Numerous people have been suggested. Among them are Apollos, Aquila and Priscilla, Silas, Philip the deacon, Timothy, and Luke. Of all these the one who seems most likely is the gifted and ingenious teacher, Apollos of Alexandria. The allegorical interpretations of the Old Testament are much like those earlier developed by Philo of Alexandria. The description of Apollos given in Acts 18:24 seems to fit the author very well. However, the early church had many extremely able people who are completely unknown to us today.

This essay or sermon was written during a time when the Christians were suffering persecution. They had gone through an earlier period of suffering (10:32). This suggests a date near the end of Domitian's rule, about the same time as the "Revelation to John." It was probably written chiefly for the church at Rome, although the author doubtless had in mind all Christian groups.

263

It could hardly be called the letter to the Romans since there already existed Paul's message to the church there. To call it 2 Romans would imply that Paul was the author. Christianity had come to be thought of as the new Israel of God. This may be why the title, "To the Hebrews" was given. It is quite probable that the author gave no title to his writing. Since he makes a comparison between the Hebrew and Christian religions and a title such as was given to Paul's letters—to the Galatians, to the Philippians—seemed desirable, the expression, "to the Hebrews" came to be used.

The group for which this writing was intended was made up of second or third generation Christians. Their parents or grandparents had embraced Christianity enthusiastically, gladly suffering for their new religion. But a generation or two later the distinctive values of Christianity tended to be forgotten. The enthusiasm had begun to disappear.

These people needed to rediscover the importance of their religion, to be made to realize the consequences of being lukewarm to Christianity. They should be carrying the banner toward a bright new world. They should be world leaders. In government and in business people looked to Rome for guidance. All roads led to Rome. Would not the Christian world also be depending upon Rome! The church there should be leading, instructing others. Although the "Gospel according to Mark" and the prison letters of Paul had been written in Rome, they were not the product of the Roman church. "For though by this time you ought to be teachers, you need some one to teach you again the first principles of God's word. You need milk, not solid food" (5:12).

Therefore the writer proceeded to point out the value of Christianity by comparing it with the next greatest religion, Judaism. Judaism was the only other religion that believed in one supreme God, the only other faith that considered itself to be a revelation from God. The motto of this epistle is "Jesus is better." The importance of Christianity centers around the personality of Jesus Christ, "the pioneer and perfecter of our faith" (12:2). "In many and various ways God spoke of old to our fathers by the prophets; but in these last days he has spoken to us by a Son" (1:1-2). This is the perfection of God's revelation. Christianity

264

was not founded by an angel or a prophet, but the Son of God himself. Christ "reflects the glory of God and bears the very stamp of his nature" (1:3). Like the rabbis, the author used numerous verses from the Hebrew scriptures to support his arguments. We doubtless would not agree with the use of some of these quotations. Seven verses are cited to prove that the Son is superior to angels. "Therefore we must pay the closest attention to what we have heard. . . . How shall we escape if we neglect such a great salvation?" (2:1-3). "Because he himself has suffered and been tempted, he is able to help those who are tempted" (2:18).

The Jews have every right to be proud of Moses the founder of their religion, "yet Jesus has been counted worthy of . . . much more glory than Moses" (3:3). Moses was God's servant; Christ his son. Other writers called Jesus a prophet. Only the writer of the letter to the Hebrews calls him a priest, the high priest. A priest was one who spoke to God for the people, brought people to God. Jesus could do this more than any previous priest, for he "has passed through the heavens" (4:14), and is "at the right hand of the Majesty on high" (1:3). Jesus also understands us: "We have not a high priest who is unable to sympathize with our weaknesses, but one who in every respect has been tempted as we are, yet without sinning" (4:15). Thus he is completely fitted to deal with human weakness. He is far superior to any priest in the Hebrew tradition. He does not even fit into the Levitical priesthood started by Aaron.

"Thou art a priest forever after the order of Melchizedek" (5:6). The author applies this statement of Psalm 110:4 to Jesus. Other than this reference in the Psalms the only previous mention of Melchizedek is the story given in Genesis 14:17-20. The first verses of the seventh chapter of Hebrews retell this story. The Hebrew priests were extremely proud of their ancestry; in fact all Hebrews were. But no vital statistics are given for Melchizedek. "He is without father or mother or genealogy, and has neither beginning of days nor end of life" (7:3). At this point he resembles the Son of God. He represents a timeless priesthood. He was greater than the ancestor of all the Hebrews, Abraham. Did not Abraham acknowledge his greatness by giving Melchizedek a tithe of his spoils? Did not he bless Abraham? It is always the greater who blesses the lesser. Since Aaron and all the Hebrew priests were descendants of Abraham, the Christians, whose priesthood is after the order of Melchizedek, have a greater priesthood.

Christianity has done away with both the Levite priesthood and the Jewish law which was produced by the priests. Jesus, our Lord and high priest, was not a member of the tribe of Levi which was supposed to produce all the priests, but of the tribe of Judah. The author does not feel that the priesthood or the Jewish law were evil, but that they were a weak, shadowy forerunner of something much better. We now have one "who has become a priest, not according to a legal requirement concerning bodily descent but by the power of an indestructible life" (7:16). The weakness of the law has been set aside, and "a better hope is introduced, through which we draw near to God" (7:19). As the 110th Psalm was considered by various New Testament writers to refer to the Messiah, so the writer of Hebrews keeps applying the fourth verse to Jesus, "Thou art a priest for ever." Death interrupted the service of former priests, but Christ "holds his priesthood permanently, because he continues for ever" (7:24). None of the imperfections of other priests is to be found in our high priest.

In his conviction that the Jewish religion was but "a copy and shadow" of the much superior religion founded by the Son of God, the writer notes that our priest ministers not in a tabernacle made by men, but in a heavenly sanctuary. The Hebrew religion, with its sacrifices, was based upon a covenant. Jeremiah had said, "The days will come, says the Lord, when I will establish a new covenant with the House of Israel" (Jer. 31:31-34). This, says the writer to the Hebrews, makes the old covenant obsolete. Christ "is the mediator of a new covenant" (9:15). The author does not say that the new covenant does away with sacrifice, but Christ the high priest is himself the sacrifice. As the blood of sacrifices was used to purify the Hebrew worshippers, "how much more shall the blood of Christ, who through the eternal Spirit offered himself without blemish to God, purify your conscience from dead works to serve the living God" (9:14). This better sacrifice has brought God and man into a new relationship. The repeated sacrifices of the Hebrew religion had little value, "for it is impossible that the blood of bulls and goats should take away sin" (10:4). But the single offering of his life by Christ has brought about the forgiveness of sin. His was the perfect sacrifice.

Having proved to his satisfaction that Christianity has a better founder, high priest, sanctuary, covenant and sacrifice than the world's next best religion, our author proceeds to warn of the punishment deserved by "the man who has spurned the Son of God" (10:29). With warning and rebuke he gives encouragement and assurance. "Let us consider how to stir up one another to love and good works" (10:24). "It is a fearful thing to fall into the hands of the living God" (10:31).

The real Christian is a man of faith who does not "shrink back." Faith is loyalty to unseen reality. "Now faith is the assurance of things hoped for, the conviction of things not seen" (11:1). Men of faith are those who live by a conviction that God is winning, that he created the universe and will eventually have a good world. Such people are acceptable to God. The author then proceeds to call a roll of Old Testament characters who lived by faith. "These all died in faith, not having received what was promised, but having seen it and greeted it from afar" (11:13). They never turned back but kept looking ahead. As did these people, we must keep our faith, "looking to Jesus the pioneer and perfecter of our faith, who for the joy that was set before him endured the cross, despising the shame, and is seated at the right hand of the throne of God" (12:2).

We should not expect to have an easier life than did Jesus. We have not shed our blood as he did. The author even suggests that the suffering his readers were experiencing was discipline from God. Value can come to us through this. With analogies from the Hebrew scriptures the author predicts dire consequences for those who do not obey the will of God. To "neglect such a great salvation," "to fall away from the living God," brings dire consequences, "for our God is a consuming fire" (12:29). "Let us be grateful for receiving a kingdom that cannot be shaken" (12:28).

It is possible that the last chapter of Hebrews had another author. It differs from the preceding chapters, although the writer again backs up his statements with Old Testament quotations. It is more like a letter than the first twelve chapters. It is largely a group of moralizing exhortations. Christians must lead the new life shown to them. "Let brotherly love continue" (13:1). "Do not neglect to do good and to share what you have, for such sacrifices are pleasing to God" (13:16). "Obey your leaders and submit to them" (13:17). However, the permanence of Christ and things Christian as compared to the temporary aspects of the Hebrew religion is summed up in the well-known statement, "Jesus Christ is the same yesterday and today and forever" (13:8).

The importance of worship is emphasized in Hebrews more than in any other New Testament book. To the author religion chiefly means access to God. This can be obtained through worship. "Let us then with confidence draw near to the throne of grace, that we may receive mercy and find grace to help in time of need" (4:16).

Despite the author's insistence that Christianity is the best religion, he does not think of earlier religion as bad. Rather, it prepared men for Christianity. There is a definite continuity of history. Men have always been seeking for God, hoping for a better understanding, living by a faith that something better lay ahead. Christianity is the fulfilling of these hopes, the achievement of this faith.

For Class Discussion

1. Which term better describes Jesus, prophet or priest?
2. What is the value of sacrifice? How does Jesus fit this?
3. How does the author's concept of faith differ from that of other New Testament writers?
4. What does the author mean by "salvation?"
5. If you were to write today on a comparison of Christianity with Judaism what points would you emphasize?

Assignment

1. In what five ways does the author of "Hebrews" believe Christianity is better than Judaism?
2. What does the author feel are the consequences of falling away from Christianity?
3. Give the author's list of heroes of faith

Supplementary Reading

1. Goodspeed, Edgar J. *An Introduction to the New Testament.* Chicago: University of Chicago Press, 1937. Chapter XVI.

2. Hunter, A. M. *Introducing the New Testament.* Philadelphia: The Westminster Press, 1946. Chapter XVI.

3. Laymon, Charles M. *Christ in the New Testament.* New York and Nashville: Abingdon Press, 1958. Chapter XIII

4. Parsons, Ernest W. *The Religion of the New Testament.* New York: Harper & Brothers, 1939. Chapter VI.

CHAPTER 38

"Be Doers of the Word"

Read 1 Peter and James

Persecution of the church brought encouragement from many sources. The church at Rome had been accused of not teaching others. It responded by producing two letters, 1 Peter and 1 Clement. Both deal with much the same subject, but 1 Clement is a long writing of 61 chapters. It lacks enthusiasm and does not make especially interesting reading. Although the Corinthian church to which it is addressed, and some others, included it in their lists of Christian writings, there was little support for making it a part of the New Testament canon. The revered name of Peter gave weight to the shorter and more interesting product of the Roman church. "The Shepherd of Hermas" was also soon produced by the church at Rome as an answer to the challenge made in Hebrews.

The Revelation to John likewise needed to be answered. Paul had instructed, "There is no authority except from God, and those that exist have been instituted by God. . . . Pay all of them their dues, taxes to whom taxes are due" (Rom. 13:1-7). But in Revelation the empire was pictured as a raging beast which should be avenged: "Repay her double for her deeds; mix a double draught for her in the cup she mixed" (18:6). This could quickly develop hatred. Christianity should be a religion of love. The church at Rome recognized a real responsibility. Revelation had called Rome, seated on her seven hills, Babylon. The signature to 1 Peter is "She who is at Babylon . . . sends you greetings" (5:13). As the Revelation had been addressed to the churches in the province of Asia, so the Roman church felt obligated to write to churches in Asia and neighboring provinces where the hatred suggested by Revelation might be developing.

By the time 1 Peter was written the apostle Peter had been

dead for many years. What right did the Roman church have to write its message as from "Peter, an apostle of Jesus Christ" (1:1)? To us this seems dishonest. To the church about A.D. 96 this was acceptable. Associating the names of famous people with current writing was common practice. Books often were known by the name of their chief characters, as Moses, Joshua, Samuel. In time people came to call the first five books of the Old Testament the books of Moses although few would think of Moses as their writer. Many Jewish and Christian writings not included in our Bible had the names of famous people attached to them: Solomon, David, Jeremiah, even Enoch and Adam. Shortly before the writing of 1 Peter a Christian message had been produced under the title, The Odes of Solomon. The Revelation to Peter has already been mentioned. Other early Christian writings were entitled, The Gospel of Peter, The Acts of Peter, The Teaching of Peter, The Preaching of Peter, and The Letters of Peter.

The church at Rome felt that it really represented Peter. His memoirs of Jesus had been written at Rome by Mark. Peter apparently had spent some time at Rome and been executed there. Rome came to be known as the city of Peter and Paul. The church at Rome had become the spokesman for Peter. It felt identified with Peter in spirit and doctrine. Certainly the outspoken Peter would not have allowed the implications of Hebrews and Revelation to go unchallenged. Therefore the little book we call 1 Peter must be written.

Of course, there are those who insist that this letter was written by the apostle. When it is pointed out that Peter the fisherman could not have written such excellent Greek as that used in 1 Peter these people reply that Silas or Silvanus, the traveling companion of Paul, could have written it for Peter. However, the whole atmosphere of the book is that of a time of persecution considerably after the death of both Peter and Silas. One who is familiar with Paul's letters will recognize that they are a part of the background of the writer of 1 Peter. The book also has a number of parallels to statements in Matthew and Luke. The book seems to have been written a little before A.D. 100. A few Bible scholars believe that this letter was written twenty years later when the church was again being persecuted, but this group has remained small.

This is a letter of Christian hope. The author points out that his Christian readers have "an inheritance which is imperishable, undefiled and unfading" (1:4) in which they should rejoice "though now for a little while you may have to suffer various trials" (1:6). "As the outcome of your faith you obtain the salvation of your souls" (1:9). In Christ you have that for which the Old Testament prophets were seeking. "You have tasted the kindness of the Lord" (2:3). Therefore grow up in your Christian living. "Love one another earnestly" (1:22). "Put away all malice and all guile and insincerity and envy and all slander" (2:1). "Once you were no people but now you are God's people" (2:10), God's new Israel, who must declare his wonders to the heathen.

Christians must "maintain good conduct among the Gentiles" (2:12). They must be subject to the emperor and his governors. "Love the brotherhood. Fear God. Honor the emperor" (2:17). In pointing out that Christ also was called upon to suffer, the author imitates statements of the Suffering Servant passage of Isaiah 53. He evidently feels that this passage can be used as a fitting description of Jesus. Servants and wives should also set a Christian example to the heathen. To all Christians the advice is given "Do not return evil for evil . . . but on the contrary bless" (3:9). "It is better to suffer for doing right . . . than for doing wrong" (3:17). To do this is to imitate Christ. There is no place in the Christian life for "licentiousness, passions, drunkenness, revels, carousing, lawless idolatry" (4:3). One should practice hospitality and use every talent he has in the service of God.

A Christian should never be a murderer or thief or wrongdoer or mischief-maker, "yet if one suffers as a Christian, let him not be ashamed, but . . . glorify God" (4:16). Such can "entrust their souls to a faithful creator" (4:19). The elders among those who hear this message should be good examples to their flocks. Thus they "will obtain the unfading crown of glory" (5:4). The Christian should not be anxious. He should be humble and watchful. Thus he can avoid the devil who is like "a roaring lion, seeking someone to devour" (5:8). Remember that others have suffered and that suffering is only temporary, for there will be an eternal glory in Christ. The writer ends his message of encouragement by expressing his hope that peace will come to "all of you that are in Christ." (5:14).

This emphasis upon Christian living was needed by the church. Most Christian thinking had been centered about what God and Christ had done, not about what Christians themselves should do. The proclamation about Christ needed to be supplemented by an examination of how the spirit of Christ in the individual affects one's own living. Moral or ethical implications of the Christian gospel needed emphasis. Kerygma is not enough; living according to the didache is essential. Christians must be told this phase of their religion.

A Christian teacher who called himself "James, a servant of God and of the Lord Jesus Christ" (1:1), but about whom we know nothing more, proceeded to do this. Judaism was facing a similar problem. After the destruction of Jerusalem in A.D. 70 the Pharisees had come to dominate Jewish thought. The emphasis of the Pharisees on form, ritual, detailed law needed to be supplemented. Since there is little in the letter of James that is distinctly Christian, some scholars think that the letter we are examining was originally a Jewish writing, a "Letter of Jacob" —James is the Greek equivalent of the Hebrew Jacob. We know of other Jewish writings that were similarly "converted" to Christian use.

Whatever its origin, this letter or sermon served a need of the church about A.D. 100. It reflects no definite situation. We do not know where it was written. Syrian Antioch has been suggested. It was not addressed to a specific limited group. Christians had come to be thought of as the new Israel of God scattered through the Mediterranean world much as the Jews had been scattered in what was called the "dispersion." Therefore James is addressed to "the twelve tribes in the dispersion" as 1 Peter was addressed "to the exiles of the dispersion."

Reading James is somewhat like reading the dictionary, or the book of Proverbs. Each book jumps from one theme to another with little or no connection. Jewish writings which did not emphasize ritual or theology came under the disapproval of the Pharisees, except for the book of Proverbs, which had been commonly accepted as a part of their scriptures. The lack of a specific theme was typical of Greek sermons, both non-Christian and Christian. Such sermons sought to have something for every hearer. The book of James is "an ethical scrapbook" full of practical suggestions. It contains a number of terms echoing Jesus' Sermon on the Mount. James is an excellent conversational sermon.

The introductory admonition of James is an emphasis similar to 1 Peter: "Count it all joy, my brethren, when you meet various trials, for you know that the testing of your faith produces steadfastness" (1:2-3). Through sincere prayer one may find the wisdom necessary to withstand trial.

Being jealous of the financially rich had injured the Christian spirit of some church members. James speaks three times of problems arising from differences of wealth. He points out that riches may be very temporary. As the grass withers, "so will the rich man fade away in the midst of his pursuits" (1:11). Deferring to the rich is sin. Sarcastically James compares the treatment sometimes given to "a man with gold rings and in fine clothing" as contrasted to that given "a poor man in shabby clothing." "Is it not the rich who oppress you, is it not they who drag you into court" (2:6)? The royal law says, " 'You shall love your neighbor as yourself' . . . if you show partiality you commit sin" (2:8-9). In his last chapter James loses all patience with the rich, too many of whom had secured their wealth by unjust means. "Come now,. you rich, weep and howl for the miseries that are coming upon you. . . . Behold, the wages of the laborers who mowed your fields, which you kept back by fraud, cry out" (5:14).

Those who steadfastly endure trial "will receive the crown of life" (1:12). One must be patient, as the farmer patiently awaits his harvest. The prophets suffered patiently. "Behold, we call those happy who were steadfast" (5:11). One should not blame God for his trials and temptations; "God . . . himself tempts no one" (1:13). God sends only that which is good. "Every good endowment and every perfect gift is from above" (1:17). We must seek self-control, for anger harms the soul.

Our religion is one of action: "visit orphans and widows in their affliction" (1:27). "Be doers of the word, and not hearers only" (1:22). "Show me your faith apart from your works, and I by my works will show you my faith" (2:18). "Faith apart from works is barren" (2:20). Twice James insists that faith without works is dead (2:17 and 2:26). A belief in monotheism and that God will reward the good and punish the bad is not enough.

James so emphasizes this that many feel he was trying to counteract a misinterpretation of Paul's statement, "We hold that a man is justified by faith apart from works of law" (Rom. 3:28). By "faith" Paul meant trust; James meant holding a concept, agreeing to a teaching. James doubtless approved Paul's emphasis upon "faith working through love" (Gal. 5:6).

"If any one thinks he is religious, and does not bridle his tongue but deceives his heart, this man's religion is vain" (1:26). By means of the tongue one can bring tremendous harm. Almost anything else can be tamed, "but no human being can tame the tongue" (3:8). "Do not speak evil against one another. . . . Who are you that you judge your neighbor" (4:11-12)?

The sin of wrong desire and covetousness brings quarrelling and war. Be humble. "Submit yourselves . . . to God. Resist the devil and he will flee from you" (4:7). Boasting and over-confidence are sinful. We must use the intelligence God has given us. "Whoever knows what is right to do and fails to do it, for him it is sin" (4:17). Absolute truthfulness is also essential. Oaths should not be used. Doubtless James felt that if one depended upon an oath to assure the truth of what he said, then omitting an oath might seem to cancel the necessity of being truthful.

Christianity includes ethics but it is never separated from God. "Is any one among you suffering? Let him pray. Is any cheerful? Let him sing praise" (5:13). This likewise applies to sickness and to sin. "The prayer of a righteous man has great power in its effects" (5:16). The letter of James ends suddenly by reemphasizing that we are our brother's keeper, that we have an obligation to bring back any one who has wandered from the truth. 1 Peter had said that "love covers a multitude of sins" (4:8). James uses the same expression in connection with this act of love.

As the author and date of this letter or sermon are unknown, so is the source of a quotation found in it. New Testament writers make a number of quotations from non-Biblical material. However, in James 4:5 we read; "do you suppose it is in vain that the scripture says, 'He yearns jealously over the spirit which he has made to dwell in us'?" Such a verse or even anything similar to it is not found in the Old Testament, the Apocrypha, or earlier New Testament writings. It is not in any Jewish writing that has survived. There are two possible answers to the problem this raises. One is that James, like many people today, quoted from memory some familiar saying which he erroneously thought was in the scriptures. The other answer is that James may have quoted from some writing, now lost, which Christians of his time considered scripture. The Council of Jamnia in A.D. 90 had specifically defined what made up the Hebrew canon, omitting the Aprocrypha. However, Christians did not feel bound by this decision. Lists of the Apocrypha did not agree. Doubtless some Christians included writings which we no longer have.

Some scholars find a similarity to the thought expressed in this verse in a lengthy statement in "The Manual of Discipline," one of the Essene books known as the Dead Sea Scrolls. An examination of the Essene literature reveals a number of expressions peculiarly similar to those used in James.

Assignment

1. From where does the author of 1 Peter send greetings? This is the cryptic name for what city?

2. Give three quotations from the book of Isaiah which the author of 1 Peter makes.

3. How did Jesus sum up his attitude toward government?

4. What use of ridicule does the author of James make?

5. What does he say about (a) the tongue, (b) faith?

6. What parallels to statements in the Sermon on the Mount do you find in James?

Supplementary Reading

1. Baker, J. Christian. *The Church Faces the World.* Philadelphia: The Westminster Press, 1961.

2. Goodspeed, Edgar J. *An Introduction to the New Testament.* Chicago: University of Chicago Press, 1937. Chapters XVII and XVIII.

3. Hunter, A. M. *Introducing the New Testament.* Philadelphia: The Westminster Press, (Rev.), 1957. Chapters XXIII and XXIV.

CHAPTER 39

"God Is Love"

Read 1, 2, and 3 John

Admiration for Christ brought many interpretations and explanations. How could the personality of Christ be understood? Attempts to solve these problems tended to break the church into dissenting groups. Some of these attempts were so at variance with the more generally accepted ideas that they came to be classed as heresies. The elemental spirits idea that had developed in Colossae was but one branch of Gnosticism. Other "know-it-all" groups had grown up as new people had been accepted into the church, and each Christian community applied its own thinking to the problems religion faced.

One of these branches of Gnosticism that developed in Asia Minor or Turkey came to be known as Docetism. The major element in this belief was that Christ was so holy that he could not have been contaminated with earthly things, that he was not a human being, did not have an earthly body. He only appeared to be human, to have a physical body. His suffering was not physical, not real. The name of the group came from the Greek verb to seem or appear. Some of the Docetists said that Christ borrowed the body of Jesus at his baptism and deserted it just before the crucifixion. The Moslem religion today teaches much the same thing about the crucifixion. The Docetists put forth their ideas in several books, some of which they claimed were written by members of the original Twelve. One of these books, the Acts of John, reported that Jesus' feet left no footprints on the ground. Sometimes he seemed tall, sometimes short. At the time of the crucifixion he was in a cave above Jerusalem talking with John. John was told that the multitude only thought they were crucifying the Christ. At another place he was reported to

277

have said, "Nothing therefore of the things they will say of me have I suffered."

Like other Gnostics the Docetists felt that they were far superior to orthodox Christians. They proclaimed, "I have fellowship with God," "I have no sin," "I am in the light." These arrogant people had got control of some of the churches and driven other Christians out. At some places they had broken away from the church.

A warning must be sent to the churches of Asia Minor about the Docetists and their fellow Gnostics. An unnamed Christian leader, so well known that he simply calls himself "the elder," composed such a warning and had representatives carry it to his "little children" of various churches. There is much in his message to suggest that it was written by the same man who wrote our Fourth Gospel. Emphasis upon love, light, life, truth is found in both writings. Eternal life could be said to be the theme of each of these. Both consider Jesus the Logos or word of life. The gospel of John was written to tell how men may have eternal life (20:31). The epistle was written to explain how they may know that they have it (5:13). The epistle might be called a postscript to the gospel. The gospel account is anti-Docetist. It emphasizes the humanity of Jesus. It notes Jesus' becoming weary (4:6), being interested in food and drink, weeping (11:35), and even on the cross exclaiming, "I thirst" (19:28).

Tradition has called the author John. An early Christian, Papias, writing between 130 and 140 points out that this was a different John from the apostle. The earliest church historian, Eusebius, writing about 325 also notes this. The author may have been the bishop of Ephesus concerned about the heresies rising in his churches.

Along with this warning, which we call 1 John, have come down to us two little cover letters. One was written to some individual church with which the author was well acquainted. It is a summary of the longer letter. In it he emphasizes the importance of love. We must all love one another. He then notes that "many deceivers have gone out into the world, men who will not acknowledge the coming of Jesus Christ in the flesh; such a one is the deceiver and the antichrist" (7). Such a person does not have the doctrine of Christ and should not be received into the house or given any greeting.

278

The other cover letter, called 3 John, is addressed to Gaius, a friend of the writer. Gaius probably belonged to the church to which 2 John was addressed. The writer is glad to learn that Gaius has remained true to the Christian doctrine and has been cordial to witnesses who have been sent to the churches. It is hoped that he will be helpful to those who are traveling for the Christian cause, evidently those who are carrying the message of 1 John. They need encouragement. However, in the church with which Gaius is acquainted there is a trouble-maker, Diotrephes. He does not acknowledge the authority of the writer, saying evil words against him. He is driving people out of the church. His example must not be followed. Those to whom 2 and 3 John are addressed are told that the writer hopes to visit them soon.

The elder begins his general message by pointing out that Christians who have had an abiding witness of Christ, even to the extent that some had seen and touched him, should have fellowship with one another. This also means fellowship "with the Father and with his Son Jesus Christ" (1:3). Such fellowship brings joy.

As the Gospel according to John says that "light has come into the world . . . men loved darkness rather than light, because their deeds were evil" (3:19), so the elder begins his message by saying that "God is light and in him is no darkness at all" (1:5). Those who say they are in the light but reject fellowship with others are liars. Those who say they have no sin not only are liars themselves, but make God a liar. The elder was generous with his use of the word, liar. "He who says 'I know him' but disobeys his commandments is a liar, and the truth is not in him" (2:4). Love is the primary command. "He who says he is in the light and hates his brother is in the darkness still" (2:9). Young and old are admonished to love the Father rather than things of the world. "The world passes away, and the lust of it; but he who does the will of God abides for ever" (2:17).

The elder attacks those who are deceiving the church: "They went out from us, but they were not of us; for if they had been of us, they would have continued with us" (2:19). They are antichrists. This writer is the only Biblical author who uses the term "antichrist" although the idea was expressed by Paul in his 2 Thessalonians. Evidently Paul's idea had been accepted, for

279

John says, "You have heard that antichrist is coming" (2:18). At such a time, it was believed, hatred and falsehood would appear and many would be led astray from the church. The elder, as did the writer of the "Revelation to John," felt that a new age was about to be ushered in, that these Docetists were antichrists, denying that Jesus is the Christ.

The faithful are children of God looking forward to the coming of Christ. At this time they will be transformed into something even greater. "He who does right is righteous" (3:7). Those who do not do right, do not love their fellow-men, are not of God, but "are the children of the devil" (3:10). However, the elder knew that to some extent we all sin. "If we say we have no sin, we deceive ourselves, and the truth is not in us" (1:8). "We know that we have passed out of death into life, because we love the brethren. He who does not love remains in death" (3:14). We should imitate Christ. "Let us not love in word or speech but in deed and in truth" (3:18). Keeping this commandment of God gives us confidence.

Again the Docetists are attacked. Those who deny that Jesus has come in the flesh are not of God. They are of the world. "We are of God. Whoever knows God listens to us" (4:6). As the author had said that God is light, now he says that "God is love" (4:8). Because of his love, God sent his Son. "If God so loved us, we also ought to love one another" (4:11). As in the gospel record it was stated that "No one has ever seen God" (1:18), so the elder repeats this statement pointing out that it is in loving one another that we find God, discover that "God abides in us" (4:12). This love gives us complete confidence. "There is no fear in love, but perfect love casts out fear" (4:18). Again the divisive, hating, Docetists are criticized: "If any one says, 'I love God,' and hates his brother, he is a liar; for he who does not love his brother whom he has seen, cannot love God whom he has not seen" (4:20). Only those who believe that Jesus is the Christ are children of God. If one loves God he must love these children of God.

The elder's concluding sentences emphasize the importance of putting confidence in him who has the name and authority of the Son of God. Thus you know "that you have eternal life" (5:13). "Eternal Life" is John's term for salvation. It is what Paul meant by "being in Christ" and the synoptic gospels called "being in the Kingdom." With great assurance the elder states, "We know that the Son of God has come and has given us understanding, to know him who is true; and we are in him who is true, in his Son Jesus Christ" (5:20). Therefore we must keep away from "idols," untrue, unreal objects of devotion.

For Class Discussion

1. How can it be said that heresies make helpful contributions?
2. John emphasized that the Christian must be willing to lay down his life for another (1 John 3:16). Is this a distinctly Christian idea, or do other religions practice it?
3. In what ways did Jesus differ from us?

Assignment

1. To whom does the author address 1 John? 2 John? 3 John?
2. What is his commandment?
3. In what terms does he define or describe God?
4. Where did we first find the anti-Christ idea?
5. What three types of people does John call liars?

Supplementary Reading

1. Goodspeed, Edgar J. *An Introduction to the New Testament* Chicago: University of Chicago Press, 1937. Chapter XX.
2. Laymon, Charles M. *Christ in the New Testament*. New York and Nashville: Abingdon Press, 1958. Chapters XI and XII.
3. Parson, Ernest W. *The Religion of the New Testament*. New York: Harper & Brothers, 1939. Pages 240-250.

CHAPTER 40

"Be a Good Minister of Christ Jesus"

Read: 1 and 2 Timothy and Titus

Paul's reputation had to be saved. Seventy-five years after Paul's death the church's greatest heretic, Marcion, claimed to be a close follower of Paul. If "birds of a feather flock together" Paul too must have been a heretic. One of the church fathers, Justin, writing at this time, uses numerous ideas and quotations from Paul but carefully avoids mentioning his name, lest Justin himself be classed as a Marcionite.

Marcion was an earnest sincere heretic. He had been brought up in Asia Minor, the son of a prominent Christian leader. In 139 he went to Rome preaching his interpretation of Christianity. He won favor there, made converts, but five years later was rejected. He spent the remainder of his life going through the Christian world organizing churches of his own. No other heretic was so enterprising, therefore so dangerous. Marcion had read descriptions of God given in the early part of the Old Testament. These pictured God as killing Er and Onan, trying to kill Moses as he was returning to Egypt, ordering Joshua to kill all the inhabitants of various Canaanite cities, killing a large number of people because they had enough curiosity to look inside the ark of the covenant. Marcion also read Jesus' portrayal of God as a kind, loving, forgiving heavenly father. He could not see any relation between these two descriptions and concluded that there were two gods, that one must choose which he would follow. Marcion had no concept of evolution. He did not know that men's understanding of God had grown, that the early writers were honest but mistaken in their picture of God. He did not realize as some Christians had, that the Hebrew people gradually grew in their religion and undestanding, that the Hebrew scriptures are a record of men's growth toward a knowledge of God and his will given by Jesus.

Because Marcion did not like the Old Testament picture of God he felt that Christians should discard the Hebrew scriptures, break away entirely from their Hebrew religious background. Since reading the scriptures was a definite part of the Christian church services, Marcion proceeded to draw up a set of Christian scriptures. Matthew, Mark and Luke were well known. John was just coming into use. Matthew had too many quotations from the Hebrew scriptures to satisfy Marcion. Mark did not give enough of the teaching of Jesus. Therefore the only gospel account Marcion would use in his Christian Bible was Luke. He even edited it at places to make it independent of the Hebrew scripture and religion. To this Marcion added the writings of Paul which he also edited. With these he included Ephesians. To round out his Christian Bible he wrote a book of his own which he called Antitheses or Contradictions. He felt that Christianity should contradict many things in the older religion. He set up the gospel as contradictory to law. The God of grace was a contradiction to the God of wrath.

There was enough truth in Marcion's teachings to make them popular. Paul and his writings must be saved for orthodox Christianity. So must the Old Testament, for most Christians found in it great values. They were sure that God had spoken through the Old Testament.

Marcionism was not the only heresy that needed to be refuted. Phases of Gnosticism were continuing to grow. Gnosticism was also undermining the Old Testament. While Marcion had been taking it too literally, Gnosticism was turning the Old Testament into myth and allegory. Marcion had taught that the world was made by an evil god. Gnosticism taught that God as a spirit is good but the world as matter is entirely evil. Since Christ would not be associated with evil he only seemed to have a body. Christians should shun the world and become ascetics, these Gnostics taught. Such heresies must also be denied. Orthodox or correct Christianity must be understood and supported.

Another problem needed attention. That was the organization of the churches. Christianity was no longer a drive to get ready

283

for the immediate return of Christ. It must settle down to a long-term proposition. The church could not continue to be held together by a new enthusiasm. It must be organized with trained and respected officers. Money must be collected and disbursed without the least breath of scandal. Great care must be taken in selecting and appointing people to the ministry. Only those of high character must be chosen.

To meet these needs of the middle of the second century, a Jewish Christian who had been shocked by Marcion's attitude toward the Old Testament and things Jewish, wrote a series of three "letters." These he entitled 1 and 2 Timothy and Titus. He was convinced that if Paul were still living he would assail Marcionism and Gnosticism in no uncertain terms. Paul had vigorously attacked the earliest form of Gnosticism in his letter to the Colossians. Therefore it seemed wise and practical to word this message as if coming from Paul. This method had been used by other writers. However, the author of these three little letters which we call the Pastorals did not succeed in copying Paul's sentence structure, style, or vocabulary. Of the 897 words he uses, 306 are not found in any of Paul's letters. The writer was an organizer, a church administrator, rather than an inspirer. There are very few people who have the ability to inspire that Paul had. Although the author made numerous personal references so that the writings would sound to be the concern and expression of Paul, he did not attempt to cover up the fact that they were produced some time between 130 and 150, long after Paul's death. In 1 Tim. 5:18 he quotes Luke 10:7 and refers to this quotation as scripture. Luke was not written until Paul had been dead twenty years. Moreover Luke was not considered scripture until Marcion put it into his collection of Christian scriptures. A few scholars believe the author of the Pastorals may have incorporated some sentences from private notes Paul had sent to Timothy and Titus.

Luke addressed both of his writings to Theophilus, an unknown and possibly imaginary character. Thus the reader had the feeling that he was looking over the shoulder of another man, that the writings were warm and personal. The writer of the Pastorals decided to do a similar thing. Next to Paul, Timothy and Titus were doubtless the chief men in founding and guiding

284

churches in Asia Minor. Paul mentions Timothy twelve times and Titus eleven in his letters. They were his closest younger friends. Therefore advice from Paul to them would be of interest to the churches in Asia Minor, the center of Christianity at this time. People were accustomed to this kind of framework for religious teaching. Both Jews and Christians used it. To people of that day it did not seem dishonest or artificial.

To continue the illusion that the teachings are Paul's, the writer in 1 Timothy represents Paul as writing after his Roman imprisonment, writing from Macedonia or Greece after leaving Timothy at Ephesus. Titus pictures Paul at liberty and planning to spend the winter in Nicopolis in northwestern Greece. Second Timothy pictures Paul in prison again, facing sentence of execution.

Were these three letters a series, one appearing after the other to reinforce certain teachings? Possibly. They may all have been sent out at one time just as Paul's genuine letters were being circulated as a unit. These were probably added to a new edition of Paul's letters. There was a very definite attempt to relate them to Paul. This was perhaps a bit overdone as in reference to "my gospel," "my sufferings." The first verse of each Timothy epistle reads, "Paul an apostle of Christ Jesus." If the Apostle Paul had been writing to a friend as close as Timothy, one whom he thought of as a son, he would not have started out by telling Timothy that he was an apostle of Christ—that was one thing Timothy definitely knew. As "Paul" the writer symbolized the great apostle, so "Timothy" and "Titus" symbolized Christian ministers to whom the letters were addressed. These letters are advice to young ministers. That is why they are called Pastorals.

Three types of church organization had developed by the time the Pastorals were written. There were churches here and there which were independent of all other churches, made their own decisions. We call these Congregational. There were groups of churches which banded together for fellowship. They sent their representatives or presbyters to meet together to decide questions pertaining to the churches. This type of government is called Presbyterian. However, the large majority of churches adopted an Episcopal type of organization. Local leaders were untrained. When they found problems they could not solve they turned to the leader of a neighboring city church, who in time came to be thought of as an overseer or bishop. When these bishops differed they took their differences to the bishop at Rome. All roads led to Rome. Rome was the authority in government and commerce. Thus eventually the bishop of Rome came to be considered the head of the church. This point had not been reached when the Pastorals were written. The church was in the process of transition from a lay to a professional ministry. Naturally some people opposed this and looked down upon professional clergy as greedy or self-righteous. This applied to ministers of all types, deacons, elders, bishops. These men must gain respect by being respectable.

The discovery of the Dead Sea scrolls indicates that a number of things we had thought of as only Christian were taught or practiced by some pre-Christian Jewish groups. The Essenes had overseers whose duties were quite similar to those of the bishops referred to in the Pastorals.

The author of the Pastorals insisted that the work of a bishop is a noble task, but the bishop also must be a noble person. His character is the important consideration. "A bishop must be above reproach, married only once, temperate, sensible, dignified, hospitable, an apt teacher, no drunkard, not violent but gentle, not quarrelsome, and no lover of money. He must manage his own household well, keeping his children submissive and respectful in every way" (1 Tim. 1:2-4). The author takes for granted that the bishop will be a married man. This does not quite sound like Paul. However it counters the asceticism of the Gnostics. Although Paul found it necessary to appoint to church office men who had very recently become Christians, that is no longer necessary and should be avoided. Otherwise the man appointed to a position over older Christians might become conceited. A bishop must also be respected, well thought of by outsiders, if the church is to have standing in its community. Second Timothy mentions only ministers without designating bishops, elders, deacons. However, in the latter part of the first chapter of Titus there is another list of qualities a bishop should possess.

Since this list is in the same paragraph with a list of qualities needed for the office of elder, there is considerable evidence to suggest that bishops and elders were the same people. Possibly bishop was a Greek term, elder a Jewish term for the same office.

In Titus we read that elders must be "men who are blameless, married only once, whose children are believers and not open to the charge of being profligate or insubordinate" (1:6). In 1 Timothy we are told that good elders who preach and teach should be well paid. Leaders should be careful about listening to criticism of such elders, although if they are guilty of sin they should be openly rebuked.

The task of the deacon is also undefined. "Deacons likewise must be serious, not double-tongued, not addicted to much wine, not greedy for gain; they must hold the mystery of the faith with a clear conscience" (1 Tim. 1:8-9).

Marcion had given women a higher position in his churches than Paul would have considered proper. Therefore the writer of the Pastorals attempts to put women "in their place." "Women should adorn themselves modestly and sensibly in seemly apparel, not with braided hair or gold or pearls or costly attire but by good deeds, as befits women who profess religion. Let a woman learn in silence with all submissiveness. I permit no woman to teach or to have authority over men" (1 Tim. 2:9-12). Churches had undertaken the support of their dependent members. These had come to include a great many widows. The writer sought to cut down this burden. Children should support their widowed mothers. "I would have younger widows marry, bear children, rule their households, and give the enemy no occasion to revile us" (5:14). This is not quite in accord with Paul's teaching. Paul thought that remarriage of widowed people was not wrong but definitely undesirable. (1 Cor. 7:40). This was because he felt that Jesus was coming back soon; people should spend their time getting ready for this rather than making love. The early return of Christ is not a concern of the writer of the Pastorals.

However, the author did make provision for the support of elderly widows. He would have a church organization of widows. "Let no one be enrolled as a widow who is under sixty years of age, or who has been married more than once, and she must be well attested for her good deeds, as one who has brought up children, shown hospitality, washed the feet of the saints, relieved the afflicted, and devoted herself to doing good in every way" (1 Tim. 5:9-10).

Second Timothy deals with the qualities of the true minister.

Sincere faith is essential. Evidently this means commitment to the Christianity taught by Paul. One's ministry must be active and courageous. "God did not give us a spirit of timidity but a spirit of power and love and self-control" (1:7). The minister must take his "share of suffering as a good soldier of Christ Jesus" (2:3). A minister must "avoid disputing about words" (2:14) as the heretics do, but rather do his best to present himself "to God as one aproved, a workman who has no need to be ashamed, rightly handling the word of truth" (2:15).

The author is quite concerned about correct doctrine. The good minister will "have nothing to do with stupid, senseless controversies; you know that they breed quarrels" (2 Tim. 2:23). People are warned "not to teach any different doctrine, not to occupy themselves with myths and endless genealogies which promote speculations rather than the divine training that is in faith; whereas the aim of our charge is love that issues from a pure heart and a good conscience and sincere faith" (1 Tim. 1:3-5). "If any one teaches otherwise and does not agree with the sound works of our Lord Jesus Christ and the teaching which accords with godliness, he is puffed up with conceit . . . he has a morbid craving for controversy and for disputes about words which produce envy, dissension, slander, base suspicions, and wrangling among men" (1 Tim. 6:3-5). One extremely important part of this true doctrine with which Marcion did not agree is that "there is one God" (1 Tim. 2:5).

A Christian's faith is shown in deeds, not words. He should have nothing to do with a man who is controversial. He should "be submissive to rulers and authorities . . . ready for any honest work . . . avoid quarreling . . . and show perfect courtesy toward all men" (Tit. 3:1-2). Seriousness, sobriety, temperance are essential. Being "addicted to much wine" is frowned upon, but medicinal wine is permitted—"a little wine for the sake of your stomach and your frequent ailments" (1 Tim. 5:23). The piety and ethics of the Jewish traditions in Christianity must be maintained. Loose living found among many Greeks must be avoided.

Paul considered the Jewish law as "our custodian until Christ came. . . but now that faith has come, we are no longer under a custodian" (Gal. 3:24-25). Marcion rejected the law as completely unworthy of the Christian, an opponent of the gospel. The author of the Pastorals contradicts Marcion but does not take quite the same approach Paul took. He says "the law is not laid down for the just, but for the lawless and disobedient, for the ungodly and sinners" (1 Tim. 1:9) and then lists the very worst categories of sinners, concluding "and whatever else is contrary to sound doctrine" (1:10). Therefore law had its place, but Christians should "avoid stupid controversies . . . and quarrels over the law" (Tit. 3:9). Although the Christian is not controlled by Jewish law he finds definite values in it. It is a part of the scriptures used by Christians and "all scripture is inspired by God and profitable for teaching, for reproof, for correction, and for training in righteousness" (2 Tim. 3:16). This, of course, is completely contrary to the insistence of Marcion.

For Class Discussion

1. Why are these three letters called Pastorals? Distinguish between the terms pastor, minister, clergyman, parson, preacher, reverend.
2. What is asceticism? Why was it practiced by some Gnostics?

Assignment

1. What have we already had about Timothy? What do we learn in Galatians and Corinthians about Titus?
2. How does 1 Tim. 5:18 indicate that Paul could not have written all the book?
3. Sum up the duty of Christian ministers as given in 1 Tim. 4:11-16 and 2 Tim. 4:1-5.
4. What attitude toward government are Christians urged to have (1 Tim. 2:1-4 and Tit. 2:15-3:11)?
5. What was Marcion's heresy?

Supplementary Reading

1. Goodspeed, Edgar J. *An Introduction to the New Testament.* Chicago: University of Chicago Press, 1937. Chapter XXI.
2. Hunter, A. M. *Introducing the New Testament.* Philadelphia: The Westminster Press, Rev., 1957. Chapter XXV.
3. Parsons, Ernest W. *The Religion of the New Testament.* New York: Harper & Brothers, 1939. Pages 233-239.
4. Titus, Eric Lane. *Essentials of New Testament Study.* New York: The Ronald Press Co., 1958. Pages 229-232.

CHAPTER 41

"Grow in the Grace and Knowledge of Our Lord"

Read Jude and 2 Peter

The church must also be saved from Docetism. The letters of John, "the elder" had attacked this heresy that held that Jesus only seemed to have a body. Doubtless many Christians were caused to turn a critical eye on this phase of Gnosticism. However, the heresy had continued to grow. Its followers had become convinced that, since the body was definitely not spiritual, what we did with our bodies was not a matter of religious concern. They did not accept the teaching of Paul that "your body is a temple of the Holy Spirit within you" (1 Cor. 6:19). They maintained that gluttony, drunkenness, sexual irregularity should not be disapproved by Christians since these were physical matters rather than spiritual. Such immoral practices among Christians had become a scandal.

This situation was so bad that a teacher named Jude, who had been contemplating writing "of our common salvation," felt called upon to warn the churches and appeal for a return to "the faith which was once for all delivered to the saints" (3). We do not know who this Jude was. Like James, he calls himself "a servant of Jesus Christ." There is added to this the phrase, "and brother of James." Could he have been a brother of the James who wrote twenty-five years earlier? Possibly the fact that these two writings begin with the same expression and make appeals for clean, ethical living caused some one later to insert this phrase. There are those who feel that this introduction was to give the writing additional weight by seeming to be associated with the brother of Jesus who at one time was the head of the church at Jerusalem. In somewhat the same way the name of Peter had been used by a Christian writer in the general letter called 1 Peter, and that of Paul a bit later by the author of the Pastorals.

Jude points out that licentious Docetists, whom he calls "ungodly persons" had got into the church for the purpose of destroying the main-line faith, even denying "our only Master and Lord, Jesus Christ" (4). The elder has said that those who deny that Jesus Christ has come in the flesh are not of God. Docetists and those who follow their heretical teachings are doomed. Jude points out that the scriptures show that God always punishes sinners. After saving the Israelites out of Egypt he "destroyed those who did not believe" (5). Even disobedient angels were punished. This is a reference to a story in the Book of Enoch, a Jewish apocalypse. Sodom and Gomorrah had also been destroyed for indulging in "unnatural lust." Docetists defile the flesh and hold angels in contempt. This is because they believe the angels assisted in the creation of the world and were therefore defiled. Jude emphasizes the evil of these Docetists by referring to a story in The Ascension of Moses, a book written about A.D. 50. The story relates that the devil tried to keep the archangel Michael from burying the body of Moses, claiming that as a part of the material world it belonged to him. Although Michael won, he showed respect to the devil as a supernatural being by merely saying "The Lord rebuke you." Men must not "revile the glorious ones" (8).

Docetists are as disrespectful as animals. "Woe to them" (11). They are as bad as Cain, Balaam, or Korah. With their carousing they bring disgrace upon Christian love feasts. Jude lines up a number of metaphors to emphasize how artificial and useless the Docetists are: "waterless clouds, carried along by winds; fruitless trees in late autumn, twice dead, uprooted; wild waves of the sea, casting up the foam of their own shame; wandering stars for whom the nether gloom of darkness has been reserved forever" (12-13). Jude borrowed the analogies of waterless clouds and wandering stars from Enoch, although the cloud analogy is also found in Prov. 25:14. His reference to wild waves seems to come from Isa. 57:20. In his condemnation of the Docetists Jude quotes Enoch as referring to them: "The Lord came . . . to convict all the ungodly of all their deeds of ungodliness . . . and of all the harsh things which ungodly sinners have spoken against him"

(14-15). He proceeds to call them a number of unflattering names.

Jude reminds his readers that the apostles at one time predicted that "in the last time there will be scoffers, following their own ungodly passions" (18). These are the Docetists, he believes. The doctrines of these people can never lead to a good life. Christians must build their lives on a foundation of sound theology, most holy faith. This will keep them in the love of God and the mercy of God expressed through Christ. They will thus be assured of eternal life. They must be concerned with the salvation of other people, never condoning sin and being sure that they do not take to themselves some of the sins of those they are helping. It is God who is able to keep Jude's readers from falling and without blemish.

Jude's little book soon became popular among orthodox Christians and was added to their lists of Christian writings. However, it did not do away with Docetism. Twenty-five years later this heresy was still prevalent. Christian leaders felt that it again must be attacked. This resulted in the writing known as 2 Peter, the last book of our New Testament to be written. It was produced a century after Paul wrote the first book, his original letter to the Thessalonians. This second attack was doubtless composed in Rome, the city of Peter and Paul. Rome was taking Christian leadership away from Ephesus and Asia Minor. It was becoming popular to write Christian books under the name of Peter. Therefore, Christians at Rome produced what they called the second letter of Peter. It makes an even stronger attempt to be considered the voice of the departed apostle Peter than 1 Peter does. Its introductory phrase reads, "Simon Peter, a servant and apostle of Jesus Christ." The style differs greatly from that of 1 Peter. Peter had come to symbolize early authoritative Christianity. He would unhesitatingly have condemned heresy. The author of this last New Testament book to be written evidently recognized that Peter had been responsible for the "Gospel According to Mark." As if it were Peter speaking, he writes, "I will see to it that after my departure you may be able at any time to recall these things" (1:15). Scholars believe that the writer of 1 Peter was referring to the same thing when he says that greetings are sent by "my son Mark" (5:13).

By 150 people were reading Paul's writings and asking what

292

had become of Paul's emphasis upon the second coming of Christ. The writer of the "Gospel According to John" had attempted to spiritualize the second coming, but Paul seemed to believe definitely in a physical return of the Lord. Second Peter 3:4 reports that scoffers are asking, "Where is the promise of his coming? For ever since the fathers [the apostles and other early Christians] fell asleep, all things have continued as they were from the beginning of creation."

A new spokesman for the church at Rome, the author of 2 Peter, answers this by pointing out that many who call themselves Christians should be very grateful that Jesus has not yet returned. He would have found them in licentious living. This would have led to their damnation. They should be grateful that God has given them a second chance. Christ will return. "Do not ignore this one fact, beloved, that with the Lord one day is as a thousand years, and a thousand years as one day. The Lord is not slow about his promise" (3:8-9).

The writer of 2 Peter notes that through the apostles a knowledge of Christ has been given which enables his readers to "escape from the corruption that is in the world because of passion, and become partakers of the divine nature" (1:4). Faith is not enough. It must be supplemented by virtue, knowledge, self-control, steadfastness, godliness, brotherly affection, and love. Docetists were not known for these virtues. These are essential to being a part of Christ's kingdom. The author shows his knowledge of the gospel records and Paul's letters. He refers to the Transfiguration account (Matt. 17:1-13) as indicating that the message of Christ has the backing of God.

As false prophets rose up in Old Testament times, so false teachers exist. Many follow the licentiousness of these teachers, the Docetists. The attacks of Jude upon the Docetists are incorporated in 2 Peter as the main part of the second chapter. People who have become Christian and then have fallen under the sway of the Docetists are worse than if they had never known the Christian message. "The last state has become worse for them than the first" (2:20).

The false teachers are considered as denying the second coming. In their insistence that the world has not changed since creation they deny the change that came about as a result of the flood of the time of Noah. A great change is in prospect. With the coming of Christ the heavens and the earth will be destroyed by fire and Christ's kingdom will be established. The old must make way for a new heaven and a new earth. This makes it all the more important that Christians should live "lives of holiness and godliness" (3:11), "without spot or blemish, and at peace" (3:14). Such lives are not led by the Docetists. God has postponed the great event of all history in order that men may have an opportunity of salvation. In this connection the author shows his respect for Paul and considers his writings as scripture. Paul had written a number of times, especially in his letter to the Romans, about the forbearance and patience of God. With this knowledge believers must exert themselves to clean Christian living, "lest you be carried away with the error of lawless men and lose your own stability" (3:17).

As this letter began with the prayer that "grace and peace be multiplied to you in the knowledge of God and of Jesus our Lord" (1:2), it concludes with the directive to "grow in the grace and knowledge of our Lord and Savior Jesus Christ" (3:18). The writer of 2 Peter did not know that he was writing the last advice to be included in the Christian scriptures, in fact the closing thought of the entire Holy Bible. If he had realized this he could not have made a more fitting ending. It is an ending that is the beginning and the continuing of the Christian life—growing in the grace and knowledge of Christ.

For Class Discussion

1. What phases of Docetism are evident today? What should be the Christian attitude?
2. What should be our attitude toward the question raised by 2 Peter, the return of Jesus?
3. How can the advice of the last verse written in our Bible be carried out?

Assignment

1. Identify: (a) Enoch, (b) Cain, (c) Balaam, (d) Korah.
2. Describe each of the heresies dealt with in the various "catholic" letters.

3. Most of Jude is repeated in 2 Peter. What two other Christian books are largely repeated in later New Testament writings?

Supplementary Reading

1. Goodspeed, Edgar J. *An Introduction to the New Testament.* Chicago: University of Chicago Press, 1937. Chapter XXII.
2. Hunter, A. M. *Introducing the New Testament.* New York: Harper & Brothers, Rev. 1957. Chapters XXVI and XXVII.
3. Parsons, Ernest W. *The Religion of the New Testament.* New York: Harper & Brothers, 1939. Pages 261-264.

Review Assignments

1. Give the root meaning of: Messiah, gospel, synoptic, atonement, repent.

2. What do you know about the authors and dates of each of the four gospel accounts? What chief sources are used in the book of Matthew? What other book did Luke write? What types of material did Luke contribute to the gospel record? In what language was the gospel account written? In what ways does the Fourth Gospel differ from the Synoptics? What is: Q, Kerygma, Didache?

3. Draw from memory a map locating: Mediterranean Sea, Dead Sea, Sea of Galilee, Nile River, Jordan River, Judea, Samaria, Galilee, Perea, Jerusalem, Bethlehem, Nazareth, Capernaum, Jericho, Caesarea Philippi, Tyre, Sidon, Caesarea, Joppa, Lydda, Damascus.

4. What three types of temptation did Jesus overcome as described in the wilderness story? Give the illustration used for each. Suggest later times when Jesus was tempted.

5. What planks for his platform did Jesus find in Isaiah 61? For each of these aims give a definite example of the church's attempt to achieve it.

6. Name ways in which Jesus came into conflict with religious authorities.

7. What three attitudes are taken toward Biblical miracles? Did Jesus break the laws of nature or utilize little understood laws? What was Jesus' attitude toward miracles done by others?

8. Suggest ways in which Jesus was ahead of his times.

9. What is the Sermon on the Mount? What general themes are discussed in it?

10. What did Jesus mean by the Kingdom? What erroneous concepts of the Kingdom did the disciples have? What erroneous concept is often held today? Explain how these ideas came into existence.

11. What did Jesus mean by the poor in spirit, the meek, "those who hunger and thirst for righteousness," the salt of the earth, the light of the world, "if your right eye cause you to sin, pluck it out," the second mile?

12. Define: Pharisee, Sadducee, Essene, Zealot, Herodian, scribe, rabbi, sanhedrin, blessed, beatitude, "the Law and the Prophets", parable.

13. List the teachings introduced by, "You have heard that it was said . . . but I say . . .". Tell in each instance in what way Jesus went beyond the Old Testament teaching. What two emphases in the teaching of Jesus are not found in the Old Testament?

14. Explain: "I have not come to abolish them, but to fulfill them."

15. In Matt. 6:1-18 at what three points did Jesus attack religious artificiality? What advice did he give in each case? What other phases of religious artificiality did Jesus attack?

16. What teachings of Jesus do we have about: treasure or wealth, giving, worry, judging or criticizing others, perseverance, false prophets, true greatness?

17. Explain: "speck in your brother's eye"; "if his son ask him for a loaf"; "grapes gathered from thorns"; "not every one who says to me, 'Lord, Lord' "; "built his house upon the rock"; "the crowds were astonished."

18. What is meant by: baptism, the Lord's Supper, sacraments, feast of the Passover, temple, synagogue, Holy Spirit, Gethsemane, the "Golden Rule," Golgotha?

19. Give the social customs reflected in each of the following parables: Soils or Sower, Tares, Leaven, Dragnet, Friend at Midnight, Lost Coin, Lost Sheep, Prodigal Son, Rich Man and Lazarus, Ten Maidens. In each of these parables what was Jesus teaching?

20. Give Jesus' attitude about: Sabbath observance, women, other nations and races, immortality, superstition, ignorance, war, prayer, forgiveness, the most important commandment.

21. In what ways has the life, teaching, and death of Jesus changed civilization? What further changes are needed before Jesus' dream of the Kingdom will be realized?

22. Identify: Elizabeth, Zechariah, Mary, Joseph, Magi, Herod the Great, Anna, Simeon, Levi, Nicodemus, Joseph of Arimathea, Simon of Cyrene, Herod Antipas, Pontius Pilate, Caiaphas, Annas.

23. Tell all you know about: John the Baptist, Judas Iscariot, Peter, Barnabas, Mark, Silas, Luke.

24. Outline the life of Paul. List his major contributions to Christianity.

25. Give: Klausner's two reasons that most Jews rejected Jesus; two things in Judaism that offended intelligent Gentiles; four things from which the Jerusalem conference said Christians must refrain; three attitudes regarding the second coming of Jesus; three attitudes regarding miracles; three types of church government; in order, the four centers of the Christian church.

26. Give the root meaning of: salvation, believe, church, sin.

27. Discuss Paul's experience at Lystra, Philippi, Athens, Corinth, Ephesus, Caesarea, Malta, Rome.

28. Give the approximate dates of the writing of 2 Peter, John, Revelation, Luke-Acts, Matthew, Mark, Thessalonians.

29. Identify: Jason, Apollos, Demetrius, Aquila, Agabus, Matthias, Felix, Festus, Gamaliel, Cornelius, Timothy, Agrippa II, Theophilus.

30. Identify: Sapphira, Rhoda, Dorcas, Tabitha, Lydia, Apphia, Priscilla, Phoebe.

31. Identify: Domitian, Nero, the Elder, Epaphras, Epaphroditus, Onesimus.

32. Identify two people by the name of: Simon, Joseph, Ananias, Judas, Philip, John, James, Jesus (not the Christ).

33. Identify: Alexandria, Tarsus, Malta, Damascus, Patmos, Cyprus, Crete, Troas.

34. Identify: "in the first book," Pentecost, Hellenists, God-fearers, devout converts, "We" passages, Macedonian vision, great commission.

35. Give: three views regarding the relation of Jesus to "James, Joses, Judas and Simon"; how Paul differed from Jesus in his presentation of the gospel; an explanation of the Christian communism of the early church; an example of putting God or conscience above government; where the word "Christian" was first used; the earlier term for Christians; two contributions to present Christian thinking found in Paul's Athens address; the way Paul's idea that he was living near the end of an age warped his view of human relations.

36. Identify the quotations: "We must obey God rather than man." "What must I do to be saved?" "It is more blessed to give than to receive." "Lord, do not hold this sin against them." "These . . . were more noble than those in Thessalonica." "I perceive that . . . you are very religious." "In him we live and move and have our being." "When I have an opportunity I will summon you." "Grow in the grace and knowledge of our Lord and Savior Jesus Christ."

37. What did Paul say about: speaking in tongues, value of the law, descendants of Abraham, meat offered to idols, Adam, cliques at Corinth, his own imprisonment, the letter from Laodicea?

38. Why were the following written: Revelation, 1 Thessalonians, 2 Thessalonians, Galatians, Corinthians, Romans, Philippians, Philemon?

39 .What thinking is represented by: Docetism, Gnosticism, Marcionism, the elemental spirits idea, Asceticism? What four problems brought about the writing of the Pastorals? What three factors influenced the character of "Revelation?" What are 2 and 3 John?

40. Discuss the problem of: how many women visited the empty tomb; the end of the book of Mark; John 7:53-8:11; the Acts account of two journeys to Jerusalem as compared to the report in Galatians; contradictions in Acts and Galatians regarding Paul's experience shortly after his conversion; Paul's four letters to the Corinthians; Romans 16; Paul's letters to the Philippians.

NAME INDEX

Aaron, 265

Abiathar, 108

Abraham, 20, 46, 48, 73, 95, 122, 131, 209, 211, 213, 225-7, 265-6, 298

Achaicus, 215

Adam, 95, 225, 227, 298

Adronicus, 224

Agabus, 230, 235, 298

Agrippa I, 184-5, 233-4

Agrippa II, 234, 298

Ahimelech, 108

Alexander (son of Simon of Cyrene), 151

Alexander the Great, 8, 78, 187, 195-6

Amos, 85, 193

Ananias, 166, 172

Ananias of Damascus, 177, 231

Andrew, 53

Anna, 43, 47, 297

Annas, 149, 164, 167, 172, 297

Antipas, 28, 34, 36, 44, 53, 150-1, 168, 184, 297

Antipater, 27, 34

Apphia, 247, 263, 298

Apollos, 214-6, 219, 298

Aquila, 203, 209, 214, 219, 224, 263, 298

Aratus, 202

Archelaus, 28, 34, 44

Archippus, 247-8

Aristarchus, 236, 247

Artemis, 220

Athanasius, 6

Augustine, 104

Augustus, 27

Balaam, 291, 294

Balthasar, 44

Barabbas, 37, 150, 159

Bar Jesus, 186

Barnabas, Joseph, 5, 17, 159, 166, 168, 178, 181-3, 185-195, 210, 237, 297

Barsabbas, Joseph, 159

Barsabbas, Judas, 159, 192

Bartimaeus, 91, 145

Bede, 8, 14

Buddha, 40

Caedmon, 8, 14

Caiaphas, 149, 164, 167, 297

Cain, 291, 294

Caligula, 184

Chaucer, 8

Chloe, 215

Claudius, 232

Clement, 5, 239, 270

Cornelius, 179-80, 183, 191, 194, 298

Coverdale, Miles, 9-10, 14

Crispus, 204

Daniel, 100, 165

David, 46, 73, 78, 108, 114-5, 156, 187

Demas, 247

Demetrius, 220, 298

Diotrephes, 279

299

Domitian, 253, 255, 259, 261, 263, 298
Dorcas, 179, 298

Elijah, 39, 54, 124
Elisha, 39, 54, 61, 116, 124
Elizabeth, 39, 41, 49, 297
Elizabeth, Queen I, 10
Enoch, 294
Epaphras, 244-5, 247, 298
Epaphroditus, 240-2, 244, 247, 298
Er, 282
Erasmus, 9
Euodia, 197
Eusebius, 6, 278
Eutychus, 229
Ezekiel, 142, 258

Felix, 232-3, 298
Festus, 233-4, 298
Fortunatus, 215

Gaius, 279
Gallio, 204
Gamaliel, 167-8, 176, 231, 298
Gandhi, M. K., 61, 117
Ganesh, 124
Gaspar, 44
Gideon, 52
Goodspeed, Edgar J., 13

Hannah, 41, 100
Hawthorne, Nathaniel, 141
Helen, 195
Herod the Great, 27-8, 34, 43-4, 179, 181, 184, 231, 297
Herodias, 36
Homer, 12
Hosea, 96

Ignatius, 248-9
Isaac, 122, 131, 211

Isaiah, 39, 115, 117, 254, 258
Isaiah, II, 92, 95, 111, 141
Ishmael, 211

Jacob, 95, 112, 122, 131, 141, 202
James (the disciple), 5-6, 53, 79, 83, 145, 158-9, 163, 184, 234
James (brother of Jesus), 47, 178, 184-5, 192-5, 210, 230, 290, 298
James, King, 11, 14
Jason, 200-1, 298
Jephthah, 52
Jeremiah, 97, 172, 266
Jerome, 7, 9, 14
Jesus,—nearly every page
Jesus Justus, 247
Joel, 162
John (the Baptist), 23, 36, 39, 48-51, 53-55, 90, 120, 142, 161, 165, 214, 297
John (the disciple), 5-6, 53, 79, 124, 145, 163-4, 167-8, 172-3, 184, 189, 297
John (the evangelist), 23-5, 127, 136-7, 141, 147-8, 161, 239, 246, 277-8, 290
John (the prophet), 254, 256-62
Jonah, 11
Joseph, 39-41, 43-7
Joseph (brother of Jesus), 47
Joseph of Arimathea, 37, 297
Josephus, Flavius, 185, 231-2
Joses, 47, 298
Joshua, 39-40, 114, 170, 282
Jotham, 69
Judah, 266
Judas (brother of Jesus), 47, 298
Judas of Damascus, 177
Judas of Galilee, 54, 167
Judas Iscariot, 78, 146-9, 152, 158-60, 177, 192, 297
Jude, 5-6, 290-2

Julius Caesar, 27
Junias, 224
Justin, 4, 282

Klausner, Joseph, 154, 159, 297
Korah, 291, 294

Lamech, 61
Lazarus (in Jesus' parable), 76, 92, 132
Lester, Murial, 162
Levi, 36, 266, 297
Luke, 20-3, 25, 39-44, 46, 48, 50-1, 75-6, 90, 119, 128, 146, 155-6, 161, 167, 169-73, 182, 185, 187-8, 190, 192-204, 209, 219-20, 224, 229-31, 236-9, 247, 250, 257, 263, 296
Luther, Martin, 9
Lydia, 196-8, 298

Marcion, 4, 14, 212, 282-4, 287-9
Mark, 15-23, 36, 38, 44-48, 51, 108, 119, 121, 123, 140, 142, 184-5, 187, 190, 194-5, 207, 238, 247
Mary (mother of Jesus), 40-1, 158, 297
Mary (of Bethany), 127
Mary Magdalene, 37
Mary, Queen, 10
Matthew, 18-23, 25, 43-4
Matthew, Thomas, 10
Matthias, 159-60, 298
Melchior, 44
Melchizedek, 265-6
Micah, 87, 115, 117, 155
Moffatt, James, 13
Mohammed, 124
Moses, 19, 29, 56, 59, 73, 95-6, 106, 124, 126, 147, 170-2, 187, 211, 265, 271, 282, 291

Naaman, 54
Nathan, 46, 68
Nehemiah, 100
Nero, 15, 203, 253, 259, 298
Newton, Isaac, 57
Nicodemus, 91, 297
Noah, 294

Onan, 282
Onesimus, 247-9, 298
Origen, 5-6, 263

Papias, 16, 278
Paul, 3-5, 7, 17, 21-2, 46, 57, 60-1, 84, 97, 131, 134, 137-8, 147, 152, 157, 159, 162, 167, 171, 173, 175-6, 182-3, 185-207, 209-251, 256-7, 259, 263-4, 270-1, 282-294, 297-8
Peter, 5-7, 15-17, 53, 108, 115, 118, 127, 141, 145, 149-50, 158, 162-9, 171-4, 178-184, 186, 189, 191, 194, 196, 210, 215-7, 270-1, 290, 292, 297
Philemon, 247-9
Philip (the deacon), 170, 172-3, 180-1, 191, 210, 263
Philip (son of Herod the Great), 28, 34, 184, 234
Philip of Macedon, 196
Phillips, J. B., 13
Philo, 263
Phoebe, 223-4, 298
Polycarp, 242
Pontius Pilate, 28, 37, 150-1, 168, 297
Priscilla, 203, 209, 214, 219, 224, 263, 298

Queen of Sheba, 173

Rhine, Joseph B., 102, 104
Rhoda, 298

Rogers, John, 10
Rufus, 151

Samson, 40
Samuel, 40, 100, 114, 130
Sapphira, 168, 177, 298
Saul, 114, 130, 176
Saul — see Paul
Shakespeare, William, 13
Silas (Silvanus), 192, 194-5, 197-201, 204-5, 263, 271, 297
Simeon, 43, 47, 297
Simon of Cyrene, 37, 151, 297
Simon (brother of Jesus), 47, 298
Simon the Samaritan, 124, 172-4
Simon the tanner, 180
Solomon, 46, 78, 173
Sopater, 201
Sosthenes, 204
Stephanes, 215
Stephen, 170-1, 174-5, 178, 181, 187, 298

Synthyche, 197

Tabitha, 179, 298
Theophilus, 22, 25, 257, 284, 298
Theudas, 167
Thomas, 174
Timothy, 194, 198-9, 201, 204-5, 230, 240, 263, 824-5, 298
Titus, 210, 219-20, 284-5
Tychicus, 244, 247, 249
Tyndale, William, 9-11

Weymouth, R. F., 13
Wilhelm (William), 39
Wycliffe, John, 8, 12, 14

Zacchaeus, 91, 145
Zebedee, 36, 163
Zechariah (father of John), 39-41, 48-9, 297
Zechariah (Old Testament prophet), 145